BRAIN FITNESS

BY THE SAME AUTHOR

Death in the Locker Room: Steroids, Cocaine, and Sports

Death in the Locker Room II: Drugs and Sports

The "E" Factor

Seven Anti-Aging Secrets

Stopping the Clock

The Science of Anti-Aging Medicine

Advances in Anti-Aging Medicine

Anti-Aging Medical Therapeutics, Vol. I

Anti-Aging Medical Therapeutics, Vol. II

BRAIN FITNESS

ANTI-AGING STRATEGIES FOR ACHIEVING SUPER MIND POWER

Robert M. Goldman, M.D., D.O., Ph.D.

with Ronald Klatz, M.D., D.O., and Lisa Berger

DOUBLEDAY

NEW YORK LONDON TORONTO SYDNEY AUCKLAND

A MAIN STREET BOOK
PUBLISHED BY DOUBLEDAY
a division of Random House, Inc.
1540 Broadway, New York, New York 10036

MAIN STREET BOOKS, DOUBLEDAY, and the portrayal of a building with a tree are trademarks of Doubleday, a division of Random House, Inc.

Book design by Chris Welch

Brain Fitness was originally published in hardcover by Doubleday in 1999.

The Library of Congress has cataloged the Doubleday edition as follows:

Goldman, Robert, 1955–
Brain fitness: anti-aging strategies for achieving super mind power / Robert M. Goldman with Ronald Klatz and Lisa Berger.—1st ed.
p. cm.
Includes bibliographical references and index.
1. Cognition—Age factors. 2. Memory—Age factors. 3. Sleep—Age factors.
4. Stress management. 5. Aging. 6. Aging—Prevention.
I. Klatz, Ronald, 1955– . II. Berger, Lisa. III. Title.
BF724.55.A35G64 1999
153.1′2—dc21 98-18785
CIP

ISBN 0-385-48869-6

Printed in the United States of America
First Main Street Books Edition: January 2000
1 3 5 7 9 10 8 6 4 2

To all the great scientists past, present, and future seeking to unlock the secrets of the human brain, and to my parents Arnold and Alice and grandmother Rose, who shaped my mind and being.

ACKNOWLEDGMENTS

There were many challenges with this project, especially since I was induced to present scientific information from a personal angle revealing private past life experiences. I would like to thank my collaborators, Dr. Ronald Klatz and Lisa Berger, for their astute insight and professionalism, my publisher Doubleday and Judith Kern, and book agent Gail Ross. My thanks to the following individuals who provided information, data, personal interviews, and ancillary support for the project.

Arnold Schwarzenegger, William Shatner, Dan Rutz (CNN), Dr. Tom Deters (*Muscle and Fitness*), Jack LaLanne, Dr. Vernon Howard (Harvard University), Don Yaeger (*Sports Illustrated*), Dr. Ben Weider, John Abdo, Dr. Thomas Allen, Neil Spruce, Phil Broxham, Stedman Graham, Anthony Barone, Lyle Hurd, Dr. Dharma Singh Khalsa, Dr. Eric Braverman, Dr. Steven Sinatra, Dr. Steven Novil, Dr. Thierry Hertoghe, Dr. Vincent Giampapa, Dr. Kelvin Brockbank, Dr. Michael Taylor, Dr. Aftab Ahmed, Warren Preis, Phil Scotti, Bob Brahm, Perris Calderon, Dr. Michael Crohn, Joe Shultz, Leslie

Cohen, Alan Tamshen, Martin Silverberg, Steven Speigle, Glen Braswell, Ali Berman, Ben Lew, Bryon Klein, Paul and Sandy Bernstein, Mauricio Fernandez, June Colbert, Paul Chua, Darryll and Jo Burleigh, Chan Boon Young, G. K. Goh, Leong Wah Kheong, Yew Lin Goh, T. T. Duarai, Ron Ooi, Andy Handayanto, Ali Kahn, Alan and Cory Dropkin, Mark Brun, Will and Norm Dabish, Rob Romano, Pam Kagan, Joe Vitale, Dr. Steve and Claire Bernstein, Jerry and Goldie Klatz, Sparky Bernstein, Harry Schwartz, Dr. Nick DeNubulie, Bob Delmontique, Dr. Dari Ann Ungaretti, Royalynn Aldrich, Graham and Kathryn Putnam, Steve Groshek, Eve Magnet, Paul and Mark Goldman, Susan Greenberg, Dr. Brad Grant, Judy Heifitz, Dr. Harold Hakes, Dr. Deborah Heath, Alex Thomson, Dr. Arthur Heath, Louis Habash, Kenny Wong, Peter Julian, Sumner and Georgia Katz, Joy Knapp, Mitch Kaufman, Leon Locke, Dr. Ron Lawrence, Jim Lorimer, Jake Steinfeld, Dr. Alan Mintz, John Adams, Gary Vogel, Jim and Debbi Manion, Sandi Renalli, Dr. Art Nahas, Tony Little, Dr. Rafael Santonja, Richard Ornstein, Stu Grannen, Joe Partipilo, Javier Pollock, Tom Purvis, Glen Pollock, Brenda Payne, Kim Bardley, Jeff Plitt, Bob Dee, Mel Rich, Steve Stern, Eric Perle, Dr. Tom Rasandich, Arlene Robins, Greg Rilmore, Rick Merner, Tim Shiner, Sylvia Lugibihl, Ida Olivos, Schinna Harris, Vicki Joy, Mildred Bonner, Dr. Jerry Rodos, Eric Roper, Amy Sklar, Steve Sokol, Steve Schussler, Larry Strickler, Dr. Phil Santiago, Anne Sobel, Lorne Caplan, David Kravitz, Gary and Tammy Strauch, Sharon Ringer, Bettie and Joseph Whitaker, Stacy Seigle, Richard Yong, Felix Lee, U Tin Maung Swe, U Hla Aung, Sudisana Sukama, Eve Taliferro, Tom Merridith, Mike Tomzak, Jay and Tracy Tuerk, Titus and Vicki Marincas, George and Maria Iusco, Dr. Bob Voy, Carole Weidman, Eric Weider, Joe Weider, Ross Love, Joanna Gravitt, Ken Berdy, Dave Zelon, Nancy Smith, Pamela Travis, Isabella Wilson, Mary Ellen Maunz, Lisa Meacham, and Debra Battjes.

CONTENTS

INTRODUCTION. DR. BOB'S SUPER MIND POWER 1

Exceptional Super Mind Power 4

ONE. WISE UP: RAISE YOUR INTELLIGENCE 9

Lessons from Seattle and Baltimore 10

The Seattle Longitudinal Study 13

The Baltimore Longitudinal Study of Aging (BLSA) 14

What's Your Intelligence Profile? 15

A Personal Mental Agility Program 21

Assess How You Learn Best 23

Assess Your Thought Process 26

Capture New Information 29

Cement Your Sharpened Intelligence 36

Exercise to Pump Up Learning 39

A Cognitive Cocktail 41

TWO. DETAIL POWER: IMPROVING RECALL AND FIGHTING MEMORY LOSS 45

A Memory Acid Test 46

Recognizing Old Friends, Reliving Good Times 47

Kinds of Memory 49

Your Aging Memory: What Goes, What Stays, What Gets Better 52

Brain Foods 55

The Glory of Garlic 55

Try a Shot of Sugar 55

Bring On the Fat 56

Pile On the Pasta 57

A Powerful Nutrient 57

Lubricate Your Memory 58

Memory Minerals 59

Vitamin Power 60

Memory Pills 64

Hormone Therapy 68

Estrogen 69

A Mother Hormone for Men and Women 71

Human Growth Hormone (hGH) 74

Protect Yourself with Exercise 76

Smell Your Way to a Better Memory 79

Memory Builders 81

Memory Poisons 82

On the Horizon: A Well-Tuned Mind 85

News to Watch For 86

A Personal Memory Program 88

THREE. SLEEPING BETTER: FINDING YOUR PERSONAL SLEEP POWER 95

Flying into Difficult Sleep 96

Inside Your Sleeping Brain 98

Why Do We Sleep? 102

Sleep Robbers: Varieties of Insomnia 104

The Air Robber: Sleep Apnea 107

Constant Motion: Restless Leg Syndrome 109

Sleeplessness Associated with Mental Disorders 109

Sliding Sex Hormones 110

Another Sleep-Stealing Hormone 112

Suddenly Asleep: Narcolepsy 112

Are You in Sleep Debt? 113

How Much Is Enough? 115

As You Grow Older 118

Finding Dreamland 120

Sleep Potions 125

Foods, Drinks, Herbs 125

Sleeping Pills 127

Sleep Hygiene 130

Increasing Your Personal Sleep Power 131

FOUR. BATTLING THE BRAIN BEASTS: BEATING STRESS 137

A Beast with Two Heads 140

What Stress Does to the Body 142

What Stress Does to Your Mind and Brain 146

Individual Stress Signs 151

Stress and Aging 155

Taming the Beast 158

Coping Techniques 159

Exercise 159

Diet and Nutrition 164

Relaxation and Breathing 172
Making Stress Work for You 178
How Do You Deal with Stress? 181

FIVE. CEREBRAL SECURITY: HEADING OFF ALZHEIMER'S DEMENTIA 185
Family Fears: Who, When and How It Hits 186
Am I Getting It? 188
Diagnosis Difficulties 188
Solving Mysteries About Causes 191
Stressed-out Brain Cells 194
A Virus Involved? 195
The American Way of Eating 195
Poison Minerals 197
An Electricity Connection? 198
Ways to Protect Yourself 199
Solid Protection: Low Blood Pressure, Lowered Stroke Risk 199
The Nun Study 201
More Protection: Antioxidants 205
Anti-Inflammatories: NSAIDs 206
A Lifesaving Hormone? 207
Help from DHEA 210
Less Fat, More Fish 211
A Long Shot: The Nicotine Patch 212
Use It or Lose It: Education 213
Slowing It Down 215
The Calcium Route 216
Going After Free Radicals 217
New Compounds 220
On the Horizon 222

SIX. THE EMOTIONAL BRAIN: SEXUAL STIM 227
Sex Hormones 231
The Take-Charge Hormone: Testosterone 233

The Sap of Life: Estrogen 236
His and Hers 239
More Hormones to Muddy Your Relationships 241
Luteinizing Hormone Releasing Hormone (LHRH) 242
Progesterone 243
Prolactin 243
Oxytocin 243
Vasopressin 244
DHEA (Dehydroepiandrosterone) 244
Pheromones 245
PEA (Phenylethylamine) 246
Mastering Your Emotions 246
How to Find Happiness 246
Eating for a Better Sex Life 248
Cultivating Emotional Smarts 252
Hormonal Heads-Up 253
Acknowledge Strengths 253
Sexual Savvy 253

SEVEN. MIND CALM: HOPE FOR THE WORRIED WELL 257
Shades of Blue 258
Secrets of Serotonin 261
An Essential Lubricant 263
Herbal Relief 265
Sweat Out the Sadness 266
It's Not Always Depression: Attention Deficit Disorder 268
Getting Control 271
Always on Edge 273
Headaches and Migraines 276
The Hangover Headache 277
Lighten Up: Fighting Tension Headaches 278
Hitting Back: Treatment 278
When to See a Doctor 281
Headache Facts 282

Don't Ignore That Head Bang 282

APPENDIX A: GLOSSARY 288

APPENDIX B: NUTRITIONAL NOOTROPICS 302

APPENDIX C: SPECIAL BRAIN NUTRIENT PROGRAMS 304

APPENDIX D: MEDICAL CENTERS SPECIALIZING IN TREATMENTS FOR COGNITIVE ENHANCEMENT AND ANTI-AGING 308

APPENDIX E: SUGGESTIONS FOR FURTHER INFORMATION AND SUPPORT 310

APPENDIX F: KIDS' BRAIN FITNESS 313

APPENDIX G: THE AMERICAN ACADEMY OF ANTI-AGING MEDICINE 316

APPENDIX H: NEW BRAIN FITNESS RESEARCH 320

INDEX 335

ABOUT THE AUTHORS 345

A NOTE TO THE READER

The information here is intended to complement your personal knowledge and your doctor's care. The suggestions in this book should not replace the advice of your personal physician. You should consult with your doctor before making any changes in the care or treatment of a medical condition. Much of the information in this book is general and may not apply to your particular circumstances, so if you develop any medical problems or symptoms, talk to your doctor first.

BRAIN FITNESS

Introduction

DR. BOB'S SUPER MIND POWER

We all want to be smarter and more alert, to require less sleep and better handle the stresses and strains that life throws our way. I have always been fascinated with how powerful the mind can make us feel and how far the inner self can be pushed. The mind is so closely linked to the body that you really can think yourself fat, thin, sick, healthy, poor, rich, a loser, or a winner.

Having competed for many years on the world level as a strength athlete, and having studied the martial arts since my teens, I have long experienced the Super Powers of the Mind. When I set world records, I did not accomplish that goal with body or muscle power but with the power of my mind. When I performed karate board or brick breaks, it was my mind and inner *chi* that allowed my hand to pass so easily through those barriers. The more I challenged my body and mind, the more respect I gained for this intricately tuned synergy the Greeks spoke of centuries ago. The mind-body link is a reality, and I wanted to learn every technique of how to meld the two, and so increase my brainpower, memory, concentration, focus, imagination, and creativity. That was the impetus for writing this book, putting together a "user's manual" for building Super Mind Power.

As a young child, I marveled at my grandmother Rose. She came to this country at age twelve not knowing the language and with no money or family support, but she had the mental power and fortitude to raise and protect eight children. It was the force of her mind and personality that forged the bond among scores of grandchildren, great-grandchildren, and even great-great-grandchildren. At the end of her life, at ninety-five, she still possessed wit, concentration, and humor. Her selective hearing could filter out useless gossip and pick out important conversations twenty-five yards away. She was my first exposure to someone who had a natural Super Mind Power.

When I was a teenager, I marveled at the astounding concentration of martial arts masters. Though slight of build, they could exert enormous power and literally propel much larger, heavier opponents across the room with a single stroke. It was not their physical strength but Super Mind Power that enabled them to complete these feats. One of my early teachers was a Chinese gung fu master who, though he weighed only 130 pounds soaking wet, could move like lightning, with such force and concentration that he was almost a blur. When I was training for the Olympic wrestling team, his concentration and mind-body kinesthetic sense were so developed that he was able, in a matter of hours, to learn all the freestyle Olympic wrestling maneuvers I knew.

When I was competing in the 1970s, I and every athlete I knew looked up to Olympic gold medal winner Dan Gable as the ultimate mind power athlete. His drive was so intense, and his concentration and skills were so developed, that he was virtually unbeatable. And he used these same skills for years as he became the winningest collegiate wrestling coach in American history. It was Dan's super brainpower that allowed him to mold himself into the ultimate physical machine and to teach those skills to others.

Since age four, I have studied art. I began with gifted children's classes at the Pratt Institute in New York, and as an adult, went on to establish my own museum of fine art, the Institute Museum of Chicago. Art is the true mirror into the hearts and minds of people in the past, and what makes art so fascinating is that it provides a window into the soul of the creator. As I have learned about art, I have realized that there are many different types of intelligences and mental skills. For instance, there is the ability of a Leonardo or a Michelangelo to visualize complex three-dimensional images. I recall as a child forcing myself to create three-dimensional characters to train my imagination and creative skills. I did this almost daily for entertainment. In hindsight, I know that this childhood game helped me to enhance my powers of visualization and concentration. But how do we unlock the creative instincts that are within each of us? Here again, Super Mind Power is the tool, and its secrets

THE MOVIE STAR MIND

Jake Steinfeld, who has trained numerous movie stars, has noticed that they think differently: "Very successful movie stars are very focused individuals . . . my goal has been mental motivation but my technique has always been fitness. I use what I call a positive psyche or negative psyche. With people like Steven Spielberg I use a positive psyche, and would say, 'Okay, buddy, let's go twenty-five reps or push-ups or whatever,' and be encouraging him, saying, 'You're doing great,' and patting him on the back and making him feel good. But with some people, like Bette Midler, I use a negative psyche. I would tell Bette, 'Okay, let's get down for twenty-five push-ups,' and she'd give me a look and a couple of choice words and say, 'Hey, chief, I ain't doing them, I'll do ten,' and I'd tell her, 'It's up to you, you got a big movie coming up, do just ten.' Then she'd give me this zingaroo look, and end up doing fifty."

have been used by masters for centuries. Now you, too, can develop your own Super Mind Power program.

The most important organ we possess is the brain. It is our conscious mind and all the memories, power, and sensations that make us human. Our remarkable brainpower elevates us from other species and makes each of us very special. And, like our muscles, which can be made stronger with focused, consistent effort, our brains, too, have this plastic quality and can be molded.

Beginning with our earliest life experiences, our brains begin to process and store amazing quantities of data, which allow us to perform tasks that, while very human, exceed anything that can be done on the most powerful computer. But how do we tap into this enormous data bank of potential? Thomas Edison said it best: "Genius is one per cent inspiration and ninety-nine per cent perspiration." Our ability to focus with determined effort can raise each of us above the crowd.

EXCEPTIONAL SUPER MIND POWER

In the late 1980s, I founded the National Academy of Sports Medicine, which today is the premier personal fitness trainer certification organization. As I have watched the organization grow, I have been fascinated by what trainers of the stars do for clients in terms of mental training and exercises. I have taken my experiences with these trainers and detailed their lessons in this book so that you, too, can learn about these special mind programs. Read about what trainer to the stars Jake Steinfeld did to get Harrison Ford, Steven Spielberg, Priscilla Presley, and Bette Midler ready for career challenges, and techniques employed by Michael Jordan's trainer gave him for an injury-free body and mind find history-making career.

What mental powers make people rich, successful, or powerful? It is their drive, ambition, concentration, and determination that bring them to the pinnacle of their careers. Consider basketball phenom

Michael Jordan. What separates him from other players? He is not taller, stronger, younger, or even faster. No. But he does have the Super Mind Power that enables him to fly above his opponents. He has the unbending will to win and focus, and that makes him the best. Is techno whiz Bill Gates the smartest nerd in town? Not necessarily. But his Super Mind Power has made him so focused that he has crushed all competition and all obstacles in his way. In the coming chapters, you will read about how these people and others have developed their Super Mind Powers.

Arnold Schwarzenegger was just another block of muscle when he came onto the movie scene. But with his Super Mind Power—his staggering drive and determination—he was able to turn himself from the greatest bodybuilder of all time into one of the most powerful individuals in the movie industry. I have seen his mind power at work. Having served with him on the President's Council on Physical Fitness and Sports, I witnessed his remarkable memory for names and faces. He could work a room like no other person, not only greeting every individual by name but also recounting minute details of past encounters and personal habits. You will be reading about some of his other super mind skills.

Super Mind Power is not only *how much* we remember but *what* we remember. For instance, it is the extraordinary empathy of Oprah Winfrey, and her ability to connect with individuals and with the masses. It is the ability to tap into our creative selves as, for example, Al Pacino, Robert DeNiro, and Meryl Streep do when they transform themselves into characters. This feat takes not only intense dedication but tedious hard work and arduous repetition. Their mind power includes the ability to suspend their egos to adapt to the mood, manner, and very essence of fictional characters.

Another example of Super Mind Power is the brilliant and fluid stream of comic genius within Robin Williams, Whoopi Goldberg, and Billy Crystal. They have trained their minds, memory, and creative talents to be able to improvise, but it has taken years of mind power training to make this ability look simple and effortless. Tiger

Woods may well be on his way to becoming the greatest golfer in history because of his Super Mind Power—his ability to focus, concentrate, and hone his talent with constant practice.

The idea of Super Mind Power has enthralled us since childhood. This is the appeal of superheroes, from Superman to Batman to an array of other comic book heroes. And for each superhero, there has been a supervillain—a brilliant Lex Luthor or Darth Vader who has tantalized us with his possible mental powers. It has always been the Super Mind Power of the characters, more than their physical power, that has captured our imaginations. Today, the popularity of shows like *Star Trek*, movies like *E.T.*, and alien creatures like those in *Independence Day* attests to our fascination with intelligence and the power of mind over matter. Similarly, the universal appeal of vampires, black magic, crystals, and ghosts speaks to our interest in the power of the mind to control others or read thoughts. We love the idea that our minds can move mountains, so to speak.

Each of us wants to learn our own secret brain-enhancing techniques. For some, this is what drives religious devotion. Intense faith has enabled people to walk again, regain hearing and vision, and make chronic pain disappear. Hindus and monks undergo great trials of pain and deprivation, armed only with their mental powers. The powers of the mind have given them strength and made "miracles" happen.

The goal of this book is to help you learn the Super Mind Power techniques of the superstars, the supersuccessful, the superpowerful. It will give you ideas for ways to change your life by turbocharging your mind and brain to increase your memory, concentration, focus, determination, discipline, imagination, creativity, and energy, while decreasing your fatigue, stress, and need to sleep. Learn which supernutrients can power up your mind and which new super brain medications are out there to pump up your thinking power. Learn how a supernap can quick-charge your mind and how special anti-stress techniques can rejuvenate your cerebral core. And learn about the latest advances in preventing Alzheimer's and other mental diseases.

Advances in science and medicine are all around us. Computer capabilities are doubling every eighteen months, and medical knowledge is doubling every three and a half years. In just twenty years, we will know much more than we do now about how to live longer and better. In 1799, the average life span was 25 years—as it had been for centuries before. But today we age very differently.

By 1899, just a century ago, the average life span had reached 48 years. Now it is almost 80 years, and scientists are predicting that average life spans will reach 120 to 150 years by the year 2049. When the first United States census was taken in 1790, half the population was under age sixteen. In 1990, less than one-quarter of the population was under sixteen. It is predicted by the U.S. Census Bureau that by the year 2025, the country will have two sixty-five-year-olds for every teenager. The percentage of Americans over age sixty-five has risen 300 percent in the last century; those aged sixty-five to seventy-four up 800 percent; those seventy-five to eighty-four up 1,300 percent; and the number of those over eighty-five has increased by 2,500 percent!

We are all definitely living longer, but how do we keep our minds young? How do we preserve and protect our experiences and wisdom? What are we going to do with the growing number of years in our lives? You want to have the mental mind power to participate in all that's ahead.

We are living in an exciting time of history. The advent of the new science of antiaging medicine means that aging is not inevitable, and you need not lose your memory, concentration, focus, and happiness as you age. Along with Dr. Ronald Klatz, I am one of the original twelve physicians who created the American Academy of Anti-Aging Medicine, the world's first medical society of physicians and scientists dedicated to combating the degenerative disease of aging. Since its inception in 1993, it has grown to over 6,500 members in more than fifty nations. It is showing the world that we can change the way our bodies and minds age if we use the secrets of Super Mind Power.

With the mind-boggling advances in gene therapy, nanotechnology, genetic engineering, organ regeneration, and drug development, we are going to live longer and healthier, and we need a Super Mind to help us take advantage of these added years.

The greatest tragedy for anyone is loss of memories, for these are our most valuable possessions. They are the core of our personal identity, and there is a lot you can do to protect yourself from "mind robbers," and losing these irreplaceable valuables.

In this book there are self-tests, brain booster information charts, and numerous quizzes to help you gauge where your mind power is now and what you might do to enhance your performance. There is also information about the new and exciting brain medications now under development, which may soon be available so that everyone can boost their brainpower.

The programs and techniques in *Brain Fitness* are your protective barrier against the greatest team of thieves of all time—age and deterioration—which are out to steal your greatest possession, your mind. Learn the secrets of Super Mind Power!

One

WISE UP

RAISE YOUR INTELLIGENCE

Over the past decade, I have been faced with a daunting task: taking an idea about a revolutionary medical device for protecting the brain during trauma from conception to the marketplace. The idea grew out of discoveries about how cold temperatures can prevent brain damage when trauma like stroke or cardiac arrest has disrupted a person's oxygen supply. My partner, Dr. Ronald Klatz, and I have devoted years to inventing the Brain Cooling Device, which consists of a neck-stabilizing plate and a helmet that is fitted over an accident victim's head and filled with a coolant, and the Brain Resuscitation Device, which delivers vital nutrients and oxygen through the carotid arteries to the brain. We named the umbrella company that would develop and promote these innovations Life Resuscitation Technologies, Inc. (LRT).

Our venture required a wide assortment of skills and knowledge. For starters, while we had built a prototype of the device, we needed to refine the technology so that it could be manufactured for prospective users, such as hospitals, ambulance companies, and the military. I had to learn about the patenting process, steps for government approval, components and manufacturing, corporate structures and financing options, and licensing, marketing, and joint ventures. I also had to do a crash course on securities law and corporate structure, and master an array of sophisticated business development skills.

The prospect of all this learning and intellectual fine-tuning was more appealing than daunting. I knew from my brain studies what was possible: Regardless of my grades in school or my I.Q. score, my mind was quite capable of becoming stronger, faster, and capturing more knowledge. Not only could I add to the contents of my mind, but I also could alter the *structure* of my brain so that it worked more efficiently and processed more information.

LESSONS FROM SEATTLE AND BALTIMORE

A compelling source of information about the brain's intellectual capacities comes from two studies that have been under way for the past forty years. The Seattle Longitudinal Study and the Baltimore Longitudinal Study on Aging have been tracking thousands of people throughout their lives, chronicling the changes brought about by aging in their physical, emotional, and mental health. Longitudinal studies are relatively rare because they require a continuous stream of resources to track people year after year. Most scientific and medical studies are cross-sectional or case studies, meaning that they look at different people at the same time. A cross-sectional study on aging might compare a thirty-year-old woman with a seventy-year-old woman to arrive at its conclusions, while a longitudinal study would follow one woman from age thirty to age seventy. As you can imagine, results from longitudinal studies open fascinating windows onto how our bodies and minds change with time.

The Seattle and Baltimore studies have slightly different participants and methods. For example, the Baltimore study did not include women until 1978, and the Seattle study has worked with subgroups of volunteers to train people in order to change their mental aging patterns. Still, the studies share conclusions about how our brains and minds age, and what we can do about it.

Basic to everyone's findings is a belief in the brain's ability to mold or alter its structure—what scientists call its plasticity. An infant's brain has plasticlike qualities, and as the child grows its brain creates new nerve connections and strengthened communication pathways. But the idea that an adult's brain can also do this is relatively new.

For many years, the brain was considered to be hardwired, much like a computer, with its connections and chips molded permanently in place and incapable of alteration. It turns out, however, that the brain is quite capable of expansion well into adulthood. Certain physical and mental activities can noticeably alter the brain. Neurons, the brain's nerve cells, can grow larger, and the connectors between neurons, called synapses, can become stronger and multiply.

Scientists have seen this happen. Researchers at the Salk Institute for Biological Studies in La Jolla, California, put rats in what's called an enriched environment, meaning that they were surrounded by lots of stimulation. The rodents had ample space to run around, and toys and games to play with. Brain studies of rats that had spent time in this environment revealed that the animals had developed 15 percent more brain cells in the regions that control memory and learning. And the mice *acted* smarter, too, running mazes faster and more efficiently.

Results showing that the brain can lay down new wiring also come from a study done by Dr. Michael Merzenich at the University of California at San Francisco. Dr. Merzenich has been working with musicians who suffer from a condition called focal dystonia, which is caused by the brain merging nerve connections so that one neural path controls the muscles of two fingers. A guitar player, for instance, may find that continuous practice makes it impossible for him to move two fingers independently. To help musicians regain control and separate the merged neurons, Dr. Merzenich has been teaching them various muscle exercises.

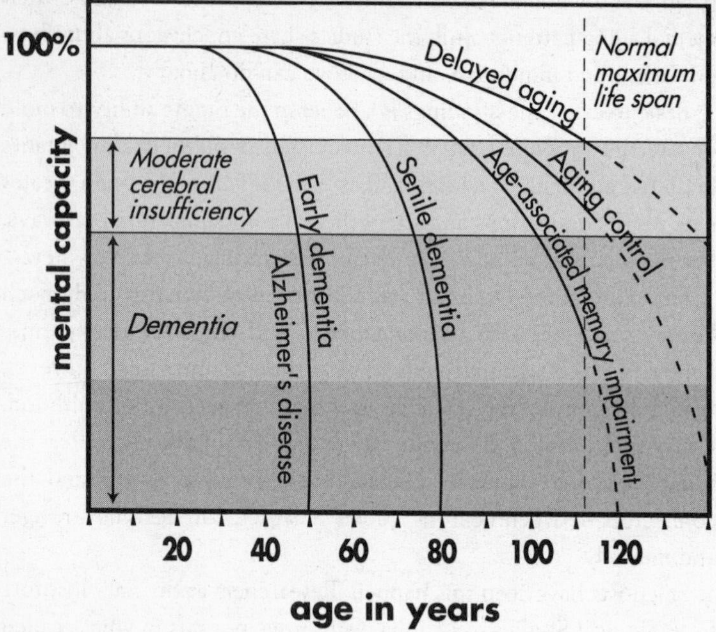

Adapted from *Smart Drugs II* (1993)

In a more startling experiment, Dr. Merzenich taught a monkey to touch a spinning disk with only its three middle fingers. The monkey repeated this action many times, and when Merzenich later examined its brain, he discovered that the area of the cortex responsible for transmitting responses from those fingers had grown.

The scientists conducting the Seattle and Baltimore longitudinal studies have witnessed what happens to people when their brains become stronger—they remember more, can think more quickly and efficiently, and develop a better grasp of elusive concepts. The studies have shown that deliberate, methodical mental training or exercises can make a demonstrable difference in people's lives. They have proved that the adage "use it or lose it" refers as much to the brain as to any other organ.

The Seattle Longitudinal Study

Since 1956, the Seattle study has been watching people aged twenty to ninety, whose numbers now top 5,000. Launched by K. Warner Schaie, who has since become director of the Gerontology Center at Pennsylvania State University, the study has also trained and tested smaller groups of people to see if mental functions could be improved. Dr. Schaie and his wife, Sherry Willis, looked at 229 people over sixty-five years old and found that over a period of about fourteen years, approximately half showed deterioration in two types of thinking. They had lost some inductive reasoning power—that is, their ability to solve problems—and spatial orientation skills—their ability to read a map or piece together objects. Half the group had maintained their thinking skills.

Dr. Schaie and Dr. Willis gave the entire group about five hours of "mental training." This consisted of exercises in learning spatial relationships, solving problems, and honing verbal and memory skills. Then everybody was retested. About half of the group whose thinking had not declined showed marked improvement, but the more stunning results came from the people whose abilities had slipped. A full 40 percent of them regained what they had lost over the fourteen years, and, even more incredible, they retained their revived thinking skills for years to come. Even seven years after the training, follow-up tests showed that they had retained what they had learned.

In examining the huge pool of people in the Seattle study, Dr. Schaie has discovered common elements among those who are the sharpest mentally. Those people who aren't missing a mental beat in their senior years share these qualities:

- Regularly do a variety of activities, such as reading, traveling, attending cultural events, joining professional associations and clubs, pursuing further education
- Open to and quickly able to grasp new ideas

- Flexible and willing to change
- Married to a bright spouse
- Above-average education and income
- Free of chronic diseases
- Satisfied with personal or professional accomplishments

On the other hand, Dr. Schaie found that the attitudes or activities common to people who suffered mental deterioration through the years included strict adherence to a routine and dissatisfaction with life.

The Baltimore Longitudinal Study of Aging (BLSA)

Like the Seattle study, the Baltimore study has been monitoring a large group of people since the mid-1950s. The BLSA, organized and run by the National Institute on Aging, has recruited more than 2,400 people between twenty years old and ninety years old. Every two years or so, participants travel to Baltimore for two days of physical, psychological, and mental function tests. The BLSA gerontologists have developed a wealth of data about how people age, not only physically and emotionally but cognitively (their thought processes), too. Leonard Hayflick, a cell biologist and one of the founders of the National Institute on Aging, summarized the BLSA findings on cognition in his book *How and Why We Age.* Here's what the BLSA has found about our minds and intellects.

- Top mental performance scores were achieved by people in every age group.
- Some people with high scores showed no mental decline at any age.
- There was no relationship between intellectual performance and high blood pressure.
- Vocabulary scores did not change with age.
- Short-term memory declines with age.

- Test scores for logic decline after age seventy only for some people.
- The ability to learn oral material begins to decline in people over age seventy.
- People over age sixty make more mistakes in verbal learning than younger adults.

WHAT'S YOUR INTELLIGENCE PROFILE?

While many people realize that a person's mental abilities and learning cannot be summed up in a single number, standard I.Q. tests—either the Stanford-Binet Intelligence Scale or the Weschler Intelligence Scale for Children—are still the most widely used intelligence measurements in the United States. Intelligence quotient tests have been criticized for all sorts of reasons, such as racial and gender bias. But for me, one of their biggest flaws is that they have little real-life application. They may be useful for predicting academic success, but they cannot predict whether a person will be a good parent, have a successful career, or can even manage a family budget.

While school systems continue to use I.Q. tests, social scientists and neuroscientists have been exploring the kinds of intelligence that play a significant role in the day-to-day life of adults. These are intelligences or mental talents that are not only innate and present in all of us to one degree or another, but that can be strengthened or improved upon. Many intelligence experts have found that the brain's plasticity enables it not only to compensate for damage but also to quicken and strengthen its processing.

The idea that we possess many intelligences has been most thoroughly developed by Howard Gardner, Ph.D., a professor at the Graduate School of Education at Harvard University, in his seminal book, *Frames of Mind.* Dr. Gardner, by applying knowledge of brain development, especially discoveries about the brain's plasticity and neuroanatomy, has identified seven "frames" or types of intelligence. Each intelligence has a neurological root, that is, a discrete region of the brain that directs it. Each of the intelligences is relatively independent and can be molded or combined with others according to the demands of a person's life or culture.

The essence of an intelligence, says Dr. Gardner, is the ability to resolve genuine problems or difficulties and the ability to find or create problems, which becomes the basis for learning.

Dr. Gardner has found that everyone has a distinctive "intellectual profile." We all possess talents and cognitive abilities that predominate or stand out and, even more important, are worthy of continuing development. Although asserting that scientists will never come up with a single list of *all* human intelligences, Dr. Gardner identifies the basic seven:

- Linguistic. This is language ability in both speaking and writing, including grammar, syntax, and vocabulary, and an ease with foreign languages. People with this intelligence are natural writers, poets, public speakers or debaters, lawyers, teachers, or scholars. They have a good verbal memory as well as a good memory for personal experiences.
- Musical. This is the ability to recognize and use pitch, tone, and rhythm. People with this intelligence learn music easily and may play an instrument, sing, compose, or all three. Or they may be devoted listeners to music and sharp at picking out rhythms and tonal patterns.
- Logical-Mathematical. This is the ability to handle long strings of reasoning, to do complicated mental calculations, and to understand and manipulate abstractions. It is unusual for these people to be talented in finance or law. They prefer working with abstractions and solving problems and might be mathematicians or physicists.
- Spatial. This is the ability to recognize and mentally manipulate shapes and to move objects, to create mental images, and to accurately perceive the visual world. Such people might be artists

or sculptors, architects, scientists or inventors, or great chess players.

• Bodily-Kinesthetic. This intelligence is rooted in body movements and encompasses physical coordination, fine reflexes, and skill with moving objects. These people may be accomplished swimmers, dancers, actors, or professional athletes, play a complicated instrument, or work with tools. Although this intelligence may seem to stem from the motor-sensory system, it originates in and depends on perception and the nervous system.

• Interpersonal. These people are smart about other people. They read other people well, naturally sensing moods, motivations, and temperament. They have great empathy, and may be nurses, therapists, social workers, doctors, religious or political leaders.

• Personal. This intelligence is deep self-knowledge. These people are acutely attuned to their own emotions and use this knowledge to understand their behavior. People with this intelligence may be writers, psychologists, or actors.

(Since writing *Frames of Mind,* Gardner has reportedly added an eighth, which he calls naturalistic intelligence, the ability to apply knowledge of the natural world to solving problems. A person with this talent might be a cook or farmer.)

Another expert in the field of intelligence offers a range of mental skills that, he says, are clearly applicable to everyday experiences. Robert Sternberg, a psychologist at Yale University, thinks that intelligence has three components: the internal thought process, application to a person's daily environment, and the application of new learning. Sternberg is a firm believer in intelligence as a practical talent that affects a person's daily work life.

His three types of intelligence surface in people with different practical achievements. The person with a strong internal thought process is analytical. He may do well on standard tests and assessing his abilities and those of others. The second type, who readily applies knowledge to situations, is creative. This person is great at gen-

TAKE ACTION

Pinpoint Your Multiple Intelligence

Take this quiz to see which of your talents and abilities predominate.

1. When listening to sounds outside your window, do you naturally pick out rhythms or notes?
2. Can you easily navigate using a map without turning the map to orient yourself to north?
3. Do you love to dance, and are good at it?
4. Do you easily remember verse you learned in school or snatches of a speech you heard?
5. Do you automatically feel sympathy and rapport with someone who's had a sad experience?
6. Do you find it easy to imagine distances that span light-years and galaxies?
7. Do you like reading philosophy or self-help books that encourage introspection?
8. Would you like to be a psychotherapist?
9. Can you immediately hear when a singer or musician hits a sharp or flat?
10. When listening to people talk, do you automatically hear when their grammar is incorrect?
11. Do you enjoy the complicated process of learning all the steps of a new software program?
12. Do you like to draw, even making realistic doodlings of people and objects?
13. Do you have good hand-eye coordination and like to use it?
14. Do friends often ask you for personal advice and regard you as insightful about people's behavior and emotions?

What your answers suggest: The questions you answered with a strong "yes" suggest you have a particularly strong intelligence. These questions point to these intelligences:

Questions 1 & 9: Musical
Questions 2 & 12: Spatial
Questions 3 & 13: Bodily-Kinesthetic
Questions 4 & 10: Linguistic
Questions 5 & 8: Interpersonal
Questions 6 & 11: Logical-Mathematical
Questions 7 & 14: Personal

erating new ideas and novel approaches to problems. The third type of person is strong psychologically—that is, intuitively reads people and circumstances.

None of these types of intelligence is more or less useful; they're simply different ways of looking at workaday problems. The core talent in each of them, and what distinguishes a gifted person from someone of average intelligence, is insight. What I find most intriguing about this type of insight is that Sternberg believes this key ingredient, insight, can be learned and become an integral part of someone's thinking. These are the three types of insight that can be learned:

- Selective Encoding Insight. Being able to focus on essential information. It's the kind of thinking a lawyer uses to pinpoint key evidence or a detective uses to identify important clues. To apply this insight to problem-solving, you need to recognize and define a problem, assemble accurate information about it, develop a strategy to solve it, apply all available resources to it, and finally track the progress of the solution.
- Selective Combination Insight. Being able to combine facts into a meaningful, larger perspective. It's the kind of thinking a doctor applies to drawing out a diagnosis from many symptoms or how scientists develop theories to test. To apply this insight in

order to come up with a new perspective, you need to question assumptions, take reasonable risks in suggesting new ideas, and allow yourself to make mistakes.

- Selective Comparison Insight. Being able to apply a unique perspective, either seeing known facts in a new way or seeing new facts in a known, accepted way. It's how inventors make discoveries. To apply this insight for daily accomplishments, you need to recognize your consistent strengths and weaknesses, accent your strong skills, and have confidence in your ability.

Medical school was hard for me. I did not do particularly well on tests and found memorization a struggle. I was only mildly reassured that I had made the right decision in going to medical school by a brutally honest riddle: "What do you call someone who graduates number one in the class, and what do you call someone who graduates last in the class?" The answer to both: "Doctor."

As I learned that I was not very good at multiple-choice exams, I also learned that I am pretty good at organization and coordinating and arranging many disparate elements of a large structure, whether it is a complicated treatment plan or an international corporation. While weak in theory and tending to detail, I score high on innovation and application.

As you read about intelligences and ways to beef them up, you may think that the lessons here apply mostly to children. But, while many of the discoveries about intelligence are being made by educators and tested on schoolchildren, we adults are not being overlooked. Research into the aging mind, especially the effects of disease and what's considered normal attrition, is revealing that there is much room in the grown-up brain for developing intelligences.

One busy researcher is Marilyn Albert, a Harvard professor and director of gerontology research at Massachusetts General Hospital. She has examined more than one thousand seniors over age eighty and looked at their capacity to enhance natural intelligence. She says, "Is mental exercise important for the brain? People used to ask me that years ago, and I would say we don't have enough data to say one way or another. I don't say that anymore. I tell them that's what the data look like—use it or lose it."

According to Dr. Albert, there are four key ingredients to staying smart:

- Education
- Strenuous physical activity, which improves blood flow to the brain
- Strong lungs, which helps deliver well-oxygenated blood to the brain
- Feeling a sense of purpose about one's life

A PERSONAL MENTAL AGILITY PROGRAM

Raising your intelligence requires two things: knowledge of what is possible and the drive to acquire and practice mental skills. Knowing about various kinds of intelligence, and the kind of thinking that goes into each, is a useful starting point for considering your own cerebral resources.

As I dove into the job of bringing the cerebral resuscitation device to market, I weighed my intellectual assets and my assortment of mental tools. The job ahead of me would require new learning,

DOT RICHARDSON'S MENTAL TALENT

This talented athlete and orthopedic surgeon excels in mental organization. She told *Sports Illustrated* writer Don Yager that the key to her success is compartmentalization. When she is on the softball field, she does not think about the hospital. And when she is in the hospital, she does not think about baseball. She has that ability to shut off everything except for the business at hand.

scientific and business analysis, a great deal of insight into others, and the ability to adapt to unpredictable developments. When our research team began developing devices for human resuscitation using portable technology that would employ low-temperature biology, many in the medical community thought it was science fiction. Even some experts in emergency and trauma medicine thought we were a bit crazy. But time and again, common sense and a basic scientific principle stuck in our minds: Rapid cooling of the brain is profoundly neuroprotective. Case after case of children falling through ice into frozen waters and then being revived and recovering fully, even after they had been clinically dead for thirty minutes or more, fueled the team's drive.

As we were developing our technology, other researchers were making discoveries in the medical art of suspended-animation surgery that bolstered our efforts. This type of surgery is used with patients who have an aneurysm, which is a bubble on a blood vessel in the brain. This bubble may burst at any time, making it a life-threatening condition. But an aneurysm may be buried deep within the brain and unreachable with conventional techniques. With suspended-animation surgery, a patient's core body temperature is dramatically lowered by removing blood, circulating ice water in the veins, and sometimes even packing the body in ice. The body temperature drops to the point at which there is no heartbeat or brain wave activity. This condition gives the doctor a bloodless, low-pressure environment in which to perform delicate brain surgery. Once the aneurysm is eradicated, the blood is warmed and replaced, and the patient is revived. This surgical innovation, as much as any technology, has helped convince the medical community that brain-cooling devices are a viable approach to saving people in emergencies.

Brain cooling is an example of how my thought processes work in this area of research as a mental skill set. This next section is another example. Sharpening your mental skills is not necessarily a step-by-step process but a total conditioning. Imagine going to a health club or gym equipped with free weights, weight machines, and aerobic

A CONSTANT LEARNER

Dr. Ron Lawrence, a seventy-three-year-old neurologist and founder of the American Medical Athletic Association, makes learning a constant activity. "What I do is learn something new every so often," he says. "Every month or two, I take a challenge. For instance, I have been studying calculus, which I was never very good at. I also have gotten into art—I studied oil painting and now I'm studying pastels. And I subscribe to different publications that keep me on my toes, like the *New York Review of Books.*"

machines like the StairMaster. Although as a beginner you may use the machines according to a predetermined circuit, once you have experience—many of your muscles are already well developed—you pick and choose what you need to work on. Some machines exercise a couple of muscle groups simultaneously, while a set with free weights may tax a single part of your body. So it is with a personal mental agility program.

Assess How You Learn Best

Figuring out how you learn best—how you understand and retain information—requires some reflection and taking a short quiz. Remembering certain classes in medical school, especially anatomy, I know that I learn best by watching or doing. I spent months trying to memorize the illustrations in *Gray's Anatomy,* but it was not until lab classes with a cadaver and seeing the organs, muscles, and blood vessels that my mind started clicking. Conversely, my weakest learning method is reading. I either forget what I read or remember inconsequential details.

I have also found that my long-term memory is stronger than my short-term memory and that I'm good at remembering faces and strings of numbers. Part of the potential marketing of the Brain Cooling Device required numerous presentations to groups that might provide financing and groups that might use the device, such as the Department of Defense. In these presentations, I did best explaining background and complicated figuring, and relating to individuals.

To define your learning style, first recall successful school experiences. Ask yourself which classes or subjects you did well in *and* enjoyed or found easy. As you know, it is possible to do well in a subject you find difficult by working very hard. For instance, I did well in organic chemistry, but it was a struggle and I devoted twice as much time to it as I did to other subjects.

Next ask yourself *why* you did well:

Because you found the material easy to understand?
Because the teacher explained everything well?
Because the teacher demonstrated concepts?
Because the teacher used a lot of visual or auditory props to explain things?
Because you were very motivated to do well and worked extra diligently?
Because you liked doing the homework and required reading?
Because you are good at the particular type of test given in the class?
Because the class included a lot of lab work?
Because you enjoyed debating the subject with other students?

The point of these questions is to find out which style of learning predominates in your mind. There are four styles, and while you use all of them at one time or another, or sometimes combine styles, you tend to prefer one of them as you absorb new information. Here they are.

- Auditory learning. You learn by listening to people talk, whether it's a lecture, on television, or from the radio. It's not that your hearing is supersensitive but that you seem to retain whatever comes through your ears, seemingly without effort. You can be sitting in a meeting doodling while you are listening and afterward remember everything that was said. If you're this kind of learner, you can't take in new information with the television or radio going in the background—too much distraction.

- Hands-on learning. You learn by doing. Elaborate explanations may go over your head, but once you actually duplicate the physical motions required in a process or construction of something, it's locked into your mind. This duplicating action may require copying mathematical figuring someone has done, actually clicking through the steps in a software program to know how to use it, or playing a sport you're trying to learn instead of listening to an instructor. If you are this kind of learner, you like to understand the *why* behind things and keep trying things. Another term for this kind of learning is "procedural," meaning that you want to know the process or inner workings of whatever you are learning about.
- Verbal learning. If you learn this way, you take in information primarily by reading. This kind of learning is also called declarative—that is, it involves absorbing many facts. You think in sentences and your learning is sometimes sharpened if you restate, explain aloud, or write down something you have read.
- Visual learning. If this is your style, you like to *see* information. Demonstrations, firsthand experiences, movies, and pictures all provide grist for this learning style. This learning is especially lasting if it's delivered in color and with another sensual association, such as a distinctive smell, or with an emotional connection. What is acquired in this type of learning is often big-picture impressions as opposed to detailed renderings of a subject.

When you learn well, you remember. But your memory, like your learning, has long suits and short suits. If you want to sharpen just your memory, take a look at Chapter Two. In the present context, with memory as an adjunct to learning, it is useful to understand that you tend to favor a particular type of memory. The main categories of memory are:

- Numbers and data
- Words
- Proper nouns, such as names and places
- General information and concepts

Go through the same process with memory that you did with learning. Recall what has stayed in your mind and use memory cues to jar what you have forgotten in order to pinpoint what your memory grabs first and keeps longest. Once you have identified your predominant learning style and memory ability, you know the kind of situation to seek out or construct for peak learning.

One last piece of advice to enhance your learning: Assume the right frame of mind. Prime yourself to learn by controlling physiological distractions. Put another way, do not let your body's reaction to stress or pressure affect what your mind is doing. Use deep breathing (Chapter Four explains this technique) to suppress distracting hormonal action. Relax large muscle groups—head, neck, back, abdomen—to improve concentration. Make yourself physically comfortable in your surroundings and clothing so that you are not interrupted by annoyances.

Finally, keep your mind flexible and confident. Very little in this world is rocket science. You can master almost anything you put your mind to. Often, insecurities and doubts have no more substance than your imaginings. Shrug them off. Believe that you can step up to the task.

Assess Your Thought Process

There are a number of ways people think when confronted with new facts and ideas, new projects, and new people. How you analyze something in order to make a decision or solve a problem depends on how you process information. Young people, with a smaller database, so to speak, and fast-charging synapses, tend to be more impulsive and instinctive than adults in making decisions. Adults have more experience that they can apply to their judgments, but, as with learning, there are various ways they can consider new information and a new situation. Dr. Edward de Bono, a British educator who has written extensively on thinking and creativity, says that there are six ways of thinking:

Objectively: focusing mainly on facts, statistics, and hard information, which form the foundation for any decision or proposed solution. With this kind of thinking, you avoid making assumptions or judging something too early. You try to let the information speak for itself.

Critically: looking at a situation or problem for possible drawbacks, unwanted consequences, and trouble spots. This kind of thinking could be called "What's the downside?" It's a negative way of evaluating things.

Positively: looking at all the benefits, solutions, and new possibilities a situation or problem may provide. This kind of thinking could be called "What's the upside?" With this thinking, everything has a plus side, a silver lining.

Creatively: applying novel or unusual remedies to a situation or problem. This type of thinking is always generating new ideas. To prod this kind of thinking, de Bono uses exaggeration, reversals and opposites, and random words and word association.

Intuitively: reacting mainly according to emotions or instinct. A person thinking this way responds to a situation with his or her feelings.

Self-monitoring: examining the way you think about a problem to identify any biases or flawed assumptions. With this type of thinking, you first consider *how* you think before deciding which of the other thinking styles to apply.

I tend to be a combined objective-plus-creative thinker. I like to collect facts and hold off making any conclusions until I have a ton of information. While I am doing this, I also like to mull over far-out, even esoteric ideas about the situation. Once my company had

TAKE ACTION

Develop Your Thinking Skills

Use this exercise to develop thinking styles. For each circumstance described below, write out a way to think about it according to each of the styles.

Problem: You have just had your annual job performance evaluation and learned that your boss does not think you are productive enough. You have six months to convince her that you are. How do you do this?

Decision to make: Your teenager wants to earn and save enough money to buy a car. He has asked for a bigger allowance and help in making money. What do you do?

Tricky situation: Your neighbor's dog, which is kept in an area near your bedroom, wakes you up many nights with its barking. You've talked to your neighbor about it, but he swears that he's a light sleeper and has never heard his dog bark, and so refuses to do anything. What do you do?

a prototype for the Brain Cooling Device, I had to come up with ways to get the word out about it. I had enough information to know that medical schools, medical organizations, professional associations, and medical companies were potential users. As I was thinking about these people, I imagined myself with the device on my head. Where would I be? In a highway accident? On a back street in Bosnia? Beside a frozen lake I had fallen into? I turned my thinking to the people who would be saved by this device, and that opened a door to a whole new group of prospective supporters, endorsers, and medical researchers.

Capture New Information

With most of the thinking styles, you need to know something about the problem or decision at hand in order to consider it. You can't think positively without some information and you can't react with your emotions unless you have something to go on. So, capturing information is essential to perking up your intelligence and sharpening your thinking. It's this ability to find and master information that makes a person not only seem smart but actually function as an exceedingly bright person. There's no magic to this, but like the successful magician, you need to draw from a grab bag of gadgets. I always begin with the basics: lots of reading, selective comprehension, enhanced vocabulary, quick calculations, and sharpened listening. Then I add the stimulation of creativity.

Lots of Reading Before you skip over this, muttering to yourself that you already have too much paper to wade through, take a peek at my desk. It has almost no paper on it, and I go through dozens of journals, newspapers, and books every week. The secret to being able to read large amounts of material is learning how to scan and mentally compartmentalize the information.

What I mean by scanning is precisely what the dictionary says it means: "to look over quickly and systematically." The "quickly" part means that you do not read every word that is printed. When you are reading for information, not for enjoyment, you need to cherry-pick. Pick out only the "best" words—those that carry the most meaning—in the sentence or paragraph. At times, you can skip over sentences, particularly those that restate information, offer examples, cite sources, or serve as transitions to another point. Words like "for instance," "namely," "according to," "in summary," and "in fact" are all flags for material you can skip if you've got the main point. And do not read aloud or even say the words in your mind. Instead of getting bogged down by individual words, think of chunks of facts or ideas and read words in blocks.

The "systematically" part means that you always look in certain spots for key sentences or nuggets of information. Generally, a piece of writing is organized one of three ways: as a pyramid, with facts and arguments building to a main point; as an inverted pyramid, with a main point followed by supporting facts and arguments; and as a string of pearls, a series of ideas or facts connected by a single string or theme. Each paragraph of the writing is usually built around a central point, which is stated in either the first or the last sentence. If the paragraph has a heading, that highlights the thesis. Look for the topic sentence, or even the topic phrase, that is the heart of the paragraph. When I want to plow through a lot of material, I will limit my reading to an article's headlines, the first sentence of the main paragraphs, photo captions, and the last paragraph.

To practice your scanning skills, go through a stack of material (if you don't have a ready pile, use a couple of magazines) and read each article or piece of writing just once. Don't backtrack if you're fuzzy on a paragraph's main point—it will probably be stated a number of times and a number of ways. With a pen in hand, underline or circle the key ideas or topic sentences. When you finish reading each piece, state aloud or write out in no more than a paragraph the main points. Do this with three to five articles, depending on their length. Spend no more than half an hour on this. Put the material aside for a day, then return to the articles you read, and this time read the old way. Don't scan but go word by word. When you finish each article, compare your impression of the main point with what you gleaned from the earlier reading. I think you will find that they are pretty close, but that your second reading takes twice as long.

To categorize information, you physically organize each piece of reading. Create a simple system for organizing all that you have to go through—discrete piles or file folders will do the job. You can organize information according to subject matter, according to relative importance for you, or according to how much follow-up activity, if any, it demands.

Selective Comprehension For a better understanding of what you read, learn to ask questions. Virtually every piece of writing does two things: conveys information and expresses an author's opinions, feelings, or attitudes. There is no such thing as purely objective writing. Even the driest rendition of statistics is made subjective by what the author has chosen to include or not include. Reading comprehension is usually gummed up not by the informational content of a piece, but by the author's individual, sometimes personal, reasons for writing the piece in the first place. When you have a strong sense of the author's agenda, whether it is to promote a point of view, share new insights, or educate, you've grasped the secret of comprehension. As you read, ask yourself these questions:

What information is the author trying to convey?

What ideas is the author trying to convey?

What does the author think of this information: approve, disapprove, unsure?

What writing tricks does the author use to put forth the information and demonstrate self-expression: exaggeration, generalizations, emotional appeals, data from unreliable or outdated sources, anecdotes, use of secondhand sources, convoluted or faulty arguments?

Is the piece balanced or one-sided? If skewed, which side does it favor? Why is the author doing this?

Enhanced Vocabulary Building your vocabulary should be a lifetime habit, as regular as brushing your teeth. No one is so smart or learned that he does not need to constantly add to his personal dictionary of words. I think the mistake many people make in enhancing their vocabulary, and the reason they do not hang with it, is that they collect too many words they have little use for. When you are assembling a working vocabulary, the words stick with you. This is why young children easily learn about ten new words a day and eventually can accumulate a vocabulary of 100,000 words.

To construct your growing, working vocabulary, try these suggestions:

- Limit yourself to one new word a day. When you encounter it, jot it down anywhere. On the flap of a used envelope, the edge of a dollar bill, in the margin of a magazine. You do not have to keep this piece of paper, but writing it down will help cement it in your mind.

• Collect words related to your immediate world. For instance, words related to cooking, food, clothing, the weather, the names of everyday objects, adjectives describing people you regularly encounter, verbs or adverbs for actions you do or often see.

• Use association to remember words. You'll remember a word better if you immediately associate it with an experience or emotion. Use it in a conversation. Make up a rhyme or sing about it. Eat a distinctive food or inhale a strong smell as you are learning the word.

• Buy an unabridged thesaurus. Roget's is the best known but there are other good ones out there. This is going to be a source for many of your new words. Most people tend to recycle the same old words—I've heard experts say that we all have about a two-hundred-word working vocabulary and we simply keep stirring them around. When you hear yourself repeatedly using the same word, look in the thesaurus for an alternative you did not know.

• Buy a good dictionary (larger than pocket size; unabridged is the best) not only to look up the exact definition but also for the pronunciation guide so you can say the word aloud. This also helps seal it in your memory.

• At the end of each week, try to recall the words you have looked up and written down. If you cannot remember them, get a small spiral notebook and use it to log your growing vocabulary.

Quick Calculations Number phobia is a widespread disease. Most people's eyes glaze over when they see numbers, particularly if they are being asked to multiply, divide, or do elaborate addition or subtraction. Hand calculators, which people now use for simple figuring, have increased math aversion. I confess that numbers are not my best friends, either, but I have learned not to avoid them. Some people even think I am good with numbers because of a couple of shorthand mental calculations I have mastered. Here is how I make numbers more manageable.

- I always try to round numbers to units of ten, especially when multiplying. Tens are easy to handle. For example, 15 × 19 may look difficult. But 15 × 20 (or 15 × 10, twice) then minus 15, is an easy sum. At times, I may not get the exact total, but I'm close enough, and I don't get hung up on pinpoint accuracy. If I am balancing a corporate statement or deciding whether I have enough cash on hand to buy a tank of gas, for example, getting within a few dollars of the total is good enough for me.
- Whenever possible, I think in terms of percentages, especially when dividing. I convert fractions into the nearest simple percentage, which I find easier to understand. So when I see 3/16, I transform it to a quarter or 25 percent. A steak price that dropped 11/16, in my mind slipped three-quarters of a point.
- I break down large numbers into manageable sizes when trying to remember figures. As you probably know, there is a reason telephone numbers are seven digits. Your working memory can hold a maximum of seven units—any more and something is erased or forgotten. Putting large numbers, like phone numbers plus area codes or many measurements for home repair jobs, into smaller packages helps keep them in your active memory. This is a bunching technique.

To get comfortable with numbers, do calculations in your head when it doesn't matter. For instance, at a store checkout counter, keep a running total in your head as the clerk adds up the items. As you are pumping gas, just watch the gallon number and try to total up the dollar amount. Do these painless exercises enough times, and your addition will come pretty close to what shows on the register.

Better Listening Did you know that you are twice as likely to remember something you heard than something you read? (I think I read that.) And if you train yourself to be a sharp listener, you will pick up all sorts of information and ideas. The key to listening well is quite simple: It's paying attention. It's actually hearing what is being said and not listening with one ear as you think about something else. To do this, you must first eliminate the distracting noise that surrounds the delivery. Ignore the way the information is spoken.

Don't get sidetracked by any verbal tics, gestures, facial expressions, or body language. Listen only to the content.

As you are listening, open your mind to absorb what is being said. Do not be thinking about how you are going to respond or framing a question or whether you agree or disagree with what's being said. Interrupt only if you are totally confused and then only to ask a single question. Do not string together multiple questions—that makes the speaker say what you want to hear instead of what he wanted to say. Listen for verbal clues to unspoken messages, such as repeated words or phrases, or changes in tone of voice.

Don't jump to conclusions or automatically assume that you know what is going to be said. Listen to the entire delivery before deciding what point(s) is being made. As you do that, evaluate the speaker as a reliable source of information. How knowledgeable is this person? What is the source of his information? Does he use facts or emotions to persuade?

Puzzle Art Checkerboard

Stimulate Creativity I frequently visit Bali and find it to be one of the most artistically creative places on earth. Its culture is rich and lush, and its people, from farmer to fisherman, have a natural sense of artistry. Unfortunately, such widespread beauty and creativity are rarely seen in the West, which has lost much of its artistic innocence to its stress-filled civilization. While Bali's education system rewards innovative creativity, standardized art training, particularly when I was studying, drums this quality out of students.

American-born artist Allison Berman has learned and perfected Indonesian art techniques and uses them as inspiration for developing personal creativity. She has created a series of abstract movable pieces that she calls Puzzle Art. With these pieces, like the checkerboard illustration on the facing page, you change and create your own art. The checkerboard pattern is a current image in Balinese society. It symbolizes the balance that must be maintained between good and evil, and the dynamic equilibrium between our spiritual and animal natures. The four corners represent the four corners of the world, thus symbolizing the totality of existence.

In the checkerboard, one image is the negative of the other. With your eyes closed, convert the positive into negative, and then shift back and forth, holding each image for thirty seconds. Next, imagine the checkerboards as three-dimensional cubes, spheres, and pyramids. Juggle these three objects, shifting from positive to negative every few seconds. Metamorphose one shape into the other and improvise by inventing new shapes to add to the mix.

The nice thing about Puzzle Art is that there is no right or wrong answer and so no compulsion to achieve. When I do this imagination exercise, I think of Picasso's famous words: "I used to draw like Raphael, but it has taken me a whole lifetime to learn to draw like a child."

Cement Your Sharpened Intelligence

Experts say that people retain only about a third of the knowledge they are exposed to. I suspect that people with high functional intelligences probably hold on to more. This is where the "use it or lose it" philosophy makes a noticeable difference. There is a growing body of evidence in the scientific and medical literature showing that "brain exercise" improves a person's learning ability, memory, and mental quickness. (And, as I discuss in Chapter Five, mental exercise also wards off disease.) Declares Arnold Scheibel, director of the UCLA Brain Research Institute, "Anything that's intellectually challenging can probably serve as a kind of stimulus for dendritic growth, which means it adds to the computational reserves in your brain."

There are two kinds of learning you can stimulate with intellectual exercise. Declarative or factual learning is soaking up details about people, events, and things, and procedural learning entails the motor and perceptual skills used in activities like playing sports or a musical instrument. Declarative learning originates in the brain's hippocampus, which is also headquarters for memory and a key player in a person's emotional wiring. Scientists suspect that this intertwining of learning, memory, and emotion explains why people learn better when they have strong feelings.

You also learn better when your brain is firing on all cylinders, meaning that the nerve connections are well developed in all areas. While it is a myth that people only use 10 percent of their brain (a glimpse at a PET scan of a thinking brain dispels that notion), a person's early learning does favor certain regions. To cultivate neural connections and receptors that are underused, look for opportunities to tackle unfamiliar tasks and ways of thinking.

Here are some exercises that can stimulate areas of the brain you may not normally use. You will find that gradually these activities become easier and your thinking more fluid. As a result, when you are presented with a problem or situation you have not encountered before, you will have more mental muscle to put behind it.

- Modify habits. Wear your watch upside down and on the other wrist.
- Develop other-handedness. Use your other hand to do rote tasks such as brushing your teeth or jotting down notes or numbers.
- Tap into alternative sources of learning. If you gather information mostly by reading, explore books on tape. If the television is where you get most of your news, tap into on-line news.
- Expand your reading universe. Most people stay with a certain type of reading material, usually light fiction and popular periodicals. Pick up a copy of *Scientific American* or *Forbes* to read about something completely foreign to you.
- Play word games. Do crossword puzzles or compete with someone to see who can think of the most names in a particular category (e.g., four-legged animals, edible fruits) within a fixed time.
- Memorize a poem. Start with something short and gradually master longer ones.
- Practice your spatial skills. Buy a Rubik's cube and work on it. Instead of doodling, try sketching real-life, three-dimensional objects.
- Get a topographical map of an area you know. As you study the contours of the land, mentally picture them as they are in nature.
- Learn about a musical instrument you know very little about, for example, the recorder, harpsichord, clarinet, or drums. Listen to music that features this instrument so that you can easily identify its sound.
- Listen to a new kind of music, for example, opera, Gregorian chants, or blues.
- Don't use a calculator or computer software program to balance your checkbook. Do the math by hand.
- Watch a television movie with the sound off and try to figure out the personalities of the characters by watching their actions.

- In front of a mirror, practice facial expressions, for example, suspicion or contentment or surprise.
- Reconstruct a conversation that took place at least twenty-four hours earlier. Jot down who said what. Test yourself by asking whoever else was involved about his or her recollections of the conversation.
- Keep a dream diary (see Chapter Three for details) and think about the emotions and psychological underpinnings they stir up.
- Practice reading upside down. Start with a paragraph in a newspaper, see how long it takes you, and gradually add paragraphs as you become more adept.
- As you are drifting off to sleep, pick a year from your past and try to remember as many events from it as possible.
- Keep lists. Use a small pocket notebook to record, for instance, a food log as part of a weight-watching program or purchases you make to manage a budget.
- Whenever you have a hunch about something, write it down in order to test and develop your power of intuition.
- Expand your verbal patterns by arranging unusual sentences and phrases with magnetic word pieces (available in gift shops and stationery stores.)

MORE REPS FOR A MENTAL PLAN

Fitness guru and promoter Jake Steinfeld uses his daily exercise routine to organize and prioritize his thinking. "While I'm training and counting reps, for every repetition I set another goal for the day. So when my workout is complete, I have already visualized what I have to do that day and have already accomplished it in my mind. This keeps me not only physically fit but mentally fit and way ahead of the day, and ahead of the game."

Exercise to Pump Up Learning

Physical exercise is to your brain like octane to an engine—it revs, it pumps, it makes it hum. Aerobic conditioning, vigorous exercise that requires lots of oxygen, feeds various parts of the brain, especially the basal ganglia, cerebellum, and corpus callosum. With more oxygen comes more blood, and this heightens your ability to understand and retain new information.

Activities that demand physical coordination help energize neural growth. Studies with rats have shown this dramatically. Dr. William T. Greenough has been closely watching what exercise, as well as environment, can do to a brain. In one experiment, he divided rats into four groups and four levels of exercise. The heavily exercised rats scurried around elaborate constructions of ropes and bridges. When their brains were later examined, they had more capillaries around the neurons than the control groups—that is, their brains were getting more blood and fuel.

At the Institute for Brain, Aging and Dementia at the University of California, Irvine, rats were also put through various exercise routines. Dr. Carl Cottman discovered that both the rats doing moderate running around wheels in their cages and those treading virtually all night had richer nutrients in their brains. They had higher levels of growth factors, or neurotrophins, circulating.

Although human brains are a little trickier to study, researchers have seen proof that exercise improves mental function in people. Roberta Rikli at the Lifespan Wellness Clinic at California State University in Fullerton put thirty-one women aged fifty-seven to eighty-five on an exercise program to see if they could regain mental reaction time they had lost with age. Three times a week, the women in one group either did aerobics or walking. After three years, she measured their response time and found that the mental reactions in the second group, which did no exercise, not only did not improve but declined. The liveliest group, those who did aerobics, produced a definite improvement.

Different exercises stimulate different regions and neurological functions, so here is an assortment of activities to spread around the excitement.

- Practice handstands or floating upside down when you are in a pool.
- Take up or practice an activity that requires coordination, such as a racket sport, basketball, baseball, or ballroom dancing.
- Next time a small gadget is broken (like a clock radio or a lock) take it apart to see how it works and try to fix it or identify the broken part. Consider working toward an advanced version of this exercise—doing simple servicing on your car, such as changing oil and filters.
- Learn to juggle, beginning with just three objects, or learn to tie complicated nautical knots.
- Learn basic stretching exercises, especially for those muscle groups that you do not move much, like the toes, lower back, and neck.
- "Spin your brain" and stimulate more neural activity by doing tumbling or cartwheels or spinning your body around on one foot.
- Revive your jump-roping skills.
- Extend the amount of time you can stay underwater without breathing. Diving from the edge of the pool, swim underwater as far as you can until you need air. Do this regularly, each time going a little farther and a little longer.
- Walk backward for two blocks (don't forget to look for traffic before crossing the street) and gradually lengthen the distance you can go.

ONE MAN'S BRAIN FOOD

Neurologist Ron Lawrence believes in brain food. Knowing that the brain functions on sugar, he fills his menu with complex carbohydrates, up to six small meals a day.

- Try meditation. Sit quietly with your eyes closed, mind focused on a single sound or thought, and breathe deeply.

A Cognitive Cocktail

In times of extended mental stress such as a monthlong business project, I fortify my cognitive muscle with an assortment of supplements, which I take daily. My "cognitive cocktail" contains acetyl-l-carnitine (ALC), a natural compound that improves the energy exchange between cells and strengthens cellular communication between the brain's right and left hemispheres. ALC has been tested in a number of studies with older people showing signs of mental decline, and noticeably sharpened their thinking skills. For instance, in an experiment in Italy involving almost five hundred patients in geriatric and neurologic hospital units, ALC was given for 150 days alongside a placebo. At the end of the study, the patients receiving ALC showed "significant increases" in scores of mental function tests, and their improvements persisted even after they stopped taking the drug. Those patients who received placebos showed no significant improvement. ALC is currently being tested in clinical trials as a cognitive enhancer for Alzheimer's.

Caffeine is in my cocktail because of its stimulating effects—it's the best nonprescription "upper" available. Vitamin B complex helps me guard against nutritional deficiencies that may slow my thinking. For instance, a good supply of folic acid helps blood circulation in

DR. BOB'S COGNITIVE COCKTAIL

Acetyl-l-carnitine: 500 mg
Caffeine: 200 mg
Vitamin B complex: 100 mg
Pregnenolone: 50 mg
Green tea: 1 cup
Glucose powder: 1 tablespoon

A BRIEF REFRESHER

Everyone, regardless of age or education, can improve his or her intelligence. Each of us has natural mental talents—distinctive types of intelligences, insight, learning styles, and ways of thinking—that we can hone. To sharpen how quickly and efficiently you think, you need to constantly acquire new information and practice mental skills. Here's how.

Assess your learning strengths.

Assess your thinking strengths.

Capture new material. Read, master selective comprehension, enhance your vocabulary, do quick calculations, listen better, and stimulate creativity.

Do regular mental exercises. Memorize, get out of mental ruts by changing daily habits, learn new music, and keep lists.

Do regular physical exercises to stimulate the brain. Try jumping rope, stretching, or meditating accompanied by deep breathing techniques.

the brain, and a healthy dose of B_{12} guards against memory impairment. Another cocktail ingredient is pregnenolone, which is a steroid hormone precursor; the body uses it to make DHEA and other hormones. Scientists have called pregnenolone a "smart drug" because it appears to improve a person's memory and has no toxic side effects. All this is washed down with a cup of green tea, which is full of antioxidants, sweetened with pure glucose powder, which the body slowly breaks down for brain food.

SELECTED SOURCES

Bower, B. "Enriched mice show adult neuron boost." *Science News,* 151, 206, April 5, 1997.

Brink, S. "Smart moves: new research suggests that folks from 8 to 80 can shape up their brains with aerobic exercise." *U.S. News and World Report,* 118 (19), 76–82, May 15, 1995.

Brody, J. "Good habits outweigh genes as key to healthy old age." *New York Times,* February 28, 1996.

Dana Alliance for Brain Initiatives. *Delivering Results: A Progress Report on Brain Research, Update 1996.* The Dana Press, New York, May 1996.

Dean, W., et al. *Smart Drugs II: The Next Generation.* Health Freedom Publications, Menlo Park, California, 1993.

Gardner, H. *Frames of Mind.* Basic Books, New York, 1985.

Golden, D. "Building a better brain." *Life,* 63–69, July 1994.

Hayflick, L. *How and Why We Age.* Ballantine Books, New York, 1996.

Hultsch, D. F., et al. "Age differences in cognitive performance in later life: relationships to self-reported health and activity life style." *Journal of Gerontology,* 48 (1), P1–11, 1993.

Kotulak, R. *Inside the Brain: Revolutionary Discoveries of How the Mind Works.* Andrews and McMeel, Kansas City, Mo., 1996.

Langreth, R. "Scientists find first strong evidence mental stimulation produces brain cells." *Wall Street Journal,* April 3, 1997.

Levy, A., et al. "Aging, stress and cognitive function." *Annals of the New York Academy of Sciences,* 717, 79–88, June 30, 1994.

Salvioli, G., and Neri, M. "L-acetylcarnitine treatment of mental decline in the elderly." *Drugs Under Experimental and Clinical Research,* 20 (4), 169–76, 1994.

Schaie, K., et al. "Perceived intellectual performance change over seven years." *Journal of Gerontology,* 49 (3), 108–19, May 1994.

Siegel, J. "Educating for understanding." *Phi Delta Kappan,* 75 (7), 563–67, March 1994.

Trotter, R. J. "Three heads are better than one—triarchic theory of intelligence developed by Robert J. Sternberg." *Psychology Today,* 20, 56–63, August 1986.

Williams, P., and Lord, S. R. "Effects of group exercise on cognitive functioning and mood in older women." *Australian and New Zealand Journal of Public Health,* 21 (1), 45–52, February 1997.

Young, S., and Concar, D. "These cells were made for learning." *New Scientist,* 136 (1848), S2–9, November 21, 1992.

Two

DETAIL POWER

IMPROVING RECALL AND FIGHTING MEMORY LOSS

I suspect that many readers may turn to this chapter first. I hear more complaints about poor memory than about any other mental function. It's not just older people who are worried that misplacing their glasses or forgetting a birthday means that their memory is going. Even baby boomers and a few Gen X'ers have cornered me about the meaning of their inability to remember someone's name or their "tip-of-the-tongue" memory lapses. So, before you start reading, take this quick test of your power of recall:

> "A man from New York was driving his car on the way to a family dinner, and got on the interstate at exit 23 and got off at exit 39. At this exit, there was a roadblock and the man had to wait for construction workers to remove the barricades. Impatient to move on, he took a side road. Still, he arrived late for the family dinner."

Immediately after reading this story, repeat it aloud without looking at the written text and jot down details. Repeat it again to yourself in fifteen minutes without looking at the text and jot down what you remember. Give yourself one point if you note any of the following details.

1. New York
2. interstate
3. exit 23
4. exit 39
5. barricades
6. construction worker
7. side road
8. late for family dinner

Scoring: In your first recall, remembering five to eight of these details signals a normal memory. In the second, remembering only one or two fewer than in the first recall indicates a normal memory.

A MEMORY ACID TEST

I look forward to my high school reunions not only because I enjoyed my four years at Far Rockaway High School in Queens, New York, but equally important, because they give me a reality check on how I am aging and how my memory is holding up. Over the course of six hours, I get a snapshot of my younger self, see what time has done to my recall of faces and events, and glimpse how lifestyles have helped or hurt people's thinking.

Many people are acutely aware of their minds becoming slower and more forgetful with the years. It's not all in their imagination. Beginning around age forty, our brains react a little slower and with less exactness. In standard tests pitting the middle-aged mind against a young mind, youth generally wins. Middle-aged people asked to sit at a computer terminal and count how many red dots were flashed on the screen or to trace a complicated pattern reflected in a mirror could not match the scores of twenty-year-olds.

Yet, while our reaction times slow with the march of time, other types of mental reaction and retention hold firm. And a few skills actually improve. There is much you can do to strengthen and improve your memory.

RECOGNIZING OLD FRIENDS, RELIVING GOOD TIMES

People worry a lot about losing their memory, and for good reason. A faulty memory can make daily life frustrating and unpleasant: Losing items, forgetting names and important numbers, or not being able to recall how to do something can turn everyday activities into monumental chores. Even worse, a spotty memory can rob you of cherished, satisfying experiences. Losing the ability to recall events and people in your past can alter your personality, erasing from it a rich, textured layer of images and emotions.

While concerns about memory are understandable, they need to be balanced by the good news. Our preoccupation with deteriorat-

TAKE ACTION

Write It Down

Simply writing something down forces you to pay attention to a fact or detail. The physical process of handwriting activates an area of the brain you are not using at the time. Scientists call this encoding. In writing something down, you create the equivalent of three copies of an item to remember. You have the initial thought, the act of writing it down, and the review as you write it. This is why keeping a daily journal increases your memory stores by volumes.

ing memory has prompted scientists to find ways to improve it. Memory research has exploded in recent years into many enticing methods for enhancing it: pharmaceuticals, foods, vitamins, training, and exercises. Here are some recent findings, with more details later.

- "Brain networks can always be fine-tuned," says Dr. Charles Stevens of the Salk Institute. The strength and sharpness of your memory are affected most by factors you can control—education and intellectual activity. Researchers have found that people who are kept mentally active through constant learning and activities that stimulate their memories and knowledge have strong, sound memories. Regularly using information creates stronger connections between brain cells and permanently improves neural communication.

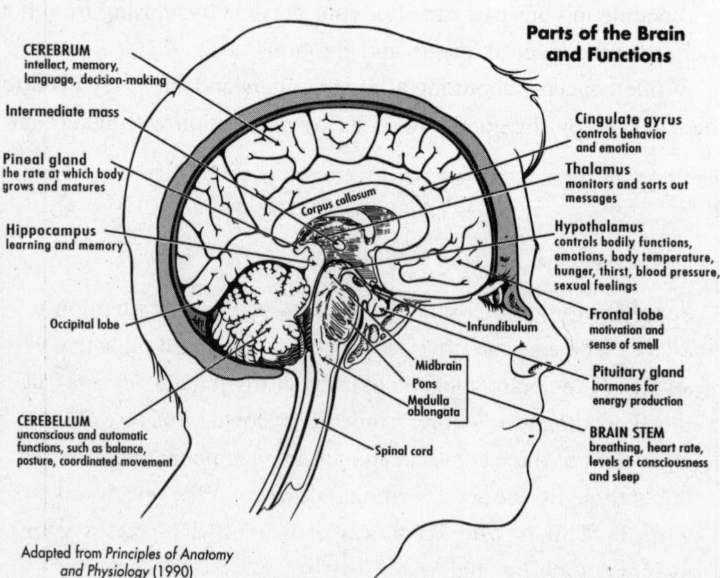

Adapted from *Principles of Anatomy and Physiology* (1990)

- Women have the edge, and they usually outscore men on all kinds of memory tests.
- Memory has a secret ingredient, best defined by the English writer Samuel Johnson. "The true art of memory is the art of attention," he said.
- Various B vitamins can have a significant impact on memory.
- Certain types of mental exercise are excellent protectors against memory loss.
- "Memory pills," which belong to a new class of pharmaceuticals, have been widely and successfully used in Europe and are now available worldwide.
- Particular foods—"smart foods"—enhance learning.

KINDS OF MEMORY

At my last reunion, I remember bumping into my locker buddy, Arthur. Since our last names were close alphabetically, our lockers were always next to each other. He gave me a hearty greeting, then rattled off a string of numbers. My expression must have been one of total perplexity because he quickly explained. "Don't you remember? That was your locker combination—you were *always* forgetting it. Good thing you had me around!" I roared with delight: He could win a TV quiz show with his long-term memory!

To improve your memory, consider which of your various memories needs the most attention. "Working memory" is how your brain translates sensory signals from what you see, hear, feel, smell, or taste into a single impression. For instance, if you smell something salty and tomato-like and then see a hot chafing dish of round, brown lumps, your brain immediately makes a connection between what you smell and what you see. This connection is working memory. It's the brain's ability to mesh together sensory clues and hold them from moment to moment. While working memory is the process the mind goes through, the thought or image it creates is short-term memory.

Working memory stores the impression of the tomato and salt smell and the bubbling, brown sight in the short-term memory bank, then taps into your long-term memory to see if this odor and sight are familiar. If so, it reports that you are smelling and seeing meatballs.

To remember a piece of information—to move it from short-term memory to long-term memory—you need to focus on it for at least eight seconds; otherwise it will evaporate. Working memory and short-term memory are like a pencil and scratch pad. Working memory jots down what you are doing from moment to moment. But since the scratch pad (short-term memory) can hold only about seven items at a time, you are constantly writing over and forgetting items you noted earlier. Exactly what ends up in long-term storage depends on how you have organized and processed the information. Repetition of and thinking about a piece of information, paying attention—what scientists call rehearsal—help send it to the long-term storage bank.

Your long-term memory bank has an assortment of deposits. There is semantic memory, which is individual facts; episodic memory, which is experiences and events; and procedural memory, which is behaviors, habits, and rote activities.

Like a pinball machine ringing with bells and lights, your memory bounces off a number of corners in the brain and triggers a chemical and electrical chain reaction. What sets off your short-term memory, scientists believe, is an electrical impulse. On the other hand, your long-term memory kicks in either because of new connections that have grown between brain cells or as the result of a chemical event involving peptides.

Of course, memories are formed every day of our lives, through conversations and experiences. While there is no way to stop the seepage of stuff into our long-term memory, we can contribute to the flow through deliberate learning. By setting out to learn something, you build memories. Educators say that learning is either declarative (also called factual or associative) or procedural. Declarative learning absorbs details about people, places, things, and events. It is highly associative, meaning that you automatically link details, which then stay together in your mind. The other type of learning, procedural, involves the perceptual and motor skills used in acquiring the knowledge of how to do things. It's activities like knowing how to dance.

Researchers have found that the chemistry of the brain changes during declarative learning, and they call this change long-term potentiation (LTP). In laboratory tests, brain cells that have been artificially stimulated react chemically with each other and appear to "remember" that stimulation, so that they continue to communicate even after the stimulus is diminished. The stimulation strengthens the connections between brain cells. In fact, the brain can grow stronger links at virtually any age—this is not a phenomenon just for youngsters. LTP may explain why practice and repetition are such successful memory enhancers. They reinforce a chain of communication that is still strong and accessible as long-term memory months or years later.

ARNOLD SCHWARZENEGGER'S AMAZING SHORT-TERM MEMORY

While attending a meeting of the President's Council on Physical Fitness in Washington, D.C., Arnold learned just minutes before the meeting that he was going to be asked to make a few remarks. Conferring with his good friend Jim Lorimer, he sketched out a list of ten topics he might talk about. Each item was numbered and they reviewed the list twice before the meeting began. When Arnold was asked to talk ten minutes later, he mentioned each topic in the order in which he and Lorimer had arranged them, and he did this without a scrap of paper to jog his memory.

YOUR AGING MEMORY: WHAT GOES, WHAT STAYS, WHAT GETS BETTER

At my high school reunion, I sought out a "girl" I had had a crush on, despite rumors at the time that she experimented with drugs. She was there, and well into her white wine. We had a brief conversation, and while she remembered my name, she clearly had no recollection of any of our times together. I drifted off to another part of the room, wondering whether the drug use, white wine, or age had eroded her memory.

Age does chip away at our memory. Starting around age twenty, your brain gradually diminishes in size and leaves you with 10 to 20 percent less gray matter by the time you are eighty. Scientists are unsure of whether this reduction is actual loss or rather shrinkage of nerve cells and glial cells. They do know that nerve cells lose receptors with age, which reduces the amount of chemical interaction between cells, and that fewer brain chemicals—neurotransmitters—are coursing through your head. Yet, researchers have found it impossible to tell exactly how these alterations affect memory and general thinking. "To this day, a connection between decreased mental function and brain cell loss has not been proven," declares Dr. Leonard Hayflick, of the University of California at San Francisco Medical School.

Not all the changes of aging bring bad news. Neurobiologists studying stroke victims and amputees suffering from phantom pain have discovered that parts of the brain can regenerate. When connections between nerve cells (synapses) are broken, the brain can grow new connections or compensate by strengthening nearby circuits. Scientists call this marvelous adaptation plasticity and herald it as a great discovery and the cause for much hope.

> Life is all memory except for the one present moment that goes by you so quick you hardly catch it going.—Tennessee Williams

TAKE ACTION

Test Your Brain Cells

Most people exaggerate their memory deficits. They know all the times they have forgotten faces and names, misplaced keys, or suffered a frustrating tip-of-the-tongue experience, but they don't remember the many times they quickly recalled a fact or detail from a long-past event. Take this test for a simple gauge of how well your memory is working. Read through this list once, turn it over, and write down as many items as you can remember.

garlic	oregano
oranges	chocolate chip cookies
flour	raspberries
tomatoes	coconut
water	hamburger
nectarines	eggplant
white wine	mustard
rice	

Scoring:

AGE	NORMAL
18–39	10 items
40–59	9 items
60–69	8 items
70+	7 items

Still, some changes in memory as we age appear to be near universal. Here's what goes and what stays.

- If speed of response is a measure, then it diminishes in everyone starting around age fifty. However, if accuracy is the measure, then it doesn't necessarily slip with age, except for long-term memory.

- The type of memory at risk as early as your forties is the immediate storage of lots of information.
- Older people need longer exposure to a sight, sound, or smell to activate sensory memory.
- A study of affluent retirees with a mean age of seventy-four found that they performed just as well in tests of word generation, paired-associate learning (how well new information is remembered), and verbal free recall as young college undergraduates. However, less educated, lower-income seniors scored lower than the college kids.
- Spatial working memory—your ability to remember where things are, which demands constant refreshing—is especially susceptible to aging. Its rapid disappearance is a sign of Alzheimer's.
- The tip-of-the-tongue phenomenon—not being able to remember a once-known, common word—is especially common among people over sixty-four.

PLUS AND MINUS

Assuming generally good health, people begin showing signs of mental aging around age sixty, and for some, there are few signs of change until their seventies or eighties. Here are the memory and learning abilities that neuroscientists and gerontology experts say people gain and lose with the years.

Plus: Vocabulary. Word generation. Paired-associate learning. Verbal free recall. Proofreading. Capacity to generate new or original ideas.

Minus: Mental response time. Speed and quality of sentence completion. Storage of lots of information. List recall. Spatial working memory. Visual-spatial response (e.g., driving reactions). Tip-of-the-tongue memory. Dream recall.

Will and discipline are part of learning and of forging strong memories, and so is a healthy brain. By that I mean taking in the necessary nutrients and doing the right exercises so that your mind functions efficiently. There is much you can do to sharpen the memory and learning skills that have slowed because they are rusty or aging. One of the first places you should look is the kitchen.

BRAIN FOODS

Scientists are just beginning to understand the strong links between nutrition and mental function, and how diet alters memory, concentration, and intellectual performance. Just as a good stew is composed of many ingredients, brain food is an assortment of nutrients, namely proteins, carbohydrates, and fats. Here are some ingredients that can spark your memory.

The Glory of Garlic

Credit the Japanese for discovering that garlic can have a noticeable effect on memory. Researchers at the University of Tokyo added aged garlic extract to the diets of mice specially bred to age quickly and found that it not only extended their lifetimes but improved their performance in the water maze, a standard learning and memory test. "These results suggest the possibility that aged garlic extract prevents physiological aging and age-related memory disorders in humans," claim the Japanese.

Try a Shot of Sugar

A dose of concentrated sugar may help short-term memory, say researchers led by Dr. Paul Gold at the University of Virginia. Twenty students were given glasses of lemonade early in the morning when their stomachs were empty, then asked to read a short passage, and forty-five minutes later they were tested on how many of seventy facts in the article they could recall. One morning they drank lemonade with sugar and on the next day lemonade with saccharin, fake sugar. On the day they had the sugared lemonade, they remembered 30 percent more. The sugar that improved their recall was not table sugar but concentrated glucose. Dr. Gold concluded in the *American Journal of Clinical Nutrition,* "Glucose enhances learning and memory in healthy aged humans and enhances several other cognitive functions in subjects with severe cognitive pathologies."

Bring On the Fat

People learn better and remember more when they have the right fat in their diets. Fats are our most concentrated form of energy, and the brain needs them to function properly. Fats are composed of a string of molecules, with the length of the string and how much hydrogen is present (this is what makes a fat "saturated") determining how the body and brain use them. Our gray matter makes especially good use of the unsaturated fat in fish oil and vegetable oil. The body breaks these down into essential fatty acids (they're called essential because the body cannot produce them but must have them in the daily diet) that feed brain cell membranes and lubricate brain workings. The brain doesn't like short-chain, saturated (highly hydrogenated) fats, like animal fat, butter, and those found in fried foods. These slow it down and do not add useful nutrients.

To test how various fats influence memory and learning, scientists in Canada put three groups of lab rats on three different diets—high unsaturated fat, high saturated fat, and normal fat—then tested them. The rats that chowed down on the saturated fat, mostly lard, performed the worst. "The results indicate that a diet high in saturated fatty acids can impair a wide range of learning and memory functions," concluded the researchers.

Pile On the Pasta

Pasta is largely carbohydrates, as you know, and when we eat them, they become part of a chain reaction that ultimately produces a brain chemical that helps you think better. This fast-thinking neurochemical is serotonin, and when it runs low you feel sluggish, maybe even depressed, and cannot concentrate well. You can help your brain produce more serotonin by feeding it tryptophan, an amino acid found in protein foods such as milk and eggs. When your brain is fed lots of carbs, which contain no tryptophan, it compensates for the chemical imbalance by increasing the tryptophan that goes into the chemical stew to generate serotonin. By eating pasta, you actually generate a higher concentration of tryptophan.

Confused? Dr. Richard Wurtman at the Department of Brain and Cognitive Sciences at MIT explains this paradox: "It seems counterintuitive that the meal that most effectively raises brain tryptophan levels is the one entirely lacking in tryptophan (that is, one containing carbohydrates but no proteins) whereas a protein-rich meal, which elevates blood tryptophan, has the opposite effect on the brain."

A POWERFUL NUTRIENT

At the reunion, I bumped into my French teacher, Mr. Darien, whose class I really enjoyed because I had a sharp verbal memory and he was an iron-fisted teacher who taught through oral rote. Every day we had to repeat verb conjugations and memorize long passages. He told us that if we listened and concentrated, years later we would still be able to rattle off the past perfect tense of "to go—*aller.*" He was right. Repetition enhances verbal memory.

Do you find yourself forgetting directions you heard only hours or days ago? This can be annoying and frustrating, and can force you to learn things twice. Today I use the same technique for remembering information that I applied in French class. I replay the sounds of the instructions in my mind, and find that I am able to remember phone numbers recited to me years ago by sounding the numbers in my mind. But the mind does not always cooperate, and knowing about citicoline would certainly have made some learning a little less trying.

Scientists in the United States and Italy have been testing citicoline, a form of choline and part of the vitamin B complex, for its effect on verbal memory. This makes sense, because they already know that choline helps the brain produce the neurochemical acetylcholine, a key ingredient in routine memory activity. In double-blind, placebo-controlled studies involving older volunteers with failing memory, from either aging or predementia, citicoline has consistently improved test scores for verbal memory as well as immediate memory and delayed logical memory, the organization of thoughts and a concept of things that occurred in the past. Choline is found in egg yolks, organ meats, beans and peas, and lecithin supplements. Lecithin, a nutritional extract, helps deliver choline to the brain. In fact, it is a better delivery system than choline supplements because it provides a steadier, longer supply of choline than the supplements.

LUBRICATE YOUR MEMORY

Another naturally occurring substance that's been shown to sharpen memory is phosphatidylserine (PS). This is a phospholipid nutrient, meaning that it's a naturally occurring lipid with both fatty and watery properties found in cell membranes. Think of it as lubrication for your mind. In more than thirty-five studies, PS has been found to stimulate people's memory of names and faces, lost objects, telephone numbers, and paragraphs they have read. In a joint study at Memory Assessment Clinics in Bethesda, Maryland, and Stanford University, 149 people were treated for what's called age-associated memory impairment, which is the memory fuzziness experienced by many people over fifty. Patients, fifty to seventy-five years old, took 100 mg of PS or a placebo three times a day for twelve weeks. The PS patients outscored their non-PS counterparts in tests of name and face memory, concentration during reading, and recall of telephone numbers and lost objects. Dr. Thomas Crook, who led the study, concluded that PS "may be a promising candidate for treating memory loss in later life." From scientists accustomed to guarded statements, that's a ringing endorsement. Not found in many foods, PS is available in dietary supplements. While recommended doses may vary, most of the studies involving PS used 300 milligrams a day.

MEMORY MINERALS

Boron, which is found in foods like apples, peaches, pears, beans, peas, lentils, nuts, and leafy vegetables, looks like a winner in memory tests. Researchers at the USDA Human Nutrition Research Center found that 3 milligrams a day improved people's alertness and learning ability.

Lack of magnesium can cloud your memory by retarding blood circulation in the brain. Scientists have had good luck with giving magnesium to memory-impaired older people who seemed to be showing signs of early Alzheimer's. You can get magnesium by eating whole wheat, almonds, cashews, and leafy green vegetables.

Zinc, a trace metal you consume when you eat shellfish, beans and peas, or dark turkey meat, can also juice up your memory. Doctors have known for a long time that a zinc deficiency, particularly in the elderly, has been linked to mental confusion and even Alzheimer's disease. Zinc's positive effects are also noteworthy. Women in studies at the University of Texas discovered that their ability to remember words and visual patterns improved when they got enough zinc into their system. The recommended daily allowance for zinc is 12–15 milligrams.

MEMORY FOODS

These foods and nutrients have been shown to boost memory in noteworthy ways:

Aged garlic. Improves spatial memory, fights age-related memory loss.

Sugar/glucose. Improves short-term memory.

Carbohydrates in pasta. Stimulates production of serotonin, which fuels learning.

Unsaturated fat in olive oil, fish oil. Strengthens general learning abilities.

Citicoline in egg yolks, organ meats. Enhances verbal memory.

Phosphatidylserine (PS) in supplements. Stimulates memory of names, faces, lost objects, and numbers.

Boron in apples, pears, beans, peas. Enhances alertness for learning.

Magnesium in whole wheat, nuts. Enhances alertness, general memory.

Zinc in shellfish, beans and peas, dark turkey meat. Aids short-term recall, word and visual memory.

VITAMIN POWER

Science is making amazing discoveries about how vitamins influence our thought processes. In recent years, vitamin supplements have been linked to better moods, higher scores on intelligence tests, more memory, and sharper attention. Some of the best vitamins and nutrients to expand your memory are members of the B complex: B_1 (thiamine), B_2 (riboflavin), B_3 (niacin), B_6 (pyridoxine), and B_{12} (cyanocobalamin), as well as choline, carnitine, and folic acid.

The harm from not getting enough vitamin B has been known for decades. Insufficient intake of niacin can foster a disease that looks like mental illness and is characterized by confusion, depression, and hallucinations. People who do not take in enough B_1 can become irritable and aggressive and exhibit personality changes. Deficiencies in B_2 may produce neurotic depression. And not enough B_{12} has long been connected with dangerous (pernicious) anemia that can lead to a host of neurological problems.

So the converse of vitamin deficiency—that higher, stronger RDA levels of B vitamins can actually strengthen your mental health—makes sense. Of the seven members of the B vitamin family, three are star memory boosters—B_1, B_6, and B_{12}.

Vitamin B_6 was the subject of a study on thinking and memory at the Jean Mayer U.S. Department of Agriculture Human Nutrition Research Center on Aging in Boston. Seventy men, aged fifty-four to eighty-one, were tested on their thinking and memory skills and then measured for levels of various B vitamins in their systems. The men with the highest concentrations of B_6 did better on the Backward Digit Span Test and the Activity Memory Test, both of which employ working memory.

Most people, says the U.S. government, do not get enough Vitamin B_6. A National Health and Nutrition Survey of almost twelve thousand people between the ages of nineteen and seventy-four revealed that 71 percent of men and 90 percent of women do not consume the recommended dietary allowance of B_6.

Older people may especially lack B_6, either because they are not getting enough in their diet or from supplements or because their bodies are not absorbing what they are consuming. Nutrient absorption is a problem as we grow older. If you find that you are consuming a reasonable amount of a vitamin or mineral but it's not showing up in your system (through blood tests), you may have to ask your doctor for vitamin injections. The recommended daily dosage for B_6 is between 1.6 and 2 milligrams, with supplemental doses going up to 200 milligrams. Rich sources of B_6, besides supplements, are yeast, sunflower seeds, wheat germ, tuna, and liver.

Another B vitamin essential for memory and concentration is B_{12}. This vitamin, like the citicoline you just read about, helps stimulate acetylcholine. A good way to pump up this neurochemical, according to Japanese researchers at the Gunma University School of Medicine, is by adding B_{12} to diets that lack the choline necessary for producing it.

You can find B_{12} in organ foods such as liver and kidneys, and in shellfish, such as clams and oysters. Vegetarians have to be especially sensitive to B_{12} intake, since it is not an ingredient in their regular diet. The recommended daily allowance for B_{12} is 2 micrograms, with the supplementary dose up to 1,000 micrograms.

Older people can suffer from what's called atrophic gastritis, meaning that they no longer produce enough stomach acid to process the vitamin B_{12} in their food. The result can be a host of symptoms, including memory loss, lack of coordination, and weakness in the limbs. You can boost vitamin B_{12} intake with milk, dairy products, eggs, meat, poultry, and shellfish, or with supplements or B_{12} shots.

Vitamin B_1 may sharpen thinking, especially in women. At England's University College Swansea, male and female students aged seventeen to twenty-seven were given huge doses (ten times the daily recommended amount) of nine vitamins or a placebo, and tested every three months for a year. At the end, the researchers discovered that the thiamin in the vitamin cocktail quickened the attention and mental reaction time of the forty-seven women in the study. The researchers, led by David Benton, were surprised by the results. "Unlike most previous studies, an unusual feature to the present study is that aspects of cognitive functioning improved only after a year of taking a high dose of vitamins," they asserted. They figured that the women showed different results from the men because their bodies respond differently to diet.

Your morning orange juice may also boost memory. Vitamin C, or ascorbic acid, is well known as an effective antioxidant, a chemical that attacks free radicals, which are unstable molecules that break down or destroy healthy cells through oxidation. Its antioxidant qualities, which fight atherosclerosis, possibly by strengthening the collagen in the arteries, may also have a direct effect on

MEALTIME BRAIN BOOSTERS

These vitamins, and the foods that deliver them, can improve various facets of your thinking:

Vitamin B_1 (whole grains, oatmeal, wheat germ, oysters, and liver): attention, reaction time

Vitamin B_6 (wheat germ, sunflower seeds, yeast, tuna, and liver): working memory

Vitamin B_{12} (clams, oysters, kidneys, and liver): concentration, mental alertness, learning

Vitamin C (oranges, strawberries, red peppers, and leafy green vegetables): general memory

thinking skills. Clearer arteries mean more blood and oxygen to the brain.

At Southampton General Hospital in England, doctors surveyed the diets and thinking abilities of 921 people over a twenty-year period and found that "cognitive function was poorest in those with the lowest vitamin C status" and suggested that "high vitamin C intake may protect against cognitive impairment."

Italian scientists are even more enthusiastic about ascorbic acid, saying that there is "substantial" evidence that it may be useful in fighting memory disorders. Drs. De Angelis and Furlan at the University of Trieste found ascorbic acid did an extraordinary job combating induced amnesia in aging mice and suggest it may be a treatment for an assortment of memory disorders.

Good food sources for vitamin C are red peppers; leafy vegetables like parsley, broccoli, and brussels sprouts; and, of course, fruits like oranges, strawberries, and papaya. The recommended daily allowance is 60 milligrams, the supplementary range between 50 and 10,000 milligrams, and a dose for peak mental performance is 1,000 milligrams per day.

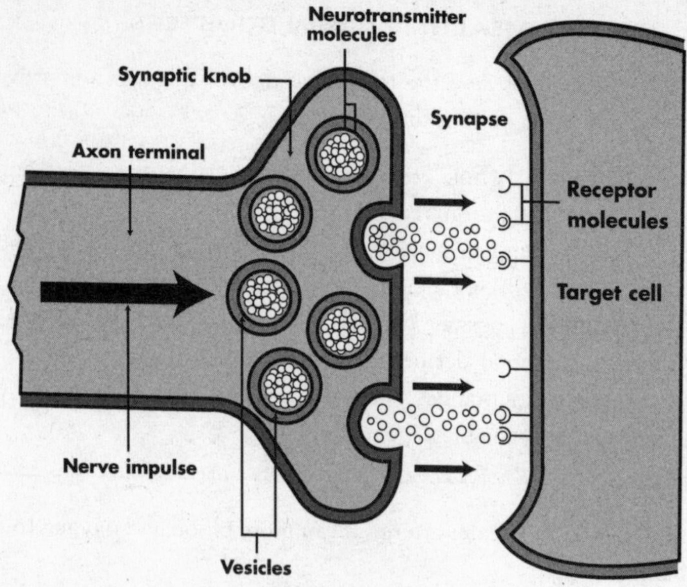

Nerve-Muscle Interface

Adapted from *The Brain and Nervous System*, AMA Home Medical Library (1991)

MEMORY PILLS

At my reunion, I had an encounter common to many. My old English class pal Debbie introduced me to her husband, and after a short chat, I moved on. Ten minutes later, I had no memory of Debbie's husband's name.

What strains my synapses are short-term memory tasks like being introduced to a group of people, then having to use their names in conversation minutes later. I know this is a common experience, and undoubtedly a big reason why pharmaceutical companies are feverishly testing an array of compounds that they hope will do for the memory what Prozac has done for depression. I recently read that more than 150 such "brain drugs" are currently under development worldwide.

What many people do not know, however, is that there are already drugs available that are designed specifically to improve mental functioning. First developed by a French scientist in the 1970s, they are common fare in Europe, Asia, and South America. This new class of drugs is called nootropics, literally meaning "toward the mind." Some people call them cognitive enhancers because they can improve learning and thinking speed, delay mental aging, and sharpen memory. For now, I will focus on what they do to memory.

Nootropics are controversial in the United States because their effects are not always consistent and experts disagree on whether they work. Those who believe they do work say that the inconclusive results are typical for a juvenile science and a new category of drugs. The skeptics point out that most of the studies have been on animals, not humans, and that the whole science of improving thinking and memory is founded on poorly understood mechanisms. Nevertheless, the experts do agree on a couple of points. For one, nootropics do not produce side effects like those of other "mind drugs," the psychotropic medications used to treat mental illnesses. They do not sedate or stimulate, as can other drugs that work on the mind. Most experts accept the evidence that they can improve some aspects of learning, but their effects are not uniform, and there is no way to predict whom they will benefit.

Still, as often happens with new medical treatments, people are forging ahead regardless of scientific debate. For instance, in Germany nootropics are widely prescribed by physicians not only for dementia but also for slight memory disturbances. The most popular of these drugs are ginkgo biloba, piracetam, pyritinol, nimodipine, and ergot alkaloids, a medicinal compound derived from fungus.

The mostly widely known cognitive enhancer, piracetam, is usually taken as a general "brain booster" for various thought processes, but it has also been successful in relieving age-associated memory impairment. One recent French study produced dramatic results.

About 135 people, aged fifty-five and older, at Grenoble University Hospital were separated into three groups and given either 2.4 grams a day of piracetam, 4.8 grams a day, or a placebo. After six weeks, the higher-dose patients generated the best scores on memory tests, even though they had the worst scores before the study.

One of the most famous studies of piracetam was done, again in France, with 225 dyslexic schoolchildren. The children took either 3.3 grams a day or a placebo for nine months. At the start of the study, all of the children had below normal reading skills, although they were of average intelligence. At the end, the children taking piracetam showed "significant improvements." They had gained 1.3 years in reading accuracy and 1.7 years in comprehension, while the youngsters taking the placebo advanced only in their reading skills.

Piracetam may even have some clout with the worst kind of memory loss, the dementia that comes with Alzheimer's. Researchers in Poland have found that high doses (2.4 grams a day) seem to stop the progression of Alzheimer's and that doses of around 800 milligrams a day improve the memory and attentiveness of epileptic patients.

Piracetam is not generally available in the United States, but you can either order it through the mail from Europe or buy it in a pharmacy without prescription in Mexico; this is perfectly legal, but for personal use only. It is sold under a variety of names, such as Nootropil and Pirroxil, usually in 400-milligram or 800-milligram capsules.

Nimodipine has also produced promising results in memory tests. This drug is a calcium channel blocker (usually prescribed for heart conditions), which means that it stops calcium from leaking into brain cells, which dilutes its effectiveness in delivering electrical signals between brain cells. A steady drip of calcium reduces its impact when sending strong individual signals. It tends to become unbalanced as people grow older. Disrupted calcium regulation in the brain is thought to be one of the underlying causes of dementia. Too much calcium kills brain cells and too little halts the growth of new cell connections. Another reason nimodipine appears to work is that it increases cerebral blood flow.

Scientists have found that nimodipine is especially useful for tasks requiring associative memory, that is, linking cause and effect. You know this kind of learning and memory well—it happens when you repeatedly burn your tongue testing fresh-from-the-oven cookies until you finally learn not to taste when they are steaming. When nimodipine tablets were given three times a day for three months to people aged sixty to seventy-five whose learning had noticeably slowed, it boosted their associative learning speed by 50 percent.

As some scientists explore new drug aids for memory, others are

TAKE ACTION

Pharmacies, over-the-counter shelves, health food stores, and mail-order catalogs offer a variety of pills that may expand your memory.

Piracetam (400–800 mg/day): memory, attentiveness, reading comprehension

Nimodipine (30–90 mg/day): associative learning and memory

Clonidine (Doses vary from .1 mg to .3 mg a day. Consult your doctor.): spatial memory, learning, recall. Side effects: sedation, low blood pressure

Pyritinol (300–600 mg/day): vitamin B_6. Helps cognitive functioning. May lower depression.

Deanol (400–800 mg/day): memory, cognitive functions

Deprenyl (10 mg/day): long-term memory, concentration, attention span

Acetyl-l-carnitine (1,000–2,000 mg/day): attention, concentration

Ginseng (500–1,000 mg/day extract): general memory, learning

Ginkgo biloba (40–120 mg/day extract): attention, concentration

reexamining known pharmaceuticals for possible benefits to learning and memory. For instance, oral doses of monosodium glutamate (MSG), which spurs the flow of certain neurochemicals, have improved memory in people with deficits caused by aging.

Clonidine, a drug prescribed for lowering blood pressure, has also been found to be useful in treating memory disorders, particularly the ability to remember where you put things (spatial memory). In studies with animals, clonidine improved the ability to learn new information (like where food was hidden) and to recall facts once known but forgotten. While nowhere near perfect as a memory drug—it has sedative side effects and the dose has to be carefully gauged—scientists are encouraged enough to put it into clinical testing.

HORMONE THERAPY

Hormones play an active role in memory. A prime example of this is what happens to a person who has low levels of thyroid hormones. With less thyroid, blood flows more slowly through the arteries, bringing few nutrients and oxygen to the brain. As a result, a person thinks and moves more slowly. And if this condition, called hypothyroidism, is not treated in time, the blood vessels of the brain age prematurely and atherosclerosis can occur. Furthermore, hypothyroidism reduces the number of dendrite connections between brain cells. Symptoms of hypothyroidism are sluggishness, slowed thinking, difficulty in concentrating, and a poor memory, especially when waking up or after resting. Not surprisingly, thyroid therapy can reverse these signs. Says Dr. Thierry Hertoghe, an internationally known expert in hormones, "Thyroid supplements are really great at magnifying the intelligence of a patient to such an extent that many physicians consider thyroid hormones to be the ultimate hormone of intelligence . . . the efficacy with which thyroid treatment reverses failing memories of people definitely low in thyroid hormones depends on when the therapy is started. In general, the sooner thyroid supplements are given, the better."

Testosterone is another memory hormone. Men and women who test better for spatial memory (the ability to manipulate precise movements in space) generally have more testosterone in their blood. According to Dr. Hertoghe, "When testosterone therapy is taken by transsexual women [women who feel themselves more as men and try medical treatment to make their bodies look more like the body of a male], these masculinized women become more proficient in spatial tasks, but lose their previous language fluence, a typical characteristic of women."

Depending on the state of your memory, you may want to think about taking aggressive action such as hormone replacement therapy. The idea of replacing hormones as they are depleted from our bodies during normal aging is widely accepted. Millions of menopausal women take estrogen, and recent investigations have shown that it not only counteracts the effects of menopause but also can sharpen slowed thinking. Another hormone, dehydroepiandrosterone (DHEA), which both men and women churn out in abundance until around age thirty, when it begins to drop off, is the latest star of hormone replacement programs. It, too, has demonstrated promise in perking up flagging memories. Human growth hormone (hGH) is another candidate for replacement therapy if you are concerned about slipping cogs.

Estrogen

Most of the research into the effects of hormones on memory has concentrated on estrogen, with good cause. Researchers around the globe are finding that estrogen can markedly sharpen a woman's thinking, and one leading researcher pinpoints its cognitive benefits on memory. Dr. Barbara Sherwin of McGill University reports there is "reason to believe that this sex steroid might enhance memory," while noting that estrogen does not impact all kinds of memory equally. In healthy young women, it appears to most benefit short- and long-term verbal memory and especially paired-associate memory, which is how well they remember new information. On the other hand, the hormone seemed to have no effect on, or sometimes weakened, spatial memory.

In one of the studies, twenty-eight women on estrogen replacement therapy (ERT) and forty-three women not on ERT were read a short paragraph and after thirty minutes asked to recall as much about it as they could. The women on estrogen remembered much more, leading the researchers to conclude that the hormone not only helped their memory but also their ability to learn new material. While Sherwin admitted that the difference in performance between the two groups of women was not huge, it was statistically significant. She said that the ERT women probably recalled telephone numbers, instructions, and directions more easily.

Some scientists have found that estrogen's influence on women's memory is apparent even during normal menstrual cycles. A study of forty-five women at the University of Western Ontario discovered that during the high-estrogen phase of their cycle, women did better on verbal fluency tests (saying as many words as possible starting with a certain letter within a certain time) than during their low-estrogen phase.

The effects of estrogen on the thought processes of postmenopausal women have been examined ever since the hormone was first synthesized. A number of tests of elderly women treated with estrogen have shown that it can produce major gains not only in verbal memory but in other kinds of mental functioning as well. Dr. Sherwin says that various studies provide "compelling evidence" of the benefits of estrogen replacement for aging minds. Researchers at Stanford University who tested the memory of 144 women aged fifty-five to ninety-three, half on estrogen and half not, found that it definitely made a difference for remembering names and faces. It is important to note that estrogen comes either in tablet form or by injection, and that scientists believe more of the hormone gets to the brain when it is delivered by injection.

In studies of estrogen and brain activity, researchers have found that estrogen has a stronger influence on mental functions governed by the left hemisphere. The left side of your brain, you might recall, directs language, verbal skills, and manual dexterity. Furthermore, a healthy circulation of estrogen through the brain stimulates the production of nerve growth factor (NGF), which the brain manufactures to protect neurons vital for memory. If there is not sufficient estrogen in the brain, NGF production drops, and memory cells weaken.

While the results of various studies have not been uniform, probably because they did not measure the same kinds or levels of estrogen, or use the same memory tests, estrogen may well help you remember an address or phone number you heard but not help you remember where you put your glasses.

Estrogen replacement therapy is not for everyone, however. Women at risk for breast cancer, in particular, should think twice about whether they want to add to the hormone that researchers have implicated as a possible contributor to cancerous cell mutations. And not as much research has been done on ERT in premenopausal women.

However, a new generation of estrogen drugs that sidestep the harmful side effects is about to hit the marketplace. Called SERM (selective estrogen-receptor modulators), these drugs are designed to deliver estrogen to the heart and bones but not the uterus and breasts. Consequently, they are showing remarkable results for fighting heart disease and osteoporosis while not raising a woman's risk of breast or uterine cancer. One SERM named raloxifene is already in clinical trials, and others are close behind.

A Mother Hormone for Men and Women

A hormone reputed to boost the memories of both men and women is DHEA, known as the mother of hormones because the body converts it into dozens of other hormones (its offspring include estrogen, androgen, testosterone, and corticosterone). DHEA is a neurosteroid hormone produced by our adrenal glands in a steady stream until around age thirty, when the flow begins to slacken. By age sixty-five, our bodies are producing a small fraction of the DHEA that they were producing in our twenties. While DHEA is usually recommended for its anti-aging powers, part of its magic, say some doctors, is that it may hike your memory.

An investigation at Bates College in Maine that looked at how various steroids affect memory found that DHEA was a standout. Researchers fed female rats six different steroids, then put them through memory and learning tests. Those on DHEA-S (the sulfate form that has solubility properties similar to plain DHEA) particularly excelled in tests of working and long-term memory. In the discussion of their findings and comparisons with other research, Drs. Cheryl Frye and Jodi Sturgis concluded, "This confirms that DHEA-S' memory enhancing effects . . . are not unique to this species, sex or memory task."

Another researcher, Eugene Roberts at the Beckman Research Institute in La Jolla, California, may have learned why DHEA works so well. In his work with rats, he discovered that DHEA stimulates production of a key brain cell messenger and the formation of branches that connect brain cells.

DHEA is no magic bullet for a failing memory, however. The research into its influence on thinking and memory has so far been limited to animals, which do not have as much of the hormone as humans, so scientists must theorize about how it could affect the *human* brain. Nevertheless, they have found that it stimulates neurite growth in animal brains. DHEA also helps balance the body's production of potentially hazardous stress hormones, called glucocorticoids. If there is an imbalance among various glucocorticoids, under stressful conditions tissues like those in the memory headquarters, the hippocampus, may suffer.

Some doctors hesitate to recommend DHEA because of uncertainty over long-term side effects. In some tests, it has produced acne and facial hair in women, and researchers have theorized that it may raise the risk for heart disease and prostate cancer in men, although there is no evidence that this happens. And a rat study has shown that at extremely high doses DHEA may cause liver problems, even cancer.

You can buy DHEA, usually in 25- or 50-milligram capsules, from nutrition stores. There are no standard doses. Most clinical studies have used daily doses of 25 to 100 mg. Getting the right dose level is important with DHEA, so you should consult a physician and have your hormone level tested before starting on it. Your optimum dose will depend on how much DHEA your body is producing nat-

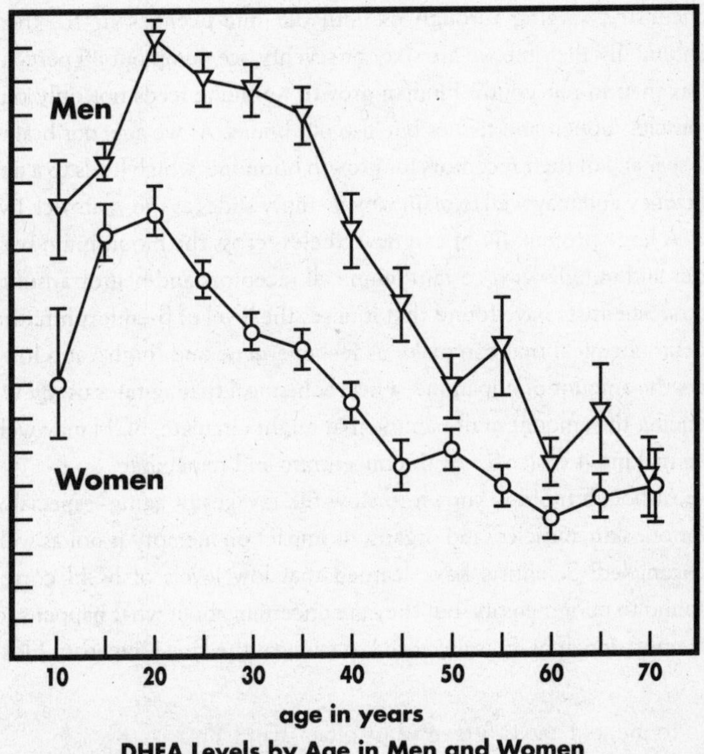

DHEA Levels by Age in Men and Women

Adapted from *Stopping the Clock* (1996)

urally, which you can find out from a blood test. Generally, women need less than men, and some people take it only every other day, particularly those who are prone to the most annoying side effect of DHEA, acnelike pimples in men and facial hair in women. For people with these complaints, a precursor of DHEA, pregnenolone, is now available, and may be even more effective in helping to replace the lost hormones of youth.

Human Growth Hormone (hGH)

As a memory tonic, human growth hormone is not uniformly potent. Like other hormones, it is essential to body development and personal chemistry, surging through us until our mid-twenties or so, then ebbing. By the time we are sixty or seventy, we pump out 80 percent less than in our youth. Human growth hormone feeds not only our muscles, bones, and tissues but also our brains. As we age, our brains lose many of their receptors for growth hormone, which leads to a deficiency and may well explain why memory slides as the years tick by.

A large protein, hGH can nevertheless cross the blood-brain barrier and mingle with certain brain cell receptors and neurotransmitters. Scientists have found that it raises the level of β-endorphin, the neurochemical that can make us feel energetic and "high," and lowers the amount of dopamine, a neurochemical that agitates us. By reducing the amount of dopamine that might circulate, hGH may well be making it easier for us to concentrate and remember.

Although hGH is known to slow the ravages of aging, especially for our skin, muscles, and organs, its impact on memory is not as well chronicled. Scientists have learned that low levels of hGH correspond to poor memory, but they are uncertain about what happens to memory when hGH is increased. A study at the Free University Hos-

> To me, old age is fifteen years older than I am.
>
> —Bernard Baruch

pital in Amsterdam found that men who had low levels of hGH had poorer iconic memory (the ability to retain a flash of information), short-term, long-term, and perceptual-motor memory than those whose pituitary did produce hGH. Yet most of the subjects had low hGH from birth, which might have also affected their brain development. More promising results have come from a study using rats at the Fujisawa Pharmaceutical Company in Japan. Here, researchers found that low levels of hGH almost definitely produced poor thinking and memory. So there's some evidence that hGH can help your memory.

Dr. Bengt-Ake Bengtsson, a Swedish endocrinologist, has been actively researching hGH and has conducted a number of studies on the use of human growth hormone, especially in adults who are deficient in it. He believes, "We are just beginning to scratch the surface of the importance of growth hormone in cognition, memory and brain function."

Human growth hormone, like estrogen, is only available through

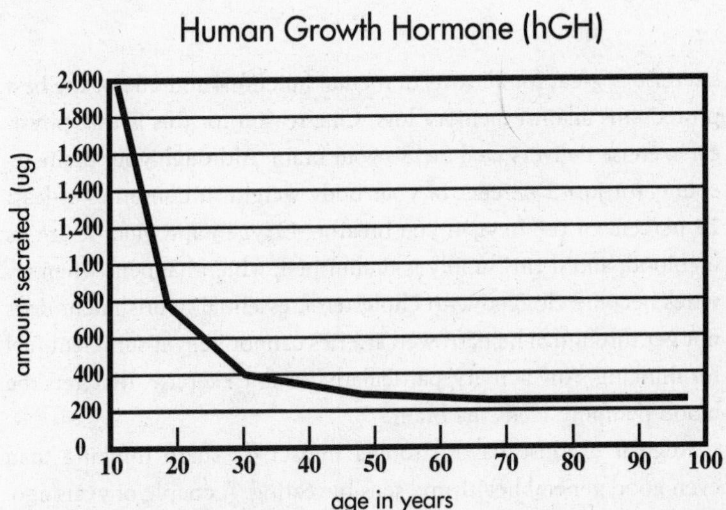

Adapted from *Grow Young with HGH* (1997)

your doctor. Before you decide to pursue any kind of hormone replacement, you need to have blood levels measured so your doctor can adjust your dosage accordingly. Another route suggested by hGH advocates is to encourage your body to produce more hGH with supplements, nutrients, and activities that spark its release. The amino acids arginine and ornithine bump up your hGH by tickling the brain's cholinergic nervous system, which uses acetylcholine to pass information along. For this reason, the supplements choline and B_5, which increase this neurotransmitter, should be taken with arginine and ornithine. Other nutrients that may increase your natural hGH are niacin, tyrosine, glutathione, and methionine.

One of the best ways to get your hGH pumping is through exercise. High-intensity exercise, such as free-weight training, multijoint training, and aerobic activities like sprinting, squash, or tennis, can boost your hGH circulation. In fact, exercise is great for your brain and memory for more than its hormone benefits.

PROTECT YOURSELF WITH EXERCISE

Exercise is great for all sorts of mental functions and one of the best protections against memory loss. One reason for this is that physical exercise delivers vital fuel to your brain. Although your brain accounts for just 2 percent of your body weight, it consumes at least 25 percent of the oxygen you breathe. Oxygen and glucose are its lifeblood, and if this supply is diminished, which happens when arteries become clogged with cholesterol, essential nourishment does not get through. The narrowed arteries cannot deliver sufficient fuel for thinking. Any activity, particularly aerobic exercise, that gets the blood pumping feeds the brain.

Regular exercise has a stronger impact on sharp thinking than even good general health and sensible eating. A couple of years ago, researchers at Scripps College in California tested 124 men and women, aged fifty-five to ninety-one, half of whom were couch potatoes and half of whom were vigorous exercisers. The sedentary group spent no more than ten minutes a week in strenuous exercise, expending few calories. The active group participated in recreational activities, gardened, climbed stairs, and walked for at least one and one-quarter hours a week, and burned at least 3,100 calories per day.

The couch potatoes and exercisers took a battery of working-memory tests that involved reading spans (recalling the last word of a sentence previously read on a computer monitor) and letter sets (holding two sets of letters in their memory and identifying which letter was unique to each). The surprise finding was that the sedentary group's good health did not make a difference in their scores, but their lack of exercise did. Although their blood pressure levels were close to those of the exercisers and they felt healthy, they could not match the scores of their active counterparts. The researchers concluded, "It appears that exercise affects the brain in ways we just don't understand. But the effect does seem to exist."

Even a relatively tame activity like walking can make a difference. A group of Japanese researchers at the St. Marianna University School of Medicine in Kawasaki have been looking at the connection between mental activity and exercise focused on walking. They gave memory tests to forty-six elderly people who walked daily and found that those who walked the farthest scored best, while those who barely walked showed signs of dementia.

One of the truest believers in the link between exercise and mental acuity is Dr. Robert Dustman, director of the Neuropsychology Research Laboratory at the Veterans Affairs Medical Center in Salt Lake City. He's been studying the effects of exercise on brain waves and mental performance for years, and has found that aerobically fit sixty-year-olds can mentally match people half their age. "On many measures, the older men in good condition scored just as well as men thirty and forty years their junior," he says. He also claims that if your mind is groggy from aging and too little exercise, you can do something about it. The mental benefits of physical activity are relatively immediate. Dustman estimates that a nonexerciser of virtually any age may begin to see results within six months.

MY FAVORITE EXERCISES FOR PEAK THINKING AND MEMORY

The exercise I use to enrich my mind depends on how sluggish I am feeling and my physical surroundings. These exercises vary in intensity and where they can be done conveniently.

- Tai chi breathing. This breathing exercise incorporates your body, breathing, and mind in four distinct stages of activity: inhalation, retention, exhalation, and pause. Stand with your heels together and your toes splayed at a 45-degree angle, knees bent, spine straight. Bring your hands together in front of you below the navel, palms up, right hand cupped in left. Empty your lungs and slowly inhale. Slowly raise your hands out to the sides, palms up, and make as wide a circle as possible as you raise them above your head. At the same time, slowly straighten your knees, hands still raised and lungs full. Tuck in your pelvis, hold, and swallow aloud. Keep your neck as stretched as possible. Slowly exhale through the nose. Gradually lower your hands, palms down, in a straight line back to the starting position, while bending your knees into a semi-squat. Empty your lungs with a final contraction. Pause to release the abdominal wall, turn palms upward, cup them, and begin again. Repeat this five times.
- Shadowboxing. Stand erect with your feet shoulder width apart. Flex your knees slightly and visualize a punching bag in front of you. Clench your right fist and punch the bag with all your might, then punch with your left fist. Alternate left and right twenty times. Move your arms in a complete motion, bringing them all the way forward and all the way back. Use your whole body. Breathe deeply.
- Conducting a mental symphony. Start humming or counting to increase your concentration and help you warm up. Standing with your feet slightly apart, arms out, elbows high and

out to the sides, trace two Cs that are back-to-back with your forearms. Do this motion at least ten times, being careful not to strain your arms. Try doing this exercise while holding light weights or full soda cans. If you do this exercise regularly, gradually increase the weights.

I still use physical activity to get my mind and memory in gear, and I believe in simplicity and efficiency. When I am reading technical material I want to remember or learning a complicated process such as how to run a software program, I take regular breaks for moderate aerobic exercise. I pedal on a stationary bike or take a brisk walk around the block. This increases the blood flow to my brain just when I need it—when I'm trying to lock information into my memory.

SMELL YOUR WAY TO A BETTER MEMORY

A pleasant, even fun way to jog your memory is through your senses of smell and sound. Did you know that when you combine learning with a sensory experience, the information stays with you longer?

According to researchers at UCLA, you can push information into your permanent memory by coupling it with a distinctive smell. The researchers separated rats into four groups and spent one day, one week, two weeks, or four weeks training them to associate an electrical shock to their feet with the smell of ammonia, then

JAKE ("BODY BY JAKE") STEINFELD'S MEMORY TRICK

"If I have to study something or memorize something, I put it into a rhyme. I make it fun for myself."

damaged the group's memory centers. When the rats that had trained for one day, one week, or two weeks were returned to the box with its electrical shocks and odor of ammonia, they showed no recollection of the surroundings, shocks, or smell. But the rats with four weeks of learning and association remembered the shocks and pungent smell.

While this study used rats, the strong ties between smell and memory hold true for people, too. At Bishop's University in Lenoxville, Canada, psychologist David G. Smith discovered that certain smells help students recall information. He gave forty-seven students a list of twenty-four words to remember while the smell of either jasmine or Lauren perfume was in the air. Later tests showed their memory to be much better when they smelled the same scent that permeated their learning session. Other odors that scientists have found to enhance learning by providing memory cues are ammonia, chocolate, and peppermint.

At the University of Cincinnati, students watched a video while breathing either different fragrances or pure air through oxygen masks. Afterward, they were asked to recall a certain line of dialogue. While the pure air did nothing to their scores, when they were tested in the presence of the odors of peppermint and lily of the valley, their scores were 25 percent higher.

I constantly practice using my sense of smell as a memory jogger. When I visit a place I have not been to for a long time, I concentrate on the smells around me to trigger old images and remember experiences. If I want to capture the essence of an experience, I seek out the most memorable smell. For instance, to recapture the feeling of my high school years, I would visit the gym to evoke the smells of sweat, polished wooden floors, and new vinyl mats. By capturing or recapturing a certain smell, you activate the elements of your memory that require detail. Paying attention is essential for a strong memory, and being attuned to your sense of smell will sharpen your ability to remember.

MEMORY BUILDERS

Here are ideas for activities that will strengthen your memory.

• You need to constantly use and stimulate your store of knowledge, language, and problem-solving skills. Activities that help are trivia games, card games, crossword puzzles, learning computer programs, and even children's word games like Botticelli ("I'm thinking of a famous person whose last name begins with R. Ask me yes or no questions to find out who").

• To sharpen your short-term memory, the next time you enter a place you have never been before, such as a new store, note the placement of ten items; leave, then return fifteen minutes later and see what you recall. You will find that the more you play this game with yourself, the more you remember.

• To remember routine things you have done, such as locking the front door or turning off the coffeepot, remind yourself aloud as you are finishing the task. Vocalizing strongly reinforces memory.

• We all know that writing things down helps us remember. What you may not know is that the *process* of writing, *not* having a written reminder to look at, cements it in our memory. So don't worry about losing your grocery list, just be sure you make one.

• Remembering names, faces, and numbers is a game of associations. When meeting someone for the first time, pick out a facial feature that you can use as a cue in the future. When you hear a name, give it a connection, which might be an alliteration ("Donna with the droopy eyes") or a context (being introduced to Tom "by the bookcase"). If you want to remember a combination or ATM number, link the numbers to a birthday, an important date in history, or an anniversary. Visualization also helps in making associations. For instance, if you want to remember that you parked in aisle 5A at the airport, think of five airplanes.

• One of the most frustrating memory lapses is the tip-of-the-tongue experience. Scientists have devoted years to discovering why people temporarily forget a well-known piece of information that seems to linger just a few inches beyond their memory's reach. While they haven't figured out why it happens (although they think that women are more susceptible than men), they suggest relaxing and forgetting about it. Dwelling on the lapse usually does not produce what you want to know.

MEMORY POISONS

It's not enough to practice and stimulate your memory, you also have to guard against assaults from harmful foods and the environment. Every day, people consume chemicals and are exposed to things like saturated fats that can poison memory. By guarding against the following poisons, you can slow or even prevent some memory loss.

Stress Stress not only hurts your physical health, it also erodes your powers of recall. While short bursts of stress can rev up your mental engine, the constant bombardment of stress hormones eventually damages brain cells. Scientists have found that stress disrupts the chemical communication that is essential to the long-term potentiation (a chemical and electrical action) that triggers learning. Stress also stimulates the flow of cortisol, a hormone that helps process carbohydrates but that in excess can damage brain cells. Glucocorticoids inhibit the brain's ability to absorb glucose, its main source of energy, and rob it of its ability to moderate other chemical signals. Consequently, brain cells become overexcited and are either damaged or killed. It is no wonder that people who live and work with constant stress say they have trouble learning and remembering.

I ease the stress that has become a regular part of my life by setting aside a time in the early evening, between my workday and nighttime reading, for what I call constructive visualization. In a quiet room, with the phone turned off and the lighting dimmed, I close my eyes and imagine an upcoming meeting, task, conversation, or phone call. I visualize the setting and the people involved and see myself going through it. I shape the ideas and sentences I am going to communicate and practice my actions and body movements. This mental rehearsal helps me not only to anticipate and control an event but also to moderate any stress associated with it. By reducing the unpredictability of my own reactions, I lower the stress factor. As a stress buster, constructive visualization is similar to meditation and aerobic exercise.

Painkillers Scientists have found that nonsteroidal anti-inflammatory drugs (what they call NSAIDs and what you know as ibuprofen) can chip away at your memory. While about 40 percent of all NSAIDs are prescribed for people over sixty-five years of age, mostly for arthritis, they have also become the drug of choice for sports enthusiasts beset by the aches and pains of physical activity. In a survey of elderly rural residents by the University of Iowa College of Medicine, people taking high doses of NSAIDs (more than 1,800 milligrams a day) were found to be at high risk for long-term memory decline. While other studies have suggested that anti-inflammatories may protect the brain from dementia, it is possible that very large doses of these drugs are harmful. Few of us can consume that much medication for any length of time and not suffer kidney damage. Nevertheless, the University of Iowa study contains a warning that we all should heed: Excessive medications can do unseen damage.

Alcohol Regular, high consumption of alcohol definitely impairs memory and thinking. When you drink too much, the ethanol is broken down into various products, particularly fatty acid ethyl esters, which in turn reduce calcium concentrations in the brain. Calcium is essential for brain cells to communicate, and so your mind begins to slow down and forget. However, there is no unequivocal scientific evidence that moderate alcohol consumption ruins recall. Some researchers have studied the effects of "medium" doses of alcohol—0.05 milligrams per kilogram of body weight—on learning and verbal recall and found that the immediate result was minimal, or memory actually improved. Some studies have shown, however, that even moderate alcohol can hurt information processing tasks.

Tap Water Tap water can be another memory poison, especially when it comes from antiquated, poorly maintained systems that contain numerous toxins. It is not unusual for tap water to contain toxic chemicals, lead, and even fecal bacteria. A much better alternative is steamed distilled water, which is also called purified, demineralized, deionized, or reverse osmosis water. Through distillation, the water is largely purified of dissolved solids, chlorine,

TAKE ACTION

Memory Poisons to Avoid

Saturated fats. Reduces the flow of oxygen-rich blood to the brain.

Stress. Creates a cascade of chemicals that kill brain cells.

Alcohol. Breaks down chemicals in the brain that are vital for communication between cells. Here I refer to alcohol as a toxin that disrupts brain chemistry.

Tap water. Odds are high that the liquid coming from your tap contains chlorine, fluorine, aluminum, lead, and bacteria.

Caffeine. In more than moderate amounts can overexcite the brain and make concentration and learning difficult. A little caffeine is a good brain stimulus; moderate amounts work to the detriment of memory.

Emotional turmoil. When the brain's emotional centers are highly activated, concentration and learning are difficult.

Medication. Medications that sedate or calm can also slow memory and learning. Drugs known to impair memory include tricyclic antidepressants, lithium, antihypertensives, antibiotics, and analgesics.

Nonsteroidal anti-inflammatory drugs. In very high doses, drugs like ibuprofen, which are used to reduce inflammation, have been linked to memory loss, particularly immediate word recall.

and toxic material. Minerals have also been removed from the water. Other types of "natural" water, such as bottled spring water or mineral water, are not as pure as distilled water.

ON THE HORIZON: A WELL-TUNED MIND

About forty years ago, an Italian biologist searching for ways to treat cancer and experimenting with how cells grow or die, discovered a protein that played a pivotal role in the development of certain glands and muscles. Later, a Swiss neurobiologist discovered that this protein also seemed essential for neurons to survive and thrive. The biologist Rita Levi-Montalcini called the protein nerve growth factor, and ever since, scientists have been captivated by its possibilities. The discovery and subsequent investigations won her and a colleague a Nobel Prize in medicine.

Nerve growth factor (NGF) is produced in the central nervous system and operates by stimulating the growth of axons and dendrites, the branches between cells and the brain's communications network. It also helps produce the neurotransmitters that are heavily involved in learning and memory. All this makes NGF as essential to a healthy brain as oil is to a well-tuned engine.

Knowing that NGF circulated in the same areas of the brain that are ruined by Alzheimer's, scientists at Johns Hopkins University and in Sweden tested whether the nutrient could stimulate a damaged or aging memory system. Researchers injected NGF into the brains of aging rats and then watched them perform in a water maze, which is a standard learning and memory test. After three weeks of receiving NGF and testing, the mentally slow rats showed distinctive improvements in their learning and memory. Furthermore, nerve cells grew in the area of the brain where the NGF had been introduced.

There is also evidence that estrogen may stimulate NGF action in the part of the brain, the cholinergic system, that is the hub and spokes of our memory apparatus. This is good news for women on hormone replacement therapy who are concerned about memory and learning abilities.

Nerve growth factor is not something you can buy at the local nutrition store or pharmacy. At present, it cannot be made into an effective drug because its molecules are too big to pass through the blood-brain barrier, the protective filter around the brain. The only way to deliver it is either through direct injection or by coupling the NGF molecules to others that can slip through, what are known as carrier molecules. For now, nerve growth factor and other members of the neurotrophin family are being clinically tested as treatments for Alzheimer's, amyotrophic lateral sclerosis, and various nerve diseases. But it's definitely on the horizon.

NEWS TO WATCH FOR

- A California company, Cortex Pharmaceuticals, is collaborating with the National Institutes of Health (NIH) to develop a memory drug called Ampalex or ampakine. In company tests, the drug was given orally to twenty-four healthy young volunteers in a double-blind, placebo-controlled study and showed remarkable results for improving learning and memory. The drug works by increasing activity in the hippocampus, which is the brain's long-term memory center, and the cerebral cortex. The NIH has recently begun enrolling patients for an early-stage clinical trial of Ampalex as a treatment for mild dementia and for people in the early stages of Alzheimer's.
- Citicoline is a nutritional supplement shown to improve learning and memory in people over age fifty, and is currently being tested for FDA approval. In a controlled study involving ninety-five people between the ages of fifty and eighty-five taking 1,000–2,000 mg per day for two or three months, the citicoline therapy improved delayed-recall memory in people with inefficient memories. People taking the higher dose showed not

only improved delayed-recall memory but also improved immediate memory.

• Researchers for the Dana Consortium on Memory Loss and Aging are coordinating with colleagues at Johns Hopkins University School of Medicine to begin testing Cognex, an Alzheimer's drug, on people with normal memories.

• A nootropic agent called huperzine A, which comes from a moss native to China, has shown promise in fighting memory disorders, particularly in Alzheimer's patients. Chinese scientists have found that the moss extract works on the chemical imbalance that is associated with Alzheimer's and has produced positive results in reversing working-memory deficits.

• A special antioxidant called a nitrone has been found to re-

HOW OLD IS YOUR MEMORY?

Read the names below, then cover them.

Barbara Cline
Henry Russell
Diane Foster
Bill Daniels
Karen Tate
Jeff Allen

Now fill in the blanks:

__________ Daniels
__________ Cline
__________ Foster
__________ Allen
__________ Tate
__________ Russell

Scoring: Under age fifty, two correct answers is average. Over age fifty, one is average.

verse age-related brain damage in animals; old rodents given the chemical did as well on a maze as young animals. Scientists at Centaur Pharmaceuticals in California are now testing an antioxidant-type drug on people.

A PERSONAL MEMORY PROGRAM

Here's what I do regularly to stimulate my memory of particular information or to sharpen my mind for better learning.

- Constructive visualization. Mental rehearsal of an event, conversation, or activity before it actually happens in order to eliminate stress of the unknown and relax. The lack of tension makes learning and remembering much easier.
- Vigorous exercise. When I am reading and trying to remember the information, I frequently take a break and do vigorous exercise. Depending on the surroundings, I may do handstand push-ups, regular push-ups, or jumping jacks, or take a brisk walk around the block a couple of times.
- Memory pills. My personal favorites are aged garlic and vitamin C.

TONY LITTLE: VISUALIZATION FOR A STRONG MEMORY

Infomercial entrepreneur and "America's Personal Trainer," Tony Little has perfected the art of visualization to boost his memory. He explains how he uses it in his TV work: "I visualize each show. I'm the only live infomercial, and the only person who can go out and make a twenty-eight-minute live situation work. I visualize exactly who I am selling to, how I'm going to sell it, what's going to be there—all that detail. I go over and over it in my mind, so by the time I do it, it's exactly right. That's why they call me One-Take Tony."

• Concentration. The weakest link in my memory chain is my tendency to be thinking of a dozen things while listening to something I need to remember. I am constantly trying to correct this by applying full-bore attention to whoever is speaking to me. This entails lots of eye contact, positioning myself so that we're face-to-face and I am not scanning the periphery, and keeping my hands and body still to eliminate distractions. I don't strain to remember exactly but let my focused attention and eventual absorption do the job.

• Memory triggers. When I want to remember something, I create a personal mnemonic device. For instance, if I want to remember to send someone a check, I move my pen to a different pocket, or if I want to remember to call someone at an appointed time, I turn my watch face to the inside of my arm.

• Articulation. When I am trying to learn or memorize complicated or technical information, I will read the material aloud or repeat aloud the facts I am trying to retain. When meeting someone for the first time, I repeat his or her name aloud and try to use it at least twice in the next minute.

• Taming anger. I have found that anger, those times when my emotions take over my mind and body, can be the biggest impediment to learning and memory. At these times, rational thinking disappears. So, whenever I feel an inkling of anger or frustration coming on, I immediately dampen it, knowing that it will block learning or remembering.

• Diet and drink. In addition to following a low-fat, high-carb, no-fried-foods, and no-red-meat diet, I consume enormous amounts of fruit and fruit drinks, and carbohydrates in the form of shredded wheat, oats, and bran. My drink of choice is bottled distilled water, and when I do drink alcohol, it is only small amounts of red or white wine.

• Breathing exercises. Deep breathing, which means breathing through the nostrils and pulling air from the lower diaphragm, helps center my thinking and concentration. As you will learn in Chapter Four, deep breathing avoids the hormonal reaction that

A BRIEF REFRESHER

There is much we can do to slow memory loss and to accentuate those facets of our memory that get better over the years. There are lots of memory boosters you can tap into. Here's a summary.

Memory foods: aged garlic, unsaturated fat found in olive oil and fish oil, and pasta

Minerals and nutrients: choline, boron, magnesium, zinc, and phosphatidylserine (PS)

Vitamins: B_1, B_6, B_{12}, C

Nootropics: piracetam, nimodipine, clonidine

Hormones: estrogen, DHEA, hGH, testosterone

Smells: chocolate, peppermint, ammonia

Exercise: Regular exercise, especially aerobic activity, delivers more oxygen to the brain and so sharpens memory.

Routines: Certain activities sharpen recall. These include writing things down, focusing for longer than eight seconds on items to be remembered, vocalizing, using associations, and regularly practicing what you want to remember.

causes panic and the fight-or-flight feeling so that you can think more clearly and learn more readily.

SELECTED SOURCES

Benton, D., et al. "The impact of long-term vitamin supplementation on cognitive functioning." *Psychopharmacology,* 117, 298–305, 1995.

Blaun, R. "How to eat smart." *Psychology Today,* May–June 1996, 35–42.

Clarkson-Smith, L., and Hartley, A. A. "Relationship between physical exercise and cognitive abilities in older adults." *Psychology and Aging,* 4 (2), 183–89, 1989.

Cohen, G. D. *The Brain in Human Aging.* Springer Publishing Co., New York, 1988.

Crook, T. H., et al. "Effects of phosphatidylserine in age-associated memory impairment." *Neurology,* 41, 644–49, 1991.

De Angelis, L., and Furlan, C. "The effects of ascorbic acid and oxiracetam on scopolamine-induced amnesia in a habituation test in aged mice." *Neurobiology of Learning and Memory,* 64, 119–24, 1995.

Deberdt, W. "Interaction between psychological and pharmacological treatment in cognitive impairment." *Life Sciences,* 55 (25–26), 2057–66, 1994.

Deyo, R. A. "Nimodipine facilities associative learning in aging rabbits." *Science,* 243 (4892), 809–12, February 10, 1989.

Fabryel, B., and Trzeciak, H. I. "Nootropics: pharmacological properties and therapeutic use." *Polish Journal of Pharmacology,* 46, 383–394, 1994.

Fackelmann, K. "Forever smart: does estrogen enhance memory?" *Science News,* 147 (5), 72–73, February 4, 1995.

Frye, C. A., and Sturgis, J. D. "Neurosteroids affect spatial/reference, working and long-term memory of female rats." *Neurobiology of Learning and Memory,* 64, 83–96, 1995.

Gale, C. R., et al. "Cognitive impairment and mortality in a cohort of elderly people." *British Medical Journal,* 312, 608–11, March 9, 1996.

Gladwell, M. "The estrogen question." *New Yorker,* June 9, 1997.

Gold, P. E. "Role of glucose in regulating the brain and cognition." *American Journal of Clinical Nutrition,* 61 (4 Suppl), 987S–95S, April 1995.

Greenwood, C. E., and Winocur, G. "Learning and memory impairment in rats fed a high saturated fat diet." *Behavioral Neural Biology,* 53 (1), 74–87, 1990.

Hayflick, L. *How and Why We Age.* Ballantine Books, New York, 1994.

Israel, L., et al. "Drug therapy and memory training programs: a double-blind randomized trial of general practice patients with age-associated memory impairment." *International Psychogeriatrics,* 6 (2), 155–70, Fall 1994.

Jaret, P. "Think fast." *Hippocrates,* April 1996, 78–79.

Kallan, C. "Probing the power of common scents." *Prevention,* 43 (10), 38–44, October 1991.

Khalsa, D. S. *Brain Longevity.* Warner Books, New York, 1997.

Klatz, R., and Kahn, C. *Grow Young with HGH.* HarperCollins, New York, 1997.

Kotulak, R. *Inside the Brain: Revolutionary Discoveries of How the Mind Works.* Andrews and McMeel, Kansas City, Mo., 1996.

Livermore, B. "Build a better brain." *Psychology Today,* 25 (5), 40–48, September–October 1992.

Martinex-Serrano, A., et al. "Long-term functional recovery from age-induced spatial memory impairments by nerve growth factor gene transfer to the rat basal forebrain." *Proceedings of the National Academy of Sciences, U.S.A.,* 93 (13), 6355–60, June 1996.

Matsuoka, N., et al. "Changes in brain somatostatin in memory-deficient rats: comparison with cholingeric markers." *Neuroscience,* 66 (3), 617–26, June 1995.

Moriguchi, T., et al. "Aged garlic extract prolongs longevity and improves spatial memory deficit in senescence-accelerated mouse." *Biological Pharmacology Bulletin,* 19 (2), 305–7, 1996.

Muller, W. E. "Glutamatergic treatment strategies for age-related memory disorders." *Life Sciences,* 55 (25–26), 2147–53, 1994.

Raloff, J. "Novel antioxidants may slow brain's aging." *Science News,* 151, January 25, 1997.

Riggs, K. M., et al. "Relations of vitamin B-12, vitamin B-6, folate and homocysteine to cognitive performance in the normative aging study." *American Journal of Clinical Nutrition,* 63, 306–14, 1996.

Saag, K. G., et al. "Nonsteroidal anti-inflammatory drugs and cognitive decline in the elderly." *Journal of Rheumatology,* 22, 2142–47, 1995.

Salaman, M. K. "Mind your brain." *Total Health,* 18 (3), 20–24, June 1996.

Sasaki, H., et al. "Vitamin B12 improves cognitive disturbance in rodents fed a choline-deficient diet." *Pharmacology Biochemistry and Behavior,* 43, 635–39, 1992.

Satoh, T., et al. "Walking exercise and improved neuropsychological functioning in elderly patients with cardiac disease." *Journal of Internal Medicine,* 238, 423–28, 1995.

Schatzl, H. "Neurotrophic factors: ready to go?" *Trends in Neuroscience,* 18 (11), 463–64, November 1995.

Shepherd, G. M. *Neurobiology.* Oxford University Press, New York, 1994.

Sherwin, B. B. "Estrogenic effects on memory in women." *Annals of the New York Academy of Sciences,* 743, 213–30, November 14, 1994.

Spiers, P. A., et al. "Citicoline improves verbal memory in aging." *Archives of Neurology,* 53 (5), 441–48, May 1996.

Stein, D. G., et al. *Brain Repair.* Oxford University Press, New York, 1995.

Stoppe, G., et al. "Reasons for prescribing cognition enhancers in primary care." *International Journal of Clinical Pharmacology and Therapeutics,* 33 (9), 486–90, 1995.

Tanouye, E. "Memory drug appears to aid rodent recall." *Wall Street Journal,* July 20, 1994.

Tracy, J. I., and Bates, M. E. "Models of functional organization as a method for detecting cognitive deficits: data from a sample of social drinkers." *Journal of Alcohol Studies,* 55 (6), 726–38, November 1994.

Werbach, M. R. *Nutritional Influences on Mental Illness: A Sourcebook of Clinical Research.* Third Line Press, Tarzana, Calif., 1991.

Young, S. N. "Some effects of dietary components (amino acids, carbohydrate, folic acid) on brain serotonin synthesis, mood and behavior." *Canadian Journal of Physiological Pharmacology*, 69, 893–903, 1991.

Zhi, Q. X., et al. "Huperzine A ameliorates the spatial working memory impairments induced by AF64A." *NeuroReport*, 6 (16), 2221–24, November 13, 1995.

Three

SLEEPING BETTER

FINDING YOUR PERSONAL SLEEP POWER

I am a reluctant sleeper and only begrudgingly hand over hours of my nighttime to unconsciousness. I like working in the quiet hours of the evening, when noises are muted and lights low. This is a serene, thoughtful time for me, when I feel full of imaginative energy. It is also when my business associates in Asia are going full blast and want to talk. As a result, my workday typically stretches into the night. At most, I get four to six hours of sleep a night, and although I awaken alert and energetic, I probably do not sleep enough. But years of conditioning, and driving to squeeze as many productive hours from the day as possible, have enabled me to get by.

I have never wanted to sleep longer, but I do want to sleep *better,* and I have developed a personal routine for improving the quality of my sleep. I will share with you what I call my Sleep Power program, but to devise your own sleep program it is useful to understand why we sleep and what happens to our minds and bodies as we sleep; to know how dreaming affects our thought process; to be able to rec-

TAKE ACTION

These little-known truths about sleep motivate me to pay attention to my sleeping habits and correct troublesome trends:

- People who sleep less at night feel more stressed during the day. According to a survey in *American Demographic* magazine, about 43 percent of adults who sleep less than six hours a night feel stressed, while just 14 percent of adults who sleep seven to eight hours a night feel stressed.
- As you age you sleep less, not because you need less sleep, but because you become a less efficient sleeper and have trouble sleeping without interruption.
- "Power naps" can compensate for shorter sleep time and produce sharper concentration and alertness.
- Physical fitness is essential if you want to stay awake for an unusually long period of time. "The only way to fight off sleep is through energetic physical activity during the critical period of the early hours of the morning," says Peretz Lavie, head of the sleep laboratory at Technion-Israel Institute of Technology in Haifa, Israel.

ognize and combat sleep disturbances and disorders; to adjust to the changes in sleep that come with age; and to follow good "sleep hygiene."

FLYING INTO DIFFICULT SLEEP

My ability to harness the lessons of Sleep Power is challenged every time I fly overseas. I travel to the Far East about every other month, and, as everyone knows, flying and sleeping are about as compatible as driving and dancing. I do a number of things to fight jet lag, to reset my sleeping times, and to minimize my body's confusion.

Even before I leave Chicago, I begin to combat jet lag. I try to schedule my travel times so that I will arrive at my destination in the early evening and can go right to bed, regardless of how much sleep I have had while traveling. The day before traveling, I eat lightly and several small meals rather than three squares. This helps me adjust to different eating times and does not overburden my digestive system with a lot of food at one time, which can make sleeping difficult. I pick my "flying wardrobe" for comfort and circulation, usually a sweat suit and cotton underwear. My carry-on luggage includes dress clothes that I put on just before landing.

As soon as I board the plane, I take off my shoes and slip on a thick pair of socks to keep me warm. When I make my reservations,, I request vegetarian meals so that my meal trays are full of sleep-inducing carbohydrates rather than lots of heavy protein, which revs up brain chemicals and delays sleep. During the flight, I avoid alcohol, including beer and wine (I'll explain later how alcohol interferes with deep sleep), and drink lots of bottled water, which counteracts the dehydrating effects of dry cabin air. Also when I make my reservations, I book a window seat—this makes me less likely to be jostled or awakened by flight attendants or other passengers going by.

I also assemble my carry-on luggage with sleep in mind, packing a toothbrush and toothpaste, dental floss, mouthwash, an eye mask, a neck-support pillow, and earplugs. Before sleeping during a flight, I go through my usual nighttime rituals, which not only makes me feel good but psychologically gets me ready for snoozing.

WEAPONS AGAINST JET LAG

Adjust eating times to coincide with destination mealtimes.
Avoid heavy meals that tie up your digestive system.
Wear clothes that are both comfortable and warm.
Avoid drinking alcohol and drink lots of water.
Honor your sleep time rituals.

INSIDE YOUR SLEEPING BRAIN

Given the prominence sleep plays in our lives, you may be surprised to learn that most medical schools offer no education on the subject. And the National Commission on Sleep Disorders Research reported in 1993 that in the entire United States it found only ten postdoctoral students and six postdoctoral fellows doing basic sleep research.

Still, we know a fair amount about the mechanics of sleep. Sleep is not a constant condition but a series of mental states and stages that vary according to brain wave activity and dreaming. Sleep has four stages plus rapid eye movement (REM) sleep—the time when we dream most vividly. Stage one begins as we fall asleep and brain waves become regular. Breathing and pulse rate slow and our skeletal muscles relax, making it impossible for us to hold our heads up. As we nod off (literally!), brain waves become slower in stage two, although we are still in light sleep and can awaken easily. Stage three and stage four are deep sleep, and our brain waves slow down but show regular spikes and "spindles," which are bursts of brain wave activity. About ninety minutes after closing our eyes, we enter rapid eye movement sleep and start dreaming. During this time, the body so completely loses its muscle tone that we become virtually paralyzed. The only reason the eyes move is that those muscles are not controlled through the spinal column but from the brain stem.

Another hallmark of REM sleep, say researchers who have studied people wired with electrodes sleeping in their labs, is sexual arousal. Men have erections and women's vaginal blood flow increases. As the night goes on, you rise and fall through sleep stages and REM sleep, with most of your REM sleep taking place at the tail end of the night. While a newborn spends about half of his daily sixteen hours of sleep in REM, adults spend only about an hour and a half out of eight hours every night in this deep dream state. Even when an adult sleeps less than eight hours, the length of the REM state is about the same.

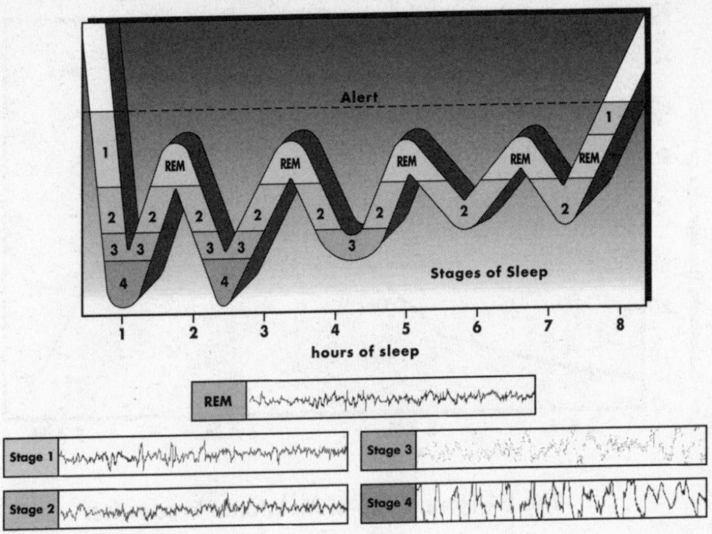

Adapted from *The Brain and Nervous System,*
AMA Home Medical Library (1991)

Sleep is vital for our body's chemistry. As we slumber, our brains are busy regulating hormones and neurochemical production. The hormone perhaps most affected by sleep is melatonin, which is produced by the pineal gland deep inside the brain. If you keep in mind that the pineal is wired to the eyes and so reacts to light and dark, it is easy to understand why melatonin production is influenced by nighttime and the seasons. Melatonin is the chemical that regulates our circadian rhythms. The dark night and the short days of winter stimulate the pineal to produce melatonin. When melatonin is circulating through our bloodstream, our bodies know it is time to sleep. As the night ends and the sun begins to rise, the pineal gradually pumps out less melatonin and we awaken. At night, the brain produces five to ten times more melatonin than during the day.

The amount of melatonin circulating in the brain affects the quality of sleep. With more melatonin comes longer and deeper sleep. Unfortunately, as we age our brains gradually make less melatonin, which partly explains the insomnia that besets older people. Ac-

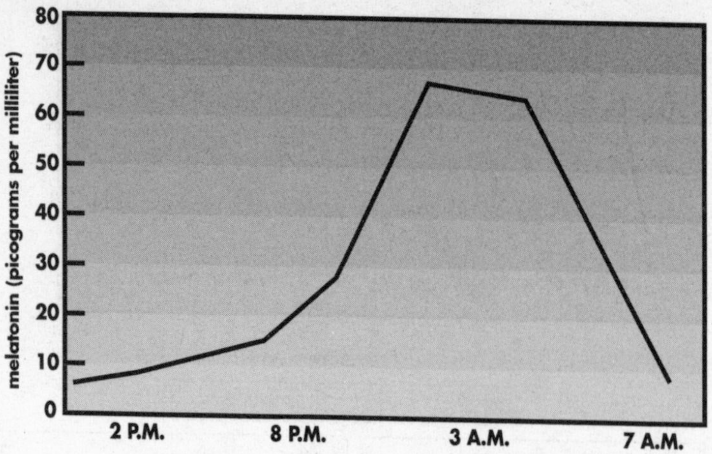

The 24-Hour Cycle of Melatonin Production

Adapted from *Stopping the Clock* (1996)

cording to a study in Israel, elderly insomniacs produce just half as much melatonin as younger people. Research with young people as well as the elderly shows that melatonin is a powerful sleep aid. Young adults at the Massachusetts Institute of Technology Clinical Research Center were given either melatonin or a placebo before an afternoon nap. Those who took the melatonin, some as little as 0.1 milligram, fell asleep within six minutes, while the placebo people needed twenty-five minutes to drop off.

Another hormone intertwined with sleeping is human growth hormone (hGH), which is made by the pituitary gland and pulses into the bloodstream in the early stages of sleep. Released in far greater quantities when we are young, hGH is converted into a growth factor that promotes bone growth. In adults, hGH is no less important, for it helps the body synthesize protein, break down body fat, build muscle, and synthesize collagen for cartilage, tendons, and ligaments. Many experts believe that hGH may be a powerful weapon against physical aging because it can produce no-

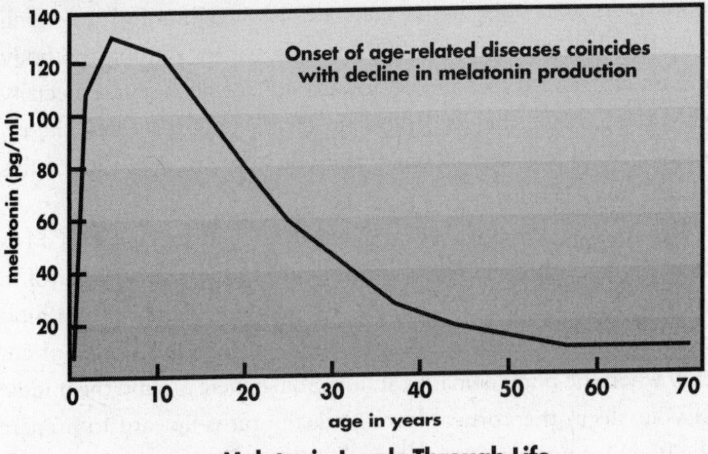

Melatonin Levels Through Life

Adapted from *Stopping the Clock* (1996)

ticeable effects on muscle mass, skin thickness, and skin elasticity. With the years, our bodies gradually generate less and less hGH. While melatonin brings on sleep, the reverse is true with hGH—that is, sleep triggers its production. The more sleep you get, the

24-Hour Plasma Cortisol

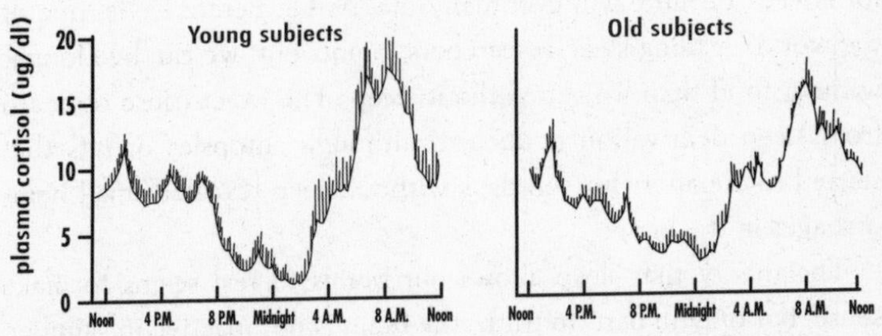

Adapted from *Hormonal Rhythmicity in Aging* (1995)

more hours your body has to generate this invigorating, anti-aging chemical. It is possible that hGH is essential for putting the body and brain chemistry in motion toward normal sleep, and especially REM sleep. Nevertheless, if you put off sleeping for a day, the release of hGH is also postponed, and you miss out on a shot of this natural body builder.

Just as you drift into sleep stages three and four, and hGH is pumping at its highest levels, the amount of the steroid cortisol in your system diminishes. Cortisol, you might remember from biology class, is produced by the adrenal glands and is a source of energy when the body demands action. Somewhere around the middle of your sleep, the cortisol level gradually turns upward to prepare the body for wakefulness and reaches its peak on awakening, when you are ready to go.

WHY DO WE SLEEP?

Despite how awful we feel without sleep and how buoyant we feel after a good night's sleep, no one knows exactly *why* we need sleep. One thing is certain: Not sleeping is fatal. Without sleep, a person's core body temperature plummets to dangerous levels, and inexplicably, the person's weight drops, even when more calories are consumed. (Remember how cold you got around 3 A.M. when pulling an all-nighter studying for an exam?) A person who is deprived of sleep for a week or more will eventually die. As Dr. Peretz Lavie, one of the world's leading sleep researchers, points out, we can live longer without food than we can without sleep. The exact cause of death from sleep deprivation is unclear, although autopsies of rats that started to die after thirteen days without sleep revealed small hemorrhages in the brain.

The theory that sleep allows our brains to rest seems to make sense, but only in part. In truth, the brain is not inactive in slumber. For one thing, it constantly monitors and regulates basic body functions. During deep dream sleep, brain waves on an electroencephalogram look the same as when a person is awake, and energy consumption and cerebral blood flow are virtually identical. Your brain is alert and scanning your surroundings, which explains why people can sleep through a jangle of noises and voices until someone speaks their name. Your brain is attuned to the sound of your name and ready to jerk awake if you are called. So much for the "restful brain" idea.

Sleep does help us conserve energy, however, and is essential to our physical health. While we sleep, our immune systems are more active and so help the body fight off disease. In animal experiments, rats deprived of sleep were much more susceptible to viruses and bacterial infections from routine, usually harmless sources. A recent study of killer T cells, which fight infection in the body, found that they are least active in insomniacs, only moderately active in depressed people, and most active in people with normal sleep habits.

That third of our life we spend in bed may also be critical for mental development, especially memory, learning, and a host of other complicated thought processes, such as making decisions and solving complex problems. Some researchers believe that the early stages of sleep are essential to our physical well-being, while REM sleep is essential to our mental well-being. When students at the Sleep Disorders Center at Laval University, Canada, enrolled in an intensive course to learn a second language, this additional brain exercise resulted in their logging more REM sleep.

In a noteworthy experiment, Dr. Carlyle Smith at Trent University in Ontario, Canada, gave four groups of students rules to a complicated logic game and a list of words to memorize, and that evening allowed each group different amounts of sleep. The next morning, everyone remembered the words, but the groups that got little or no sleep remembered 30 percent less of logic game rules than the well-rested groups. Dr. Smith believes that sleep, especially REM sleep, is essential for the absorption of new information into long-term memory.

Researchers at the University of Paris-Sud in Orsay, France, agree. In a learning study involving rats and mice, the animals spent markedly more time in paradoxical sleep (what researchers call REM sleep in animals) after they had learned new tasks. In another study by Dr. Smith, animals not allowed to sleep immediately after learning their way through a complicated maze did not retain their learning as well as animals that were allowed to sleep.

REM sleep may be especially good for perceptual learning—knowing how to act when given a visual cue. Students at the Weizmann Institute in Israel were given a simple task to learn aided by a visual cue and then allowed to sleep. During the night, some of the students were awakened during REM sleep while others dreamed on. The next morning, those students who got a full night of REM sleep performed their recently learned reaction much faster.

Problem-solving appears to be another kind of learning that is improved by dream sleep. Dr. Louis Gottschalk at the University of California, Irvine, has studied the brain metabolism of three dozen students while they were awake, sleeping, and in REM sleep. He found that intense dreaming during REM generated significant activity in the area of the brain that processes reasoning and solves problems.

Looking at all the evidence, I think Dr. Stephen LaBerge, a pioneer in sleep research, best summarized what REM sleep does for us. "REM sleep helps us adapt to our environment by improving our mood, memory and other cognitive functions through restoring certain neurochemicals that are depleted in the course of waking mental activity," he says.

SLEEP ROBBERS: VARIETIES OF INSOMNIA

Bad sleep is an almost universal affliction. While the frequent trips around half the globe upset my sleep, millions of other people lose sleep nightly because of chronic disorders such as insomnia or sleep apnea, work schedules (particularly shift work), and personal factors such as a new baby in the home or heavy alcohol consumption.

A government study of the problem has found that 40 million Americans suffer from sleep disorders and another 20 to 30 million have occasional sleep problems. Experts I know say that about one-third of the entire population suffers from frequent insomnia. Women generally have more sleeping difficulties than men, but more men experience sleep apnea, a serious breathing problem that repeatedly jerks them awake. Furthermore, people who are divorced, widowed, separated, or single experience insomnia more often than married people. Economic status makes a difference, too, with people on the lower rungs of the economic ladder reporting more insomnia than the affluent.

Insomnia is one of those silent miseries that can undermine every aspect of a person's life. Many people's slow or fuzzy thinking, quick temper, bad mood, poor reflexes, and even physical clumsiness can be traced to their sleeping habits. Nothing saps mental vigor quicker than repeated insomnia, which is why even the federal government has been concerned enough to create a national commission to study the problem. Its two-volume, almost four-hundred-page report, *Wake Up America: A National Sleep Alert* (1994), concludes, "A substantial number of Americans, perhaps the majority, are functionally handicapped by sleep deprivation on any given day."

Insomnia comes in many shapes. There is "transient" insomnia that may involve difficulty getting to sleep or staying asleep, waking in the early morning hours before the normal time, or tossing and turning all night and waking up tired. This type of insomnia lasts for only a short while and is usually the result of jet lag, an illness, medication, or stress. For most people, me included, on those nights when you cannot get to sleep or are awake in the middle of the night rehashing an argument or working out a problem, stress is the culprit.

Your sleeping environment can also disrupt your slumber—a strange bed or pillow (I know a famous author who takes a special foam pillow on all her book tours because she has difficulty sleeping without it), unusual noises (you may be used to sleeping with one

THE TUBE CAN'T HELP

If you find you cannot sleep in the middle of the night, do not resort to the late-late movie on TV. Televisions emit full-spectrum bright lights and so tend to stimulate people, not put them to sleep.

sound but kept awake by a new noise), or bright lights (when the city repaired the streetlight outside my window, it took me a week to get used to it).

When your sleeplessness lasts more than three weeks, it becomes chronic and suggests a serious medical, psychological, or behavioral cause. Medical causes could be a nighttime breathing obstruction called apnea or a movement disorder called restless leg syndrome. Psychological roots may be a psychiatric problem such as a mood or anxiety disorder, or recurring stress such as that caused by bereavement. On the behavioral front, there are many possible wellsprings of chronic insomnia: substance abuse, particularly with alcohol or smoking; or a severely disrupted circadian rhythm resulting from irregular work or personal habits.

In addition to persisting for weeks, chronic insomnia has other, telltale symptoms:

- At night, you do not fall asleep within thirty minutes.
- You wake up more than five times a night and are awake for more than thirty minutes.
- You wake up at least two hours earlier than you normally do, cannot get back to sleep, and have slept less than six and one-half hours.
- Your stage four, slow wave, sleep lasts less than fifteen minutes a night.

PRESCRIPTION AND OVER-THE-COUNTER DRUGS THAT CAN CAUSE INSOMNIA

Blood pressure medication: clonidine, beta-blockers, reserpine
Hormones: oral contraceptives, thyroid medications, cortisone, progesterone
Bronchodilators
Decongestants
Nicotine
Caffeine
Diet pills
Levodopa
Quinidine
Anacin, Excedrin, Empirin
Cold and cough medications

The Air Robber: Sleep Apnea

Sometimes insomnia is not just a sleeping problem but a symptom of some other ailment. One of the more serious medical problems it can signal is sleep apnea, an involuntary halt in breathing during sleep that can last a few seconds or as long as a minute or two. This sudden cutoff in air jerks a person awake as he or she struggles to breathe and can happen dozens of times a night. Sleep researchers have watched patients ripped from slumber even hundreds of times a night by their inability to breathe. Needless to say, come morning, the patient is exhausted from having had only fragments of solid sleep.

Sleep apnea is surprisingly common. Upwards of 4.6 million people in the United States alone have been diagnosed with the condition. Most are men. Many people who have sleep apnea know only that they are always tired and that their spouse complains they snore heavily and toss and turn in their sleep. Some people with apnea may find they are constantly waking up during the night without knowing why and believe they are suffering from simple insomnia. A friend of mine was diagnosed with apnea on a shuttle flight. Right after takeoff he fell asleep but was soon awakened by the passenger next to him, who happened to be a doctor. After explaining that his excessively loud snoring was bothering people, the doctor gave him a business card and suggested he make an appointment to be tested for a sleep disorder.

Apnea crops up most often in overweight, middle-aged men who complain of constant daytime sleepiness and accompanying psychological ailments, such as depression, irritability, and poor concentration. The main causes of apnea lie in the shape or configuration of a person's breathing passage. With obstructive sleep apnea, the airway closes because of a large bundle of tissue, the uvula, hanging in the back of the throat, or a tongue that is naturally set so far back as to block the passage, or fat deposits in the air passage.

The treatments for apnea range from simple and obvious changes in lifestyle to complex surgery. Given that so many of the men diagnosed with apnea are obese, losing weight is often the first line of treatment. Heavy drinkers are advised to cut back in order to improve the general quality of their sleep. Sleeping with the head slightly raised to prevent the tongue from collapsing into the airway may also help. But these changes alone are usually not enough.

One common treatment is to sleep wearing a device like an oxygen mask called a C-PAP, which provides continuous positive airway pressure. Even though it may irritate nasal passages, and it takes time to get used to sleeping with it, the mask has a high success rate. Surgery is another option, and can entail removing tissue to enlarge the airway passage or some type of nasal or throat reconstruction. Laser surgery to remove tissue on both sides of the uvula, and even the entire uvula itself, is done to stop snoring and may also cure the apnea. Medication for apnea is of limited value and is used only when there is a complication, like a thyroid condition or depression.

Constant Motion: Restless Leg Syndrome

Restless leg syndrome, as the name implies, is more a condition that influences sleep than a sleeping disorder in itself. Twitchy legs, the feeling that bugs are crawling around your legs, or muscle aches that make lying still impossible can get in the way of falling asleep or make staying asleep nearly impossible. The elderly suffer restless leg syndrome, or periodic limb movement disorder, more than most, and it's usually associated with another physical ailment that ruins people's sleep. With this condition, legs jerk or cramp uncontrollably while you are asleep, sometimes causing brief wakefulness, or sometimes not. Nevertheless, sleep is constantly interrupted, and the sufferer awakens tired and is sleepy during the day. Both these conditions have been linked to anemia, vitamin deficiencies, poor circulation, and kidney disease, although current thinking is that the underlying cause is hereditary. However, the problems may well be relatively mild and sporadic and may not require medical treatment. When treatment is necessary, mild tranquilizers that contain an anticonvulsant have proved effective.

Sleeplessness Associated with Mental Disorders

Insomnia can also signal a serious mental disorder. Persistent terminal insomnia—awakening in the early morning without being able to go back to sleep—is a classic indication of depression. Difficulty falling asleep or not being able to stay asleep are also associated with depression.

Other types of insomnia accompany mood disorders, particularly manic-depression. For instance, not sleeping for days, accompanied by bursts of high energy and frantic activity, can trigger a manic or psychotic episode. People who are manic sleep erratically, and often during the day but not at night.

Keep in mind that with mental disorders sleep difficulties are only

TAKE ACTION

Keep a Sleep Log

A do-it-yourself way to track the source of your sleeping problems is by keeping a sleep log.

In a spiral notebook with a page for each day, take notes from the night before: the time you went to bed, how long you think it took you to fall asleep, the number of times you woke up during the night (as well as you can remember), and the reasons (to go to the bathroom, change a sweat-soaked sleeping garment, worry about the next day's meeting). Give the night's sleep a quality grade, with "F" being agitated and exhausting and "A" being deep and refreshing. Also note mealtimes, snacks, and anything you consumed before bedtime. Include not only food and drinks but also any medication, even a simple aspirin. Make a note if you exercised before bedtime, too. If you sleep with someone, ask him or her about your sleep—whether you snored, talked or walked in your sleep, or anything else unusual. In this way you can determine which variables affect your ability to sleep and the log can be used to describe your specific habits to a doctor, if necessary.

one of many other symptoms. Insomnia alone does not necessarily mean you need psychiatric attention.

Sliding Sex Hormones

The decline in sex hormones over the years also fiddles with our sleep. During middle age, as women's estrogen drops and men's testosterone levels slide, a solid night's sleep is harder to find. Some scientists think they know precisely why.

The halt in estrogen production that comes with menopause affects every part of a woman's life, including her sleep. Nighttime hot flashes can be so severe that women find themselves taking cool showers in the middle of the night and repeatedly changing sweat-soaked bedding. Such sleeping problems can begin when a woman enters perimenopause, the time before menopause when hormone levels begin to fluctuate, which may be as early as the late thirties. About 40 percent of women over age forty experience an insomnia that many experts believe is caused by hormones in transition.

When the symptoms of menopause become unbearable, many women opt for estrogen replacement therapy (ERT). ERT deflects the physical signs of aging and the possible onset of heart disease and osteoporosis, while another of its benefits is smoothing out the ragged, disrupted sleep of the pre- and postmenopausal years. But the sleep bonus provided by ERT may, in truth, come from another hormone, progesterone, which doctors combine with estrogen for menopausal women at risk for endometrial complications.

Researchers at the Max Planck Institute in Munich, Germany, have found that progesterone has pronounced effects on different kinds of sleep. A dose of progesterone shortens the amount of sleep time before the onset of REM sleep, increases pre-REM sleep, and lengthens the time of deep sleep. Put another way, they found that progesterone can work like a mild sedative.

Men do not escape the hormonal swings that come with age. As they near their fiftieth year, testosterone levels begin to slide. While many suffer from a decreased libido and some degree of impotence, sleep problems are not common. Only a small fraction of men will experience erratic sleep and disruptive night sweats.

DHEA, a sex hormone we produce less of as we age, may help some people sleep better. Available over-the-counter, DHEA has been shown to significantly increase REM sleep in healthy men. Given a high dose, 500 mg, test patients at the Max Planck Institute in Munich stayed in deep slumber much longer than patients who did not get a nightly dose of the hormone.

Another Sleep-Stealing Hormone

Human growth hormone may be contributing to poor sleep in both men and women. Scientists have discovered that people with abnormal hGH production—either too little or too much—experience disturbed REM sleep, which doctors have been able to correct by adjusting hormone levels.

Our hormones clearly tamper with our sleep, but their influence on other parts of our lives, from how our skin ages to how well we remember, is much more pronounced. Signing up for some type of hormone replacement therapy for sleep alone makes little sense.

SUDDENLY ASLEEP: NARCOLEPSY

A much less prevalant sleeping disorder than insomnia is narcolepsy. It's as common in the general population, say sleep experts, as multiple sclerosis or Parkinson's disease. Although only 50,000 people have been diagnosed with narcolepsy, according to a U.S. government report, experts believe that 250,000 to 300,000 Americans suffer from it. This is an incurable, disabling sleep disease with four distinctive symptoms: great daytime sleepiness; episodes of muscle weakness or paralysis followed by strong emotion; hallucinations right at the beginning of sleep; and paralysis after falling asleep. Its cause is unknown, and it afflicts men and women equally. It can show up during childhood, and most people who have it show symptoms by the time they are twenty. But then it may be many years before it's officially diagnosed. Researchers say that fifteen years usually pass between the time someone begins showing signs of narcolepsy and the time when it is finally identified. Perhaps its most telltale symptom is sudden sleep—a person will be driving, in the middle of a conversation, or even eating, and suddenly fall asleep. This sudden sleep, which often occurs during times of high emotion, may last just a moment or for minutes.

Diagnosing narcolepsy is complicated and can be expensive, requiring extensive physical exams, neurological tests, and an exam used to diagnose most sleep disorders called the Multiple Sleep Latency Test (MSLT). The MSLT, which is conducted over a number of nights in a sleep lab, tells doctors how long it takes a person to fall asleep and measures the onset and length of sleep stages and REM sleep. Children with narcolepsy are often misdiagnosed as suffering from depression, mental illness, or hypothyroidism. Treatment is usually a combination of stimulant medication such as dextroamphetamines and a program of frequent daytime naps.

ARE YOU IN SLEEP DEBT?

Sometimes our sleep problems have nothing to do with biology or personal chemistry, and are purely voluntary. Many of us—most of us—at one time or another choose to deprive ourselves. And while our decision may be unavoidable as work forces us into toiling through the night, we may end up with a heavy sleep debt.

I try not to go without a night's sleep, but at times, like after a long, intercontinental flight, I have accumulated a serious "sleep debt." This is the term sleep scientists use to describe what happens after a string of nights with less-than-normal sleep time. Over a week, a sleep debt of just a few hours can have a noticeable effect and make you feel cold, weak, and irritable. Your thinking begins to suffer, too. Sleeping four hours less than usual for just one night can slow your thought processes by almost half and make it especially difficult to concentrate on a single task, such as reading a newspaper story.

The high interest we pay on our sleep debt is particularly obvious in our work lives. Given our twenty-four-hour society, lots of people work through the night answering phones, delivering pizza, servicing airplanes, talking to foreign customers, patrolling the streets, maintaining computer services, or simply working late. Shift worker blues beset millions of us. Typically, nocturnal hours reduce productivity and may stop us cold. More than half the people who work through the night, according to surveys, say they fall asleep on the job at least once a week. Working at night can also wreak havoc on people's personal lives. Night workers report three to five times more psychological problems, and the *Wake Up, America* study found that marital problems are a common fallout from nighttime jobs.

If you ever doubted the potentially disastrous consequences of lack of sleep, consider when bad accidents occur. On the Pennsylvania Turnpike and the New York Thruway, studies estimate, about half the fatal crashes are caused by sleepy drivers. The ripple effect of accidents from sleepiness can touch literally millions of people. The Exxon *Valdez* ran aground just after midnight, with the probable cause, according to the federal government, being the third mate's sleepiness. The nuclear reactor at Three Mile Island almost went into meltdown at 4 A.M. after a sleepy plant worker failed to notice that a coolant valve was stuck, and the Chernobyl reactor blew up at 1:23 A.M. When the space shuttle *Challenger* blew up, NASA workers had been getting less than six hours' sleep a night and working back-to-back twelve-hour shifts for between two and five days; one expert described them as "severely sleep deprived."

I suspect that a large segment of the population is running a sleep debt. Whenever I take an early morning flight and am aloft around 10 A.M., which should be an alert hour for most people, at least half of the coach cabin is dozing.

How can you tell if you're running a sleep debt? The National Sleep Foundation says that if you agree with any of the following statements, you may not be getting enough sleep and are therefore accumulating a debt.

1. Falling asleep is hard for me.
2. It takes me more than thirty minutes to fall asleep.
3. I have too much on my mind to go to sleep.
4. When I wake during the night, I can't go back to sleep.
5. I can't relax because I have too many worries.
6. Even when I sleep all night, I still feel tired in the morning.
7. Sometimes I am afraid to close my eyes and go to sleep.

8. I feel that I am dreaming all night long.
9. I wake up too early.
10. I am stiff and sore in the morning.
11. I feel irritable when I can't sleep.
12. I nod off when sitting in a dark room, like a movie theater, or during a business presentation.
13. I sleep for inordinate amounts of time on the weekend.

The important thing to realize about sleep debt is that you cannot bank extra hours in the sack. Getting lots of sleep one week does not mean you can sleep that much less the next week and feel fine. And the only way to *erase* an accumulated debt is with serious pillow time.

HOW MUCH IS ENOUGH?

Humans are grooved to a twenty-four-hour cycle of sleep and wakefulness, and the accompanying changes in body temperature, hormone production, and other physiological processes. By compressing or lengthening the time between light and dark, as we do when we fly across time zones, we throw our internal clocks into disarray. Flight crews and travelers have found that it takes two to three days after crossing multiple time zones to synchronize the personal wake/sleep cycle with the daylight and darkness of the new environment.

Not getting enough sleep undermines memory, learning, reasoning, math figuring, understanding of complicated verbal information, and the ability to make decisions. I can tell when I have not had enough when my speech slows and sounds clumsy. In addition, my body temperature goes on a roller-coaster ride, either rising to the point where I am flushed or dropping so much that I'm looking for another layer of clothing.

According to a Gallup poll of America's sleep habits, poor sleep hurts about half the entire population's ability to perform routine tasks at least once a week. You probably know this just by looking around at your coworkers and family members. The signs of a bad night's sleep or an accumulating sleep debt are hard to miss: One of the first clues is the loss of sense of humor, followed closely by crankiness, poor concentration, sluggishness, and forgetfulness.

Just how much sleep is enough? Put another way, how much do our brains and bodies need for peak performance? While each of us has a unique physiology and needs, researchers have put groups of people in special situations designed to reveal basic human sleep requirements. Typically, study volunteers are sequestered for weeks in windowless, soundproof rooms sealed off from natural and man-made environments so that only their individual circadian rhythms, rather than sounds, sunlight, external temperature, or normal daily routines, determine how much they sleep. When brains and bodies are free from the usual cues that tell them when to sleep and when to awaken, whether it's the sound of the eleven o'clock news on the television or the smell of morning coffee, pure biology sets the sleeping clock.

The *Wake Up, America* report noted that when a group of young people who usually sleep seven and one-half hours a night were sealed away in timeless rooms for two weeks, their average nightly sleep time rose to 8.6 hours. The notion that nine hours, not seven, is closer to our optimal shut-eye time is reinforced by other studies. Before Edison invented the lightbulb in 1879, average nightly sleep time was between nine and eleven hours.

In the Polar Psychology Project, researchers at the upper tip of Canada during the summer when the sun never sets relinquished all timekeeping devices, including the clock function on their computers, and were allowed to set their own schedules for work, recreation, and sleep. As described by Dr. Stanley Coren in *Sleep Thieves*, the researchers first kept to their usual sleeping time of seven to seven and a half hours a night. But very quickly their slumber time lengthened, and by the end of the experiment, they slept more than ten hours in every twenty-four-hour period.

Another source of clues about how much sleep we need comes

TAKE ACTION

You can conduct a personal sleeping experiment to learn how much sleep your brain and body need. First, you need to erase any sleep debt you may be laboring under. Given the pace and demands in most people's lives, odds are high that you do have a sleep debt, so devote the next two weeks to eliminating it. Add enough sleep time to your nightly pattern to pay off your debt (for many, this will consist of thirty minutes to one hour, which may be easier to tack on at the beginning of your night by going to bed earlier). A sign that you have successfully erased your debt is waking up when you want to without an alarm. (See the section on sleep debt to eliminate other indications that you are in debt.)

The actual experiment requires two weekends when you have the freedom to sleep and no morning commitments. Prepare your bedroom by eliminating any artificial or natural time cues. Unplug clocks, put away watches, keep pets out. Arrange the blinds or curtains so that they block out as much light as possible; tape them closed around the edges, if necessary. Soundproof the room as much as possible—shut windows, muffle radiators that kick on at programmed times, ask family members not to shower while you're sleeping if the noise filters through. For at least four evenings—two Fridays, two Saturdays—go to bed at your routine time and allow your body to tell you when to wake and arise (habit may push you awake at the usual time, but if you feel like sleeping more, roll over and do it). Four nights of natural sleep should give you a fairly accurate baseline figure for how much sleep your body can use.

from the animal kingdom. The animals most closely related to us physiologically, large primates, sleep much more than we do. Monkeys and large apes take ten hours a day, while gorillas need twelve hours.

One way to estimate needed sleep time is by noting how long doses of restorative sleep affect your thinking. Studies at Stanford University sleep labs, where people who normally sleep seven to eight hours a night were allowed an extra two hours' sleep whenever they chose, produced remarkable results. The subjects' mental skills became much sharper, particularly their alertness, ability to concentrate, and agility in juggling a number of demanding tasks simultaneously.

The answer to exactly how much sleep people need differs from person to person. Only you know whether after six hours a night you feel perky and ready to go or whether you are dragging after eight hours in the sack. The quality of sleep is subjective, so each of us has our own personal definition of insomnia and answer for "What is enough?"

Statistically, the odds are that your ideal number of sleep hours is close to eight, although you may well fall somewhere within a broader range. For normal, healthy adults, needed sleep time is anywhere from three hours (yes, this is the optimal amount for a very small fraction of people) to ten hours (Einstein insisted that he needed this much each night).

It may surprise you to learn that your sleep requirement does not change significantly over the years, even though, as you plow through middle age or near old age, your sleeping patterns change.

AS YOU GROW OLDER

As we grow older, we sleep differently. Although the amount of sleep each of us needs does not change, the quality of our sleep does change. Our bodies' chemistry is changing, and as a result, we spend less time in deep, delta wave sleep and more time in a light, sometimes restless sleep. We become more sensitive to our environment and so are easily awakened by sounds or lights we once slumbered through. Our sleep becomes more fragmented and we spend less time in REM sleep.

As age depletes us of hormones like melatonin, human growth hormone, estrogen, and testosterone, our internal clocks—our circadian rhythms—speed up, so we are sleepier earlier in the evening and awaken sooner. For most of our lives, the cycles of sleep and wakefulness peak twice every twenty-four hours: We are most sleepy between 2 and 4 A.M. and 2 and 4 P.M. (which is one reason the afternoon nap is such a staple in many countries—contrary to myth, people take siestas not only in warm countries but around the world) and most alert around noon and again around 7 P.M. As we age, the troughs of sleepiness shift and we become dozy closer to late morning or early evening, and wakeful in the early morning and late afternoon.

One way to reset a circadian clock knocked askew by age is with a dose of bright light. If you have ever suffered from seasonal affective disorder (SAD), the melancholy or depression that comes with the shorter daylight of winter, you know how either natural or artificial light affects you. People eager to reset their internal clocks will sit in front of strong lights (doctors specializing in treating SAD recommend some type of light box equipped with six 40-watt fluorescent tubes) for up to a few hours a day. When I'm feeling the effects of the weak winter sun, I sit in the light of two 500-watt halogen floodlights reflected off the wall by my desk. *Wake Up, America* says that exposure to bright light has been used successfully to help shift workers and NASA space shuttle crews maintain artificial sleep cycles.

Daily exercise at a set time of day can also help reset a person's circadian clock. In a recent study, both endurance and aerobic exercise helped healthy older men readjust their circadian body temperature increases and decreases, and their sleeping patterns, decreasing the incidence of insomnia. I have found vigorous walking to be very helpful in correcting a skewed circadian clock, and whenever I travel to the Far East, I start each day with a thirty- to sixty-minute brisk walk about the city.

Alterations in our lifestyle as we grow older—for instance, working less, getting into new hobbies, or personal developments such as a divorce or a child going off to college—also toy with our sleep

EXERCISE YOUR WAY TO HEALTHFUL SLEEP

There is strong evidence that exercise improves sleep. A group of forty-three people, aged fifty to seventy-six, who did no regular exercise, was put through a sleep and exercise study by scientists at Stanford University. Everyone in the group had complaints about how long it took them to fall asleep, waking up during the night, or waking too early in the morning. Twenty-four of the participants did thirty to forty minutes of low-impact aerobics four times a week, while the others were sedentary. After sixteen weeks, the people who exercised found that their sleep improved measurably. For instance, before the study, the exercise group needed almost twenty-nine minutes to fall asleep; after exercising for four months, they fell asleep in less than fifteen minutes.

patterns. Nevertheless, persistent problems with sleeping are not a natural part of aging and should not be ignored or accepted. If you find yourself on the back side of middle age with sleeping troubles, look to causes other than the calendar.

FINDING DREAMLAND

I have an active dream life involving exotic places in which I fearlessly confront perilous situations and do wondrous things like defeating monstrous apparitions and rescuing people. Dreaming, I believe, strengthens my imagination, judgment, and confidence, resolves inner conflicts, and helps me solve real-world problems. Of course, this is just an opinion, because science has little hard information about the meaning and reasons behind dreaming.

Although research into sleep and dreaming is a scientifically legitimate discipline, much of the investigation into dreaming is based

HOW OLYMPIC SOFTBALL STAR DOT RICHARDSON USES DREAMS TO PLAY BETTER

Ever since Dot Richardson was a little girl, she has used dreaming to visualize amazing feats on the ball field. For many years, she dreamed that she was playing shortstop and fielding a hard ball hit to her left. In her dream, she literally dove for the ball, stretching herself flat out, catching the ball, doing a forward roll, and then touching second base. She never actually practiced the action, she dreamed it. Then one day, as a star player on the U.S. Olympic softball team, she was playing in a national championship game in Houston and the hard drive came to her left. As she had hundreds of times in her dream, she made an amazing dive and catch, and thousands of fans went wild. They had never seen this kind of athletic skill, but for Dot, who recounted the story to *Sports Illustrated* writer Dan Yaeger, she had grooved it in her dreams, and it was as natural as trotting around the bases.

on speculation. Since we all dream—generally four to six times a night, with individual dreams lasting up to an hour—this activity deserves more scientific attention than it receives.

Our most vivid dreams take place during REM sleep, although we frequently dream throughout the night. REM dreams are not only the most complex but also bring the most refreshing sleep. As the night goes on and REM sleep consumes a larger chunk of our total sleep time, dreams grow longer, more complex, and more unusual. Dreams in early night are usually related to recent, daily events and familiar surroundings; later, our dreams are more convoluted and connected to the distant past. What you often remember are the later, flying-over-the-Grand-Canyon type of dreams rather than the dream about what you had for dinner.

While scientists argue over what dreams mean, if anything, they generally agree on how our brain manufactures them. As we drop into REM sleep, which generates distinctive brain waves, a primitive area of the brain on the brain stem starts firing electrical signals. These signals are carried by the brain chemical acetylcholine, and scientists have found that they can turn on REM sleep in cats by injecting the brain with a substance that acts like acetylcholine. Some of these signals shuttle to the thinking part of the brain and others go to where emotions originate. All the signals produce a mix of emotions and visual images that coalesce into a dream. When we forget dreams, say neurophysiologists, it is usually because our brains do not spit out enough of the chemicals needed for memory.

When it comes to what dreams mean—whether they have a point or purpose—researchers find little common ground. My dream of zooming across glassy waters watching the marine life below represents little more than random nerve impulses, according to Allan Hobson, a Harvard psychiatrist and director of the Laboratory of Neurophysiology at Massachusetts Mental Health Center and a prominent dream researcher. Hobson's book *The Dreaming Brain* revolutionized dream theory by explaining that REM sleep images are the result of a barrage of electrical impulses that our thinking brain, the cortex, has organized into loose patterns or associations to form the standard dream, which has elements of both the real and the bizarre. This dream possesses about the same amount of meaning, Hobson argues, as a hiccup. He explains, "We're not saying dreams have no meaning. We're saying dreams have meaning and they have nonsense. The problem is deciding which is which. In many instances, the meaning of dreams is so clear they hardly need interpretation. The real question arises over the idea that images in dreams are symbols. When people interpret that stuff as if it were meaningful, then sell those interpretations, it's quackery."

An alternative scientific theory about our dreams has been proposed by biologist Francis Crick, who won a Nobel Prize in medicine as one of the discoverers of DNA. He believes that dreams enable our brain to sort through and purge useless information and associations. The process helps us "unlearn" and shed some of the barrage of sensory and other information we pick up when we're awake.

Despite the debate over what dreams might mean, if anything, sleep researchers agree that they do serve an important purpose. Dreams appear to be particularly helpful in solving problems, making tough decisions, and easing emotional turmoil. Dream literature is full of famous accounts of problems solved during slumber: Jack Nicklaus's golf swing; the routes Harriet Tubman plotted for the Underground Railroad; Elias Howe's solution for designing a workable sewing machine; Robert Lewis Stevenson's plot for his story of Dr. Jekyll and Mr. Hyde; and a German scientist's discovery of the molecular structure of the benzene ring.

I find dreams very useful for solving problems, and I even keep a pad and pencil by my bed to jot down thoughts I remember between bouts of REM sleep. Most often I find myself solving organizational puzzles—arranging the corporate and marketing structure of a new company, for instance. And clearly, dream sleep helps us to untangle emotional puzzles either within ourselves and relating to our self-image or in our relationships with others. A couple of times I have gone to bed agonizing over what to do about a personal situation and found the next morning that the answer was clear. Even sleep lab researchers have testified to the emotional power of dreams. In their studies of REM sleepers, they have learned that about one-third of our dreams include feelings of anxiety and fear, and that happy thoughts come much less frequently.

Some people apply a special type of dreaming, the "lucid" dream, to their personal or professional dilemmas. Lucid dreaming entails being aware that you are dreaming as it is happening. It's being in the middle of a dream and, as you are flying, running, or whatever, knowing that it's just a dream and that you have some control over what you do. If, in the middle of a frightening dream, you can tell yourself, "This is just a dream," and dissolve the danger, then you have had a lucid dream.

TAKE ACTION

Sleep researchers offer a number of tips to improve your memory of dreams. First, realize that it is not difficult to remember your dreams—almost 90 percent of people studied in sleep labs recalled their dreams when awakened. It's important to believe that you can remember. Next, cram into your night as much REM sleep as possible, which means more sleep toward the end of the night; get up thirty minutes later. When you do awaken, do not move your head or body. Lie still and recall as many details as possible. Then write down your dream on a bedside tablet. Do this again and again. Practice sharpens your recall.

People eager to learn how to conjure up lucid dreams improve their memory of nightly dreams and go through certain mental exercises just as they are dropping off to sleep. Stephen LaBerge counts and focuses on his mental process. He repeats, "One, I'm dreaming, two, I'm dreaming," and so forth until he finds himself at fifty and really dreaming. If you think a mechanical aid might help as a biofeedback device, LaBerge has developed the NovaDream and DreamLight, which beep and flash red during REM sleep to wake the sleeper slightly so that he becomes aware when he is dreaming.

Dr. Stephen LaBerge, the Stanford University Sleep Research Center researcher who "discovered" this ability to control the actions of REM sleep, says that people use it to explore alternative ways of behaving or novel experiences without suffering consequences. Some sleepers say that lucid dreaming helps them recognize and correct unpleasant, negative emotions. During their dreams, they learn to recognize situations that will lead to trouble or possible harm, and to change what might happen and their emotional landscape. They learn to transform feelings of dread or fear into a sense of control and enjoyment.

SLEEP POTIONS

Usually when people cannot sleep, they try some kind of sleeping aid. According to the Gallup poll, about two-thirds of the people who have difficulty sleeping try an assortment of remedies, including warm baths, cutting out caffeine, relaxation, over-the-counter medicines, eating snacks, and exercise.

Foods, Drinks, Herbs

While most people know that the caffeine in coffee impedes sleep, some do not realize that the same stimulant also appears in chocolate, some soft drinks, and even over-the-counter and prescription medications. And keep in mind that caffeine flows into the bloodstream immediately, can generate a jolt within thirty minutes, and stays in the blood for up to six hours. A latte before you board a plane, for instance, may still be with you when you try to curl up.

Foods can affect your sleep, and your sleep can affect your appetite. Lack of sleep sets off a chemical chain reaction in your brain and actually stimulates your hunger, leading you to overeat. As you deprive yourself of sleep, your body begins to crave carbohydrates, which produce the brain chemical serotonin, which triggers even greater sleepiness. Thus, one danger of mixing sleep debt with eating is adding pounds. This is a common complaint of anyone pulling shift work—they eat at the wrong times, too often, and the wrong food, and so gain weight. Eating a large meal before bedtime diverts blood into the digestive system that should be circulating through your brain for its sleep activities (remember, our brains are just as active when in REM sleep as when we are awake).

If you want food that will help lull you into sleep, try what I do on these intercontinental flights. I eat starchy foods and foods with natural sweeteners. These include pastas, cereal, bread, potatoes, pretzels, cookies, fruits, and fruit juices. Calcium, which you find not only in milk and other dairy products but also in leafy green vegetables like broccoli, is another useful sleep aid. It helps soothe the neuromuscular system, stimulates the body's production of melatonin, and so acts as a natural tranquilizer. Tryptophan, an amino acid found in protein foods, helps bring on sleep by stimulating the brain's production of serotonin. While not available over-the-counter in the United States because a batch of the supplement that was contaminated badly hurt and even killed some people, it is available by prescription, and many people have found it to be a very effective sedative. One way to nudge your brain into producing tryptophan is by eating carbohydrates. By loading up on carbs, you create a shortfall of tryptophan-producing protein, and so trick your brain into spewing out more.

Since the U.S. Food and Drug Administration does not regulate herbs, there is no official approval for their use in America. However, they are widely researched and used in Europe. Particularly popular as a sleep aid is the liquid-extract form of valerian root, which is available in health food stores or in over-the-counter preparations. There are reportedly more than 150 drugs made from valerian root available in Germany alone. European scientists have been studying this herb for years, and have found that it helps reduce the amount of time it takes people to fall asleep, what's called the sleep latency period. One of the larger studies was conducted by Swiss researcher Peter Leathwood, who gave it to 128 people, who reported that it noticeably improved the quality of their sleep. There seems to be widespread agreement that it acts as a mild sedative with no side effects. Dr. Andrew Weil, author of *Spontaneous Healing,* recommends a dose of one teaspoon in warm water at bedtime.

Other herbs known for their drowsy effects include kava, which comes either in capsule form or as a liquid extract, and which Pacific islanders have been using for centuries for its calming qualities. Chamomile, especially in a tea, is famous for its sleepy influence. Lemon balm, also available in tea form, is another sedating herb. And the essence of lavender oil, according to a study reported in the

NATURAL SLEEP AIDS

Melatonin
- Dose: 0.1–10 mg/day.
- Start at the lowest dose and increase in 0.5-mg increments.
- Take on an empty stomach.
- Side effects: grogginess, mild headache, nausea, depression, lowered sex drive.

Tryptophan
- Naturally occurring in turkey and milk.
- Available by prescription.

Valerian root
- 1 tsp. liquid extract in warm water.
- No known side effects.

Kava Kava
- Follow label directions or physician instructions.

GABA: Gamma-aminobutyric acid
- A sleep aid supplement.
- Follow label directions or physician instructions.

Ethyl alcohol (*small* glass of wine prior to bedtime)

High-carbohydrate meal

Chamomile tea

Lemon balm tea

Lavender oil

Warm bath

White-noise generator

Cool bedroom

Fan directed at head of the bed

Eye mask

Earplugs

Clean towel over the pillow

Comfortable sleeping attire

prestigious English journal *Lancet,* can be as effective as a pharmaceutical sedative.

Sleeping Pills

The hot, new sleeping aid, as you probably know, is melatonin. Secreted by the pineal gland in the brain, melatonin is a hormone that regulates the body's reaction to light and dark, and so governs our circadian rhythms. It helps us know when seasons are changing, when the body is at its peak reproductive time, when to sleep, and when to wake. Darkness stimulates the production of melatonin and brightness suppresses it. As night falls, the pineal gland spits out more of this hormone, and we grow sleepy. As we age, however, the pineal gland produces less and less of the hormone. At age forty, the body produces one-sixth the melatonin it did in the teen years. Not surprisingly, elderly people with insomnia generate only a small fraction of the melatonin of a younger person with healthy sleeping patterns.

Taking melatonin to help sleep seems to make chemical sense. Swallowing a standard dose—8 milligrams—during the day can trick the body into thinking night has fallen and it is time to doze off, enabling one to nap on.

Unfortunately, not all sleep problems arise from the flow of melatonin, so it is not an effective sleep remedy for everybody. Several studies with different kinds of sleeping problems have yielded inconsistent results. The studies involved doses from 0.1 to 80 milligrams and two types of sleeper, normal sleepers whose circadian rhythms were out of sync and chronic insomniacs. While some chronic insomniacs got relief from melatonin, others did not. The best sleep from melatonin came to people suffering from jet lag, shift work adjustments, or delayed sleep onset after they took 5 milligrams a day for a month.

The bottom line on melatonin is that you have to discover whether it works for you, and experiment with various doses. However, you should avoid taking melatonin every day for prolonged periods, because taking supplements may suppress your natural production of melatonin. And be aware that in a small minority of people it can produce fatigue and even depression. If you want to try it and are not prone to these ailments, begin with a low dose (0.1–0.5 milligram) at bedtime.

Over-the-counter sleep medications can be effective without the next-morning grogginess that many people experience when taking prescription sleep aids. The secret ingredient in many of these OTC

TIPS FOR USING MELATONIN

Things to remember if you are going to use melatonin to improve your sleep:

- Sleep in total darkness or with eye shades on to maximize your body's production of melatonin.
- People under age forty produce adequate amounts of melatonin and so should take supplements only for short-term sleeping problems.
- It helps to take melatonin not only on the day of a flight but for two or three days after crossing time zones.
- Doses of melatonin as a weapon against jet lag range from 0.5 milligram to 10 milligrams a day. Lower doses produce fewer side effects. Grogginess is the most common side effect; others include mild headaches, upset stomach, lower sex drive, and depression. If unsure of your dose, start with a small amount and increase in 0.5-mg increments.
- Melatonin appears to be more effective when taken on an empty stomach, which may help rapid absorption.
- If you do not want to take melatonin supplements, certain foods increase your body's natural melatonin levels. These include rolled oats, whole brown rice, sweet corn, bananas, and tomatoes. A multivitamin high in B vitamins and calcium encourages melatonin production. Avoid consuming caffeine, which can decrease your melatonin.
- Do not take melatonin if you are pregnant, a nursing mother, taking prescription steroid drugs, or if you suffer from mental illness, severe allergies, autoimmune diseases, or immune system cancers.

remedies is antihistamines, which are usually taken for allergies and runny noses, and which also make people sleepy. A caveat that comes with these remedies is that you can build up a tolerance, so if you take them over time, their effectiveness will wear off. Also, they should not be taken if you will be driving or operating other machinery. I know a number of business executives who take them only when traveling through three or more time zones and when they will be sleeping in strange surroundings.

Some people have found that the nutritional supplement DMAE (dimethylaminoethanol) stimulates lucid dreaming. Available in capsules, tablets, and liquids, the dose ranges from 200 to 1,000 mg. As with any new supplement, talk to your doctor first and start with a low dose. Taking too much DMAE can cause cramping of your skeletal muscles.

SLEEP HYGIENE

Lots of people sleep badly because of what researchers call poor sleep hygiene. This is a stuffy way of saying that people can't sleep just anywhere or at any time and should make sure their surroundings are as conducive to snoozing as possible.

For good sleep hygiene, first turn to *where* you sleep. Make sure the room is not too warm or too cold. Check the lighting; eliminate distracting noises. You may be missing out on sleep because you associate your bedroom with more than just slumber (and, of course, sex). If your bed is also a part-time television chair, snack place, or reading table, your mind may be having a hard time thinking about sleep when the lights go out.

When you sleep or, more precisely, what you have done right before you try to sleep, may also be getting in the way. Obvious sleep robbers include an early evening nap, exercising less than two hours before bedtime, smoking (the nicotine can keep you awake), taking cold remedies that contain caffeine, or eating foods that rev up your system.

JAKE STEINFELD'S COFFIN SLEEP

The well-known personal trainer and television personality Jake Steinfeld is a most efficient sleeper. "I get about three and a half hours a night. That's basically all I need. I'm in the zone all day, and try to eat lightly before I do go to sleep, and around 6:30, so not to have too much weighing me down. But when I lay down to bed, there's no tossing and turning. I get under the covers, kiss my wife good night, and wake up the exact same way. That's why I call it the coffin sleep."

INCREASING YOUR PERSONAL SLEEP POWER

Power naps are my secret weapon. I do not use them regularly, only when I need to reset my internal clock or adjust for a bout of bad or inadequate sleep, since excess fatigue can actually keep you awake. Rarely longer than twenty minutes, my power naps are a quick drop into slow wave sleep (stage 2–4) that leaves me feeling calm yet sharp and ready for whatever is next. I think of them as I do the emergency twenty-dollar bill tucked in the bottom of my briefcase. If I spent that twenty dollars regularly, one day I would forget to replace it, then need cash and find only lint. The same is true for my power naps: As staples of my sleeping diet, they are as valuable as money in the bank.

Each time I go into a power nap I follow a routine that I believe ensures its curative power. First I adjust my clothing, which may include loosening my tie or taking off a jacket or sweater. I also take off my shoes and watch. I get as close to prone as possible, which may require sitting in a chair with my feet propped up on another chair, or stretching out on the carpeted floor of an empty office. While noise generally does not bother me, light does, so, if I cannot lower a shade or turn off a light, I get in a position that allows me to drape my forearm over my eyes. On plane trips, I carry eye shades and earplugs. As I sink into my nap, I deliberately turn my mind away from the day's concerns, and quiet my breathing and heart rate. Using the concentration I have developed from several decades of martial arts training, I focus inward, listening to my heart beat, my blood pump, my quiet breathing, and calm my mind and body. I concentrate on feeling the air move from my diaphragm to my lungs and gently slip through my nose. Every few breaths or so, I might forcefully exhale in order to accentuate that feeling of air moving through my body passages.

The essence of Sleep Power is using your slumber time for optimal mental rest and to erase the sleep debt that may be draining you. While my regime may be helpful for you, here are some other ideas to help you construct a personal sleep program.

- Body temperature leads us into sleep. We fall asleep as it drops, and it reaches its lowest point between 2 and 4 A.M. Taking a warm bath or shower before bedtime raises your body temperature so that when you go to bed, your temperature is dropping, which brings on sleep.
- Taking two baby aspirin before you go to bed increases the amount of deep-sleep time and decreases nighttime awakenings. (Be sure the aspirin is caffeine-free, and take it with water so they don't sit in your stomach undigested.)
- Keep a sleep diary, especially if you are trying to pinpoint the cause of a sleeping problem. The formal diaries that sleep researchers give their subjects contain sixteen questions that must be answered every morning. The questions include: How long did it take you to fall asleep? How many times during the night did you awaken? How rested do you feel this morning (on a six-point scale)? Did you take any naps yesterday? What foods, drinks, or medication did you take before bedtime? This provides valuable information at a medical evaluation, should one become necessary.
- Learn power napping. The secret is clearing your mind of pressing, nagging thoughts, so any rote mental activity, whether counting sheep or reliving a pleasant encounter from the day, is useful.

• Dieting changes sleeping habits significantly, making it more difficult to fall asleep and reducing the amount of slow wave sleep.

• If noise bothers you, whether it's a mate's snoring, noisy apartment pipes, or street sounds, buy a white-noise machine or

A BRIEF REFRESHER

Quality sleep is essential for good mental functioning. For garden-variety insomnia or a patch of fitful sleeping, try these remedies:

Practice good sleep hygiene. Make sure your sleeping environment is comfortable, not too warm or cold, free of distracting lights or noises, and that you have removed distractions, like reading material or a television turned on. Remove any sources of allergies, like dust.

Eat right. Starchy foods like bread, pasta, potatoes, and milk products help promote sleep because they prompt your brain to generate sleep-inducing serotonin.

Try herbal aids. Valerian root, kava, chamomile, and lavender oil help some people fall asleep more easily.

Avoid certain medications. Some prescription and over-the-counter medications can produce insomnia. These include melatonin, blood pressure medicine, decongestants, nicotine, caffeine, diet pills, and some types of cold and cough remedies.

Lower your body temperature. Sleep comes as your body temperature dips, so a warm bath or shower before sleep makes it easier for your body to cool down and drop off to sleep.

Try baby aspirin. Taking two baby aspirin without caffeine helps some people sleep.

Learn power napping. Knowing how to grab twenty minutes of restful slumber in the middle of a long day not only rejuvenates your thinking but can make it easier for you to sleep at night. Excess fatigue at bedtime can, in truth, keep you awake.

set your FM radio to a spot between stations in order to block out unwanted noise.

- If your sleeping problems stem from allergies or sinus problems, you may be reacting to dust mites in your bedding. To cut down on dust and particles, put a clean towel over your pillow.

SELECTED SOURCES

Astrom, C. "Interaction between sleep and growth hormone. Evaluated by manual polysomnography and automatic power spectrum analysis." *Acta Neurology Scandanavia,* 92 (4), 281–96, October 1995.

Borebely, A. *Secrets of Sleep.* Basic Books, New York, 1986.

Carper, J. *Stop Aging Now.* HarperCollins, New York, 1995.

Coren, S. *Sleep Thieves.* Free Press, New York, 1996.

Ezzell, C. "For a good memory, dream on." *Science News,* 142 (20), 333, November 14, 1992.

Freiss, E., et al. "DHEA administration increases rapid eye movement sleep and EEG power in the sigma frequency range." *American Journal of Physiology,* 268 (1 pt. 1), E107–13, January 1995.

Hauri, P., and Linde, S. *No More Sleepless Nights.* Wiley and Sons, New York, 1996.

Hobson, J. A. *The Dreaming Brain.* Basic Books, New York, 1988.

Karklin A., et al. "Restricted energy intake affects nocturnal body temperature and sleep patterns." *American Journal of Clinical Nutrition,* 59 (2), 346–49, February 1994.

Kate, N. T. "To reduce stress, hit the hay." *American Demographics,* 16 (9), 14–16, September 1994.

King, A. C., et al. "Moderate-intensity exercise and self-rated quality of sleep in older adults." *New England Journal of Medicine,* 277 (1), January 1, 1997.

LaBerge, S. *Lucid Dreaming.* Ballantine Books, New York, 1985.

Lavie, P. *The Enchanted World of Sleep.* Yale University Press, New Haven, Conn., 1996.

"Learning while sleeping?" *Prevention,* 42 (1), 14, January 1990.

Leathwood, P. D. "Aqueous extract of valerian root improves sleep quality in man." *Pharmacology, Biochemistry, and Behavior,* 17 (1), 65–71, July 1982.

Morin, C. M. *Relief from Insomnia.* Doubleday, New York, 1996.

National Commission on Sleep Disorders Research. *Wake Up, America: A National*

Sleep Alert. Vols. 1 and 2. Government Printing Office, Washington, D.C., September 1994.

National Sleep Foundation, 1367 Connecticut Ave. NW, Washington, D.C., 20036.

Weil, A. *Spontaneous Healing.* Alfred A. Knopf, New York, 1995.

Four

BATTLING THE BRAIN BEASTS

BEATING STRESS

I probably experience as much stress as any professional or entrepreneur who is constantly juggling the demands of healthy living and a competitive workplace. Most of my stress comes from external sources like my responsibilities in international sports federations, medical technology companies, and the American Academy of Anti-Aging Medicine. Sure, I have internal stress, which is mostly generated by managing a staff spread over four continents and worries about being overextended. But my greatest stress comes from my tendency to be a perfectionist. Over the years, however, I have learned to contain my psychological and emotional stress as long as I maintain certain habits and routines.

In truth, I frequently find stress to be invigorating, and rather than deplete my inner resources, it energizes me. While I know it can be a destructive beast, I have found that it can be tamed, given the right regimen. What especially concerns me is how stress affects the mind and brain. While most people are familiar with what stress does to the cardiovascular and digestive systems, especially its role in heart conditions and stomach ailments, I focus on its influence on my intellectual, emotional, and mental health. Stress for me is like a sports car: If I drive it right, it's fast and fun. If not, it can be scary, even deadly.

Let me take you to an international bodybuilding competition—a Mr. Universe Championship that was held in Spain—for a rarefied look at both the harmful and the productive power of stress. A world-class sports competition, especially one where the standard of excellence depends squarely on one's body, is a crucible for a host of stressors. The athletes, as well as officials like myself, must cope with demands on their professional skills, psychological smarts, emotional stability, and physical stamina. While everyone has a personal coping style, with personal and professional lives often in flux, you may find it useful to read about new ways of coping.

The ballroom at the Melia Castilla Hotel was a tense scene. Beneath a glittering chandelier dozens of muscled men wearing only swimsuit briefs were pacing, jogging in place, or talking in small clusters. On the bare raised stage were two beam scales operated by men in official blue blazers and scrutinized by grim-faced coaches in sweat suits. It was weighing-in time for the Mr. Universe World Body Building Championships and an exceedingly stressful time for the representatives from more than sixty nations as well as officials like myself.

The 170 athletes were anxious about making their weight class and whether they would be chosen for the random drug tests. My edginess had to do with professional pressures. I was attending the championship as chairman of the International Medical Commission and Medical and Doping Committee for the International Federation of Body Builders (IFBB). My chief responsibility was the event's drug testing, overseeing everything from the random selection of test participants to testing protocols to disqualifying athletes who tested positive. If anything went wrong—a sample lost, contamination, any type of misunderstanding—it was my reputation that could suffer.

International sporting events are high-stress occasions, and this one was no different. For the next two days, stress would bombard both participants and officials. We all would feel the tension of psychological pressures and physical demands. Bodybuilding is an especially stressful sport psychologically because an athlete's skills and achievements are all focused on his body. The bodybuilder's "sport" is the perfection of his physique, and so flaws or failures become intensely personal. Self-image and self-confidence are tested to the maximum. Bodybuilders never get a break from their sport, for they live with the object of their striving every hour of every day. Obsessive thinking, with all the ills it can attract, is not uncommon.

Competition, because it generates excitement and anxiety, presents an athlete with both good and bad stress. The lack of control athletes may feel about an event adds another layer of psychological stress. The outcome resulting from years of training and personal sacrifice is in the hands of judges, the sanctioning organization, and sponsors.

Physically, competing requires a person to make severe demands on his body—micromanaging his diet, sleep, and training regimen. Many feel they must finely hone their metabolism, which can strain normal body chemistry. And, as you will read, personal chemistry drives a person's response to stress.

A person's environment can also intensify anxiety. The athletes at this competition had come from around the world. Very little of their surroundings was familiar to them, and for many, this was their first big-time, foreign competition.

While I had attended numerous such events, ever since I was recruited by Dr. Ben Weider for the IFBB years before, I would be stretched by a job where I was always on call. My workday would begin before sunrise and extend long into the evening, and I had to be

> Mental toughness is many things and rather difficult to explain. Its qualities are sacrifice and self-denial. Also, most importantly, it is combined with a perfectly disciplined will that refuses to give in. It's a state of mind—you could call it character in action.
>
> —Coach Vince Lombardi, Green Bay Packers

THE MOST STRESSFUL OCCUPATIONS

Experts say that people working in these occupations are most prone to stress-related illness. While other occupations may be more stressful, they involve a higher level of control, as in the case of a corporate CEO which reduces the effects of stress.

Construction worker
Secretary
Laboratory technician
Waiter or waitress
Machine operator
Farmworker
House painter
Midlevel manager
Foreman/supervisor

always available to attend meetings, make decisions, or resolve disagreements.

A BEAST WITH TWO HEADS

It's impossible to be alive and not know what stress feels like. While it is the rare person whose experience with stress is limited to occasional encounters or situations, most of us know it as a beast always lurking nearby. Although stress usually causes discomfort and can undermine a person's physical and psychological health, it also has a beneficial side. Stress can be harnessed to fuel success and achievement.

Although many people regard it as a sensation to be eliminated or managed, this is true only part of the time. Stress can be a pleasant experience, one to be savored. Stress researchers are well aware of its appeal. Hans Selye, the Austrian physiologist who popularized the concept and study of stress, distinguished between two types:

DAMAGE STRESS CAN DO TO A BODY

- Cause mineral depletion. The stress of extra work can produce a 33 percent drop in mineral content (magnesium) in the blood. Magnesium is necessary to maintain blood pH balance.
- Increase physical craving for carbohydrates by releasing more neuropeptide Y, an amino acid peptide that helps regulate feeding behavior.
- Burn the "youth" hormone DHEA. High cortisol levels, which is detrimental over time, are accompanied by low DHEA.
- Compromise the blood-brain barrier. Researchers concerned about protecting soldiers from the effects of chemical warfare have found that stress may compromise the blood-brain barrier, which protects the brain from toxic molecules. Studies with rats have shown that physical stress makes the brain more susceptible to damaging chemicals.

distress and eustress. (An early study on hormones led Selye to apply the label "stress" to a general area of medical investigation, borrowing the word from physics, where it refers to the interaction between a force and resistance to it. Selye later confessed that had his English been better, he would have called the concept strain.)

HOW TO NOT FALL APART

"I think people get older when they are not challenged. You have to be challenged, you have to have what we call eustress. Without some positive stress, you literally fall apart. When you get all the stresses taken off, and you're sitting in a chair watching the boob tube, that's when problems develop." —Ron Lawrence, M.D., Ph.D., founder of the American Medical Athletic Association

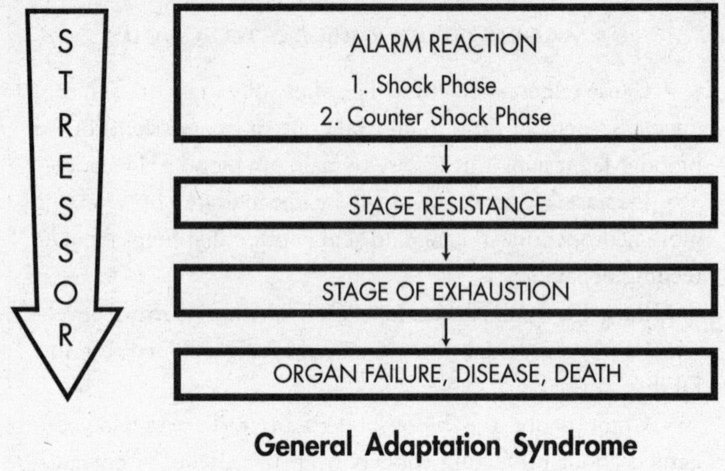

General Adaptation Syndrome

Adapted from *Stopping the Clock* (1996)

Eustress (*eu* means "good" in Greek) is pleasant stress that doesn't damage a person's health. It's the feeling of being captivated by someone and falling in love, playing a flawless game of tennis, receiving an award for a professional achievement, listening to your child play in a music recital, and even reading an exciting book. This is all stress at its best.

WHAT STRESS DOES TO THE BODY

Many people confuse stress with its symptoms. My medical training makes me look at stress as a physiological rather than a purely psychological event. To define it, I defer to Hans Selye, who described it as "the nonspecific (that is, common) result of any demand upon the body, be it mental or somatic." "Somatic" comes from the Latin word *soma*, meaning "body." Put another way, it's how the body reacts to forces either from within it, like a thought or emotion, or from outside it, like a physical threat.

So what does your body do? As soon as the brain realizes that a demand is being made on the body, it signals various glands to pump more hormones to deal with the situation. The signal goes to the director of the endocrine system, the pituitary gland. The pituitary gland releases three hormones: vasopressin, which raises blood pressure, and two stress hormones, ACTH (adrenocorticotropic hormone) and TTH (thyrotropic hormone). The stress hormones go to work: The ACTH spurs on the adrenal cortex and the TTH gooses the thyroid. The thyroid gland, which is in the throat, regulates your metabolism—how quickly you burn up oxygen and other energy resources—with the hormone thyroxine. Farther south, on top of your kidneys, the adrenals pump out two more hormones—adrenaline and noradrenaline (also called epinephrine and norepinephrine).

Adrenaline provides the energy to help the body respond. It produces more red and white blood cells to fight any incoming infection; increases blood sugar level to feed cells; elevates blood pressure so that the heart pumps faster to deliver more blood and oxygen to muscles and tissues; and stimulates the central nervous system. You start to breathe faster and your muscles tense.

Meanwhile, the ACTH has stirred up other hormones from the adrenals, namely a type of corticoid called glucocorticoids, which are stress hormones. Sometimes, glucocorticoids are referred to as corticosteroids. Cortisone is a kind of glucocorticoid that our body can convert into cortisol. (Another term for cortisol is "hydrocortisone.")

If this sounds familiar, there's a reason. While you don't exactly feel this waterfall of hormones, you know the sensations it causes—fear, excitement, panic, or variations on these feelings. In flight or fight stress response, blood is shunted from the stomach to the legs so you can run away. It goes to deep muscle for "flight," away from skin surfaces, which is why you sweat and get cold fear. The constricted blood vessels cut down on circulation, which can make you feel "cold fear." As the blood leaves your stomach, you may feel nauseous or the classic "butterflies." The quickened heartbeat and increased blood to your muscles can make you flush. This is pure stress, also known as the fight-or-flight feeling. Every system in your body braces for action.

My most vivid experience with fight or flight occurred while waterskiing in Jamaica. I was waiting to make a run, standing chest-deep in water, my feet set into the skis, when the motorboat driver yelled at me, "Freeze! Water snake!" For a second, I was a statue, and then, without thinking, I launched myself out of the skis, propelling myself almost ten feet into the air and into the boat. It was a high jump from a dead start that even an Olympian would have difficulty executing! And I'm sure I could never do it again without a huge shot of stress chemicals.

Dr. Selye dubbed this first stage of stress the alarm reaction. Often as not, the body's alarm bells clang for a brief time and then calm down when the threat diminishes, entering into the counter shock phase. However, if the threat continues, the body resists or adapts. If it resists, hormones and energy sources stay on alert status as the body depletes its stores of vitamin C, vitamin E, and B vitamins, and demands more calcium, magnesium, phosphorus, and potassium. To produce more hormones and antibodies, the body breaks down protein. The price the body pays for resistance is high—it loses weight and develops infections as its weapons weaken.

Adapting to the stress reaction is costly. The body tries to adjust to the surging hormones, elevated blood pressure, and altered body chemistry, but over time, it shows the effects of the constant pressure. It develops a stress disease, namely:

- Peptic ulcers in the stomach and upper intestine
- High blood pressure
- Heart trouble
- Nervous conditions
- Premature aging of the brain and nervous system

In the end, the body yells "Uncle!" and becomes totally exhausted. In the exhaustion stage of stress, the glands shrink and hormone production drops, the immune system produces fewer white blood cells, blood pressure rises, and the stomach churns out more acid.

The coup de grâce of the exhaustion stage is brain cell death. The unrelenting flow of cortisol lets too much calcium enter the brain, depletes it of glucose, eats up the antioxidants that fight destructive free radicals, and ultimately kills neurons. The end result may be cancer, stroke, heart attack, or kidney or liver damage, or all of these things.

As you will see from the following chart, hormone action also includes feedback mechanisms. Certain hormones counterbalance others; as one rises, another falls, or when one reaches optimal output, it may then cease circulating. Hormones do a balancing act so that just the right mixture is provided for the event at hand. Selye dubbed this entire process the general adaptation syndrome, giving us a precise description of what stress can do to our body. What it does to our brain is equally dramatic.

CHANGES IN PLASMA CONCENTRATIONS IN ADAPTIVE AND STRESS-ASSOCIATED CONDITIONS

		Counterregulatory Hormones			
Condition or Activity	**Insulin**	**Glucagon**	**Growth Hormone**	**Epinephrine**	**Cortisol**
Consumption of:					
Glucose	↑	↓	↓	NC	NC
Protein	↑	↑	↑	NC	NC
Mixed meal	↑	NC	NC	NC	NC
Starvation	↓	↑	NC	↑/NC	↓
Acute hypoglycemia	↓	↑	↑	↑	↑
Exercise	↓	↑	↑	↑	↑
Fever	↓	↑	↑	↑	↑
Surgery/trauma	↓	↑/NC	↑	↑	↑
Heart attack	↓	↑	↑	↑	↑
Most other stress states	↓	↑	↑/NC	↑ (rapid,brief)	↑ (slow,chronic)

↑ = increase; ↓ = decrease; NC = no consistent, lasting change

Adapted from *Hormones and Aging* (1995).

EFFECTS OF STRESS FROM OVERWORK

A study of 248 automotive workers compared hours worked during the week with mental function. Researchers from Boston University School of Medicine found that increased overtime was directly linked with poor performance on tests of attention and decision-making, and increased people's feelings of depression, fatigue, and confusion.

WHAT STRESS DOES TO YOUR MIND AND BRAIN

The judges at the bodybuilding competition began reading out the numbers of the athletes to be drug-tested. With each number, the room rippled with sighs of relief or bursts of nervous laughter. Virtually all the competitors were uneasy, worrying about themselves and their friends. Athletes who had never even touched a steroid fretted about false positives, although highly unlikely, or having consumed a banned substance unknowingly.

The selected athletes were isolated in a special waiting area where they were given bottled water. No coaches, friends, or other athletes were allowed into this area, only officials and interpreters, if necessary. The language barrier raised everyone's stress hormones: Competitors quickly became frustrated if they didn't understand a procedure or felt they were being misunderstood, and the other officials and I struggled to ensure that no one was offended. Each athlete was escorted to a bathroom stall to produce a urine sample. On top of the fear caused by being singled out and separated from coaches and friends, the pressure on the athletes increased as they were expected to urinate on command.

The psychological impact of stress is no less powerful than the physical onslaught. Stress churns up emotions, muddles thinking, fogs concentration, and eats at memory. Just as some people are physically energized by stress chemicals, others thrive on the mental pressure of stress.

Stress clearly can influence how people think, and memory is especially affected. For memory, stress is a good-news, bad-news story. Scientists believe that mild stress helps memory but that intense, constant stress hurts it. Memory is briefly sharpened by adrenaline, then crumbles if the hormone bath continues. At the outset, stress helps strengthen *explicit* memory, the memory of precise facts or images, or what's called flashbulb memory. But over time, memory deteriorates under stress. Scientists say the cause of the memory loss lies in the hippocampus. Stress chemicals in this part of the brain disrupt long-term potentiation, the chemical chain reaction that enables us to convert short-term memories into something more lasting. Brain scans have confirmed this theory. Scans of people who have suffered long periods of stress—children who have been abused and Vietnam veterans with post-traumatic stress disorder—reveal that their hippocampus has shrunk.

The person who responds well to stress may find his or her performance and abilities enhanced. The ability to think ahead many steps, learn quickly, concentrate calmly, apply sound judgment, and act decisively may come as naturally as breathing.

For some athletes, crowds, noise, and being the center of attention are enormously depleting, while other competitors seem to feed off the chaos and cacophony. Trained as a world-class athlete, Arnold Schwarzenegger has learned to adapt his ability to draw energy from large crowds to all facets of his life. The stress of many people's simultaneous demands, for instance when he's managing media interviews, stimulates instead of depletes him.

Outside the sports world, people who can adjust to and feed off the demands and pressure made on them are considered to have "hardiness." At the other end of the spectrum are people who react negatively to psychological stress and, as a result, develop related illnesses, such as an addiction, depression, or other psychiatric disorders.

In the late 1970s, Suzanne Kobasa, a researcher at the University

THE HARDY, STRESS-RESISTANT PERSONALITY

Commitment: is actively, enthusiastically involved in professional and personal life.

Control: can determine the direction and substance of one's life.

Challenge: views change as positive and is flexible about making adjustments.

of Chicago, began a three-year study of executives at Illinois Bell and how their personalities influenced their reactions to stress. She followed more than 160 managers, monitoring their physical health and the level of stress in their lives. All the men lived stressful lives and scored high on the scale of stressful life events (see page 150 for more on this). At the end of the study, Kobasa discovered that more than half the executives lived under constant stress but never got sick, while the rest of those studied routinely fell sick after experiencing a stressful event.

The difference between the two groups, she found, was in their personalities and attitudes. The executives who easily weathered stressful events possessed a quality of "hardiness," which consisted of three characteristics: commitment, control, and challenge. The hardy execs showed a strong commitment; they felt good about themselves and about their lives. They also felt in control of their working and personal lives, and they viewed change and readjustments as positive challenges. These three qualities, Kobasa concluded, determined whether a manager would develop a stress-related illness or not.

Ever since this groundbreaking study, numerous other scientists have explored what makes some people more resistant than others to stress. Some disagree with Kobasa's findings and point out the obvious limitations in her study—the target group was middle-class men, the information on physical illness was self-reported, and the

HOW MICHAEL JORDAN FEEDS ON STRESS

Stress energizes the world's best basketball player. Michael Jordan has told observers that when the clock is down to the last two minutes, the fans are roaring, and he has to make a game-winning shot, he hears nothing. His entire mind and body are tuned to what is happening inside the lines of the court. He blocks out everything and swishes through a three-pointer.

three qualities overlap. However, Kobasa has lots of company in her assertion that an individual's feeling of control over his life makes him better able to cope with stress.

In the world of bodybuilding, as well as in other sports, hardiness is frequently translated into a state of peak performance. It is that wonderful feeling of competence, power, and control in the middle of extreme stress that is known as "being in the zone." Athletes often find the zone when they are competing, but other people achieve it when, in the process of pushing themselves, they discover how to harness feelings of anxiety and arousal into productive, satisfying action. The salesperson who smoothly closes a big deal, the accountant who deftly executes a complicated audit, the lawyer who flawlessly remembers dozens of relevant cases—for a brief, shining moment or two, these people are in the zone.

Hardiness, like finding the zone, depends on achieving a sense of control. And this feeling of control alters your perceptions and your actions. While stress revs up your mind, being hardy or in the zone seems to put everything into slow motion so that you can focus and concentrate better. You see relationships more clearly, whether the distance between you and a tennis ball or the significance of a jumble of numbers. Your senses are heightened so that colors are sharper, sounds are more distinct, and your sense of touch more sensitive. It is as if the stress chemicals in your body have moved from

TAKE ACTION

Signs of Stress

If some of these statements ring true to you, you may well be suffering from major stress:

My sore back is becoming a regular backache.
My parents are always nagging me about something.
I had a fight with my best friend and we're still not talking.
I haven't had satisfying sex in months.
I am drinking three or more glasses of alcoholic beverage a night.
I never have time to eat a decent lunch.
My favorite jeans are too tight.
I can't sleep at night because of noisy neighbors.
The roof and gutters on my house need repair.
I have a credit card bill that I can't afford to pay.
My spouse wants to quit his/her job.
My spouse is spending too much.
If my child gets sick, day care becomes a crisis.
My child is not doing well in school.
I keep hearing rumors of layoffs at work.
It's hard for me to work because the phone keeps ringing.
I have little say over my priorities at work.
I don't feel safe at home unless all my doors and windows are locked.

your racing heart and tense muscles to your ears, eyes, fingertips, and the motor center of your brain.

Developing hardiness or finding the zone is not a matter of chance. As you will find later in this chapter, there are skills you can develop, attitudes you can cultivate, routines you can incorporate, and activities you can practice that are the raw material for the hardy personality or the zoned-in athlete.

INDIVIDUAL STRESS SIGNS

When Dr. Ben Weider recruited me for the IFBB, my book on the dangers of athletes using banned drugs, *Death in the Locker Room,* had just made a big splash and I had become a recognized expert on the subject. Dr. Weider felt it was time for the bodybuilding federation to seriously attack the drug problem, and he asked me to develop a worldwide education and testing program. Despite my medical studies, sports medicine fellowship, and a doctorate in androgen steroid chemistry, this was the first time I had been asked to apply my knowledge of medicine and drugs to creating a program for hundreds of medical professionals and athletes. Since the IFBB did not have any standing active medical committees, devising and implementing all the protocols and procedures fell to me. I had to establish relationships with Olympic testing labs around the world, design testing protocols, develop informational materials and documents, and institute a program to educate other medical professionals on drug abuse and testing.

For the first four years, I personally conducted the bulk of the testing while creating a system so that each of the 164 member nations of the federation would be able to do its own testing. Much of my work involved devising procedures for on-site testing protocols and strict quality control, and initiating partnerships with Olympic lab testing facilities around the world.

My procedures are continually scrutinized by participants, government officials, and the media, especially at international competitions with athletes from different cultures where national reputations are sometimes fragile. This Mr. Universe contest had drawn men from sixty countries and so put my system in the spotlight. Each step had to move as smoothly as a tango. Bodybuilders, like athletes in other sports that require muscle or strength, know that they are often under a cloud of suspicion of drug abuse. We know our integrity is sometimes doubted, and so we insist that our drug-testing program be very rigorous and very public.

Wherever I went during the two days of the competition, people asked me about testing procedures, test results, and plans for future tests of more substances. I felt as if I were always under a microscope. I know my stress signals well: Early signs are light muscle twitches in my face and elsewhere. With persistent stress, my appetite disappears and may not return for days. In a hot climate, I sweat much more than usual, and dehydration and dry mouth set in. Another sign is bad sleep; I cannot seem to drop into REM sleep, and I wake up ragged and weary.

Some situations are stressful for virtually everyone. It is the rare person who doesn't feel the chemistry of the adrenals when he or she speaks before a large group, gets into a heated argument, tells a lie, or enters a new social situation. Experts looking for ways to measure psychological stress have compiled lists of common experiences and assigned them values according to how stressful they are. Perhaps the best-known list was devised by Thomas Holmes and Richard Rahe in 1967 and called the Social Readjustment Rating Scale but known today as the Life Events Scale. Holmes and Rahe identified forty-three events by monitoring about five thousand patients and looking at what events in their lives preceded an illness. The most stressful life event, and at the top of the list, is death of a spouse, which has a value of 100. At the bottom is a minor violation of the law, such as a traffic ticket, which has an 11 point value.

Other items on the list, in order of stress magnitude, include divorce, being jailed, personal injury or illness, getting fired, trouble with in-laws, outstanding personal achievement, and a vacation.

What all these events have in common is the element of change. The researchers found that even happy or enjoyable experiences that involve some type of change are a source of stress. Since the Life Events Scale was devised, other researchers have developed alternative ways of measuring stress. Richard Lazarus and his colleagues at the University of California at Berkeley strongly believe that a person's perception of what is stressful can be more powerful than the situation would seem to justify, and that major events over

HASSLES SCALE

These daily hassles are most frequently cited as stressful by people, according to the textbook *Health Psychology, Second Edition,* by Linda Brannon and Jess Feist (Wadsworth Publishing Co., 1992). The number is the percentage of people out of 100 who checked the experience.

Concerns about weight	52.4%
Health of a family member	48.1
Rising prices of common goods	43.7
Home maintenance	42.8
Too many things to do	38.6
Misplacing or losing things	38.1
Yard work or outside home maintenance	38.1
Property, investment, or taxes	37.6
Crime	37.1
Physical appearance	35.9

which we have little control do not seem to be as stressful as some minor situations that require us to make a decision.

So Lazarus and friends developed the Hassles and Uplifts Scales—117 daily life events, both positive and negative, surrounding work, family, relationships, personal health, and chance occurrences. How a person reacts to ordinary hassles, especially, can offer a good barometer for stress-related illnesses such as depression. (Experts argue over whether positive, uplifting events can feed stress—some found that they do in women but not in men—and so this half of the scale is often disregarded.)

The key to the Hassles Scale is the rating. For each hassle that has occurred within the past month, a person has to indicate how often it occurred, how severe the event was on a three-point scale, and its intensity, which is frequency multiplied by severity.

The point of the Hassles Scale is that the experiences must be not only vaguely unpleasant but also persistent, so that they create a vicious cycle. The hassle fuels the stress, which makes even more ordinary events also stressful. Pretty soon, the smallest annoyance is producing a major psychological and physiological reaction.

Each of us has particular vulnerabilities. While loss of privacy and being a public person for a couple of days is stressful to me, your pivot point is probably something else. It's useful if each of us knows our personal stress points and can recognize when our bodies are resisting stress or showing signs of exhaustion from constantly battling it. I have a friend who plays professional football who years ago developed a duodenal ulcer and colitis, two classic stress disorders. Although the conditions were treated, they flare up every now and then and my friend uses these flare-ups as an early warning system for stress. Oftentimes, his gut will ache long before he realizes that some unidentified stressful situation is bothering him, and his sensitive stomach alerts him to a condition he needs to address.

Dr. Herbert Benson, a pioneer in stress-fighting techniques and author of one of the most successful books on coping with stress, *The Relaxation Response,* says that there are a variety of individual signs that warn of serious, illness-threatening stress. They fall into four realms: physical, behavioral, emotional, and cognitive.

Physical Symptoms

Headaches
Indigestion
Stomachaches
Sweaty palms
Sleep difficulties
Dizziness
Tight neck, shoulders
Racing heart
Restlessness
Tiredness
Ringing in ears
Back pain

Behavioral Symptoms

Excess smoking
Bossiness
Grinding of teeth at night
Overuse of alcohol

Compulsive gum chewing
Attitude critical of others
Compulsive eating
Inability to get things done

Emotional Symptoms

Crying
Nervousness, anxiety
Boredom—no meaning to anything
Edginess—ready to explode
Feeling powerless to change things
Overwhelming sense of pressure
Anger
Loneliness
Unhappiness for no reason
Easily upset

Cognitive Symptoms

Trouble thinking clearly
Forgetfulness
Lack of creativity
Memory loss
Inability to make decisions
Thoughts of running away
Constant worry
Loss of sense of humor

STRESS AND AGING

The age of The Men's Universe competition participants ranged from early twenties to late forties, with one athlete from Turkey in his fifties who looks great and is still competitive. By striving to maintain their muscles, middle-aged bodybuilders are slowing their

JAKE ("BODY BY JAKE") STEINFELD THRIVES ON STRESS

I have learned to thrive on stress and not let it beat me down. Rather, I go the other way. If there is a challenge, rather than avoiding it or going around it, I deal with it, go through it, and move on to the next.

mental aging. The reason is clear. As people age, they become less active, causing them to lose muscle mass (the first area to go is around the shoulders and chest). As a result, they lose strength and bone density, exercise less, and put on more body fat. This drop-off in exercise means less oxygen rushing to the brain, and so thinking starts to slow.

I have found that the athletes who stay in the sport longer are motivated by repeated success, and one quality that makes them successful is their ability to deflect the corrosion that comes with constant stress. This also seems to slow their aging. Athletes in their forties have an aura of relaxed self-confidence. Their muscles are limber and supple. They move through their routines smoothly and seamlessly, without any of the hurried movements that suggest anxiety.

Some scientists now believe that the aging process is propelled, and may even be accelerated, by stress. It may be no coincidence that the ravages of aging—heart disease, hypertension, cancer, diabetes, osteoporosis, weakened immune system, dementia—are also the legacy of years of stress. Even the superficial signs of aging, like wrinkles and loss of muscle strength, can be tied to stress.

Decades of wear and tear from stress hormones flushing through every organ of our bodies slowly breaks us down. The chemical reactions that stress puts in motion may well make our bodies and minds react older than they are. Too much stress ages us prematurely. Here are some ways that stress wears us down.

- The body requires more time to return to normal temperature (98.6°) after being warmed or chilled.
- Heart functions such as heart rate, blood pressure, and cardiac muscle strength weaken, so that physical exercise is more difficult.
- There is less sprouting of new brain cell branches.
- The brain depletes oxygen and nutrients more quickly, which can make it more susceptible to strokes.

- Heart and blood vessels become less sensitive to stress hormones, so it takes a larger shot of hormones to react to an emergency or fast-changing situation.
- The body is less able to immediately halt production of stress hormones, so they are in circulation longer to do more damage. Moreover, oversecretion may happen when not under stress.

The life and times of the Pacific salmon is a vivid example of what a large shot of stress hormones can do to a body. As you may know, these fish swim miles up freshwater streams, jumping dams and waterfalls in order to spawn. As they make their way upstream, they develop peptic ulcers, their muscles shrink, their immune systems collapse, they develop tumors, and they generate abnormally high levels of glucocorticoids. After spawning, they die. The deathblow comes from a burst of hormones that floods and kills the brain.

Dr. Robert Sapolsky, a neuroscientist at Stanford University and a leading stress researcher, firmly believes that stress hormones speed up the aging process, and not just in the body but also in the brain. He has found that glucocorticoids have a particularly nasty effect on the hippocampus, the part of the brain in charge of learning and memory.

One by-product of the rush of hormones that comes with stress and aging is a spurt of free radicals, which are renegade molecules that damage and kill neurons and other cells in the body. Free radicals are produced by the chain of chemical reactions set off by the stress hormones. Glucocorticoids, especially cortisol, can do even more damage by interrupting the body's production of antibodies, and some scientists think that they actually destroy antibodies that circulate in the blood.

As we know, some of us age more slowly and better than others. For some people, the flow of our aging stress hormones is not as damaging. Sapolsky has a theory about this, too. In his studies with rats, he has found that the animals that were petted soon after birth did not experience the same cascade of damaging hormones as those that were not touched. By petting the animals, the researchers seemed to make them resistant to the biological actions of stress. This discovery may well help us adults. While we can't turn back the clock to ask for a more nurturing childhood, it does suggest that psychology and mental wellness can have a powerful influence on how our brain copes with stress.

The flip side of the connection between stress and aging is that we may dramatically slow the aging process by moderating how we respond to stressful forces and learning to check spurts of the stress hormones that age us.

TAMING THE BEAST

During the competition, I woke early to get in a workout—a fast-clip walk—before the day's events. My goal on these walks is to raise my heart rate to 140–160 beats a minute for at least forty minutes; if I am feeling stressed-out, I stretch my walk to ninety minutes.

Another element of my stress-reduction exercise is cross-training, an anaerobic activity, such as working with weights, that allows me to put the physical activity on autopilot and concentrate on the mental side of stress. (While walking, an aerobic exercise, stimulates circulation and oxygen flow, the anaerobic action of working with weights is not as cardiovascular and focuses more on muscle development.) No matter where I travel, I can always find a couple of two- to five-pound hand weights. I also carry with me a compact exercise gym in the form of rubber surgical tubing. An even smaller version is powerbands, which look like big, thick rubber bands. When weight machines are not available, the surgical tubing or powerbands enable me to still do speed training and resistance training. This helps me maintain lean muscle mass, which normally I would lose on an extended, overseas, high-stress trip.

As I flex various muscle groups, I let my mind wander into nagging problems and play what I call the retrospect/prospect game. I recall a past event or situation that caused me great stress and relive the feelings, then reflect on how that great load produces no anxiety today. Next I turn to a current source of stress and put it into perspective, and know that it, too, will fade.

Learning to tame stress is a lifetime occupation. This is not a one-time skill like learning to play bridge, but a continuing education that we perfect as we grow older. I am much more concerned with chronic stress than acute stress. I believe that quick bursts of stress, which are often triggered by external, uncontrollable events and dissipate in a short time, are much less harmful than persistent stress. We need to constantly battle the stress that eats at us for weeks and months, flooding our brains with high levels of corrosive hormones.

Coping Techniques

There are a variety of weapons for taming this beast. At one time or another, I use most of them: exercise, diet and nutritional supplements, vitamins and herbs, social support, and what I call whole-body activities—meditation, breathing exercises, muscle relaxation, martial arts, and cognitive exercises. None of these, however, works alone. An exercise program is useless if your diet is loaded with unhealthful food, and meditation without relaxation is virtually impossible. To manage and harness your body's and brain's reaction to stress, you need a full-court press—to apply an all-around assault on every sign of stress.

Exercise

You may be surprised to learn that doctors disagree on whether physical exercise can reduce the harmful effects of stress. Ever since joggers launched the fitness boom in the 1980s, exercise has been hailed as a modern cure-all, and many people have assumed that

JUST A LITTLE BIT WILL DO YOU

You don't have to go overboard to reap the benefits of exercise. A study involving more than 13,000 people (10,200 men and 3,100 women) compared the effects of different exercise intensities. The people, all in good health, were grouped into one of five categories, from sedentary to mildly active on up to intensely active, and followed for eight years. At the end of the eight-year study, the researchers at the Cooper Aerobics Institute in Dallas compared mortality rates (the ultimate measure of health) and found the biggest difference in longevity between the least active people and the next level up, the moderately active. These in the next level, the very active, did not show significant longevity over the moderately active. Sedentary women had the highest mortality levels—4.6 times higher than women who exercised the most. Among men, the couch potatoes had 3.9 times more deaths than the vigorous exercisers. The difference in exercise ranged from no exercise (sedentary) to thirty to sixty minutes of brisk walking a day. Notably, the researchers did not see any benefits beyond this level of exercise.

stress illnesses have been just one of its targets. It turns out that only certain types of exercise lower stress, and that only certain types of stress are best battled by exercise.

The good news for many people will be finding that moderate activity may well be a better stress buster than extreme exercise. Put another way, brisk walking for an hour probably reduces stress better than running a marathon, and forty minutes of stretching and floor exercises is probably better than speed walking. For ordinary folks, this means you do not have to be a seasoned athlete or in prime shape to use exercise to lower stress.

A number of studies show that moderate exercise can influence a person's mood and feelings of stress more than sweating and straining. A four-month study by University of Massachusetts scientists, including *Relaxation Response* author Herbert Benson, of 135 middle-aged people compared the benefits of moderate-intensity walking, low-intensity walking, and low-intensity walking with tai chi-type relaxation exercises. For the women, the hands-down winner for easing tension, depression, and anger was the low-intensity walking plus tai chi. Scientists elsewhere have come up with similar results.

At Wonkwang University School of Medicine in Korea, researchers looked at a group of men learning the martial art of qigong, which revolves around breathing exercises. The researchers took blood samples at various points in the men's workouts and found at the midpoint of the training and afterward that stress hormone levels declined.

Moderate exercise successfully combats stress because of what it *doesn't* do—it does not set off a stream of stress hormones like cortisol and ACTH. It eases stress, say experts, because it creates a mental time-out from the worries and pressures that cause stress. When exercise is a calming distraction, the mind slows down and the body quiets and our whole system ceases its stressful churning.

Here are some guidelines for moderate exercise, which I define as a brisk activity for forty minutes, three to five times a week.

- Do a repetitive, relaxing activity like riding a stationary bicycle, walking, or swimming easy laps.
- Find an activity that requires enough concentration or distraction so that stressful thoughts are forgotten, like a crossword puzzle or videogame.
- Alternate or combine the two types of physical activity, aerobic and anaerobic, to avoid boredom and increase benefits. Aerobic exercises, which use large muscle groups and a strong stream of oxygen over a steady period of time, are running, walking, bicycling, and swimming. Anaerobic exercises, which use fast muscles for quick bursts of energy, are working with weights and sprinting. Many activities, like team sports or tennis, combine the two.

For any type of exercise to be an effective buffer against stress, it has to be a constant in your life. This is not like a crash diet that you go on for a few weeks or months and, having hit a target weight, abandon. Even moderate exercise needs to be constant. Researchers who have plotted the benefits of physical activity have discovered that it takes ten weeks or more before they see results like improvements in mood and a milder reaction to normal stressors.

If you're the kind of person who, like me, enjoys vigorous exercise, you still can reap stress-lowering benefits. For certain types of stress, a long, sweaty workout is just what the doctor ordered. Let me explain why. A big source of stress for many people is their weight and self-image. They're always on a diet, worry about whether clothes will fit, and think of themselves as overweight. Whether in fact they are is irrelevant. They feel this way and so every time they pass a mirror or think about trying on a bathing suit or what they'll eat for dinner, their stress hormones rise. For these people, vigorous, pound-shedding exercise is a great stress reducer. A demanding workout can also siphon off the stress of anger, frustration, and aggression. Going for a long run or pounding a tennis ball may relieve stress because it offers an outlet for an overflow of stress hormones.

Some medical people insist that the best way to stress-proof yourself is through aerobic conditioning, like jogging at least a couple of miles three to five times a week. The theory behind this school of exercise is that endurance exercise teaches your body to take in and efficiently use more oxygen. So, in times of stress, when the heart starts racing and the muscles are priming for action, the aerobically conditioned person is better equipped to meet the sudden demand for more air.

One expert has found that intense exercise eases stress by improving feelings of well-being. Dr. Steven Petruzzello at the University of Illinois at Urbana-Champaign has been studying what exercise does to people's anxiety levels for many years, and has found that really pushing on the exercise equipment produces improvement in people's moods. In one study, he compared people who did no exercise with people who did moderate cycling with people who did high-intensity cycling. He tested the cyclists' anxiety levels after exercising and found that those who worked the hardest and consumed the most oxygen not only felt less anxiety but had stronger positive feelings.

The cherry on the sundae, so to speak, for lots of dedicated exercisers and athletes is the flip side of stress reducing: generating beta-endorphins, the brain's own "feel good" chemicals. These neuropeptides are the body's natural painkillers and energizers. (The word "endorphin" comes from "endogenous," meaning "produced within," and "morphine," although this brain chemical is two hundred times more potent than morphine.) The body starts producing endorphins about twenty minutes into a vigorous workout and spews them out for hours afterward.

Unfortunately, endorphins are a bit unpredictable—not all exercisers experience the rush, and sometimes its effect is limited. Exercise physiologist Peter Farrell has suggested that we have two endorphin systems—one for the body and one for the brain—and that the blood-brain barrier prevents mingling. So, high blood levels of endorphins may act as a natural painkiller for the body but do not necessarily seep into the brain and produce the famous euphoria. Still, runners and extreme-sports fanatics wax poetic about the endorphin high, and often push themselves to the outer limits to achieve it.

One way to incorporate high-intensity exercise with the stress reduction benefits from moderate activity is to add a few minutes of relaxation to your workout time. For instance, after a strenuous workout in the weight room, I spend ten to fifteen minutes gently pedaling a stationary bicycle. During this time, my muscles relax and my mind calms down.

Regardless of whether you prefer moderate exercise or want to throw yourself into intense workouts, you should do some type of physical activity. There is little disagreement among the experts about regular physical exercise effectively diminishing stress. Study after study has found that people who exercise regularly are more re-

TAKE ACTION

Do a Walking Workout

Walking is a constant in my workout regime, threaded through a lifetime of athletic accomplishments including martial arts expertise and world strength records. Here's how I make walking a regular part of my life and keep from losing motivation or getting bored.

- Try to walk at least once a day.
- Walk to your favorite music with a sports headset.
- Build up your walking routine, going faster, farther, and more frequently.
- Keep a walking journal to record your progress.
- Set immediate and long-term walking goals.
- Reward yourself with nonfood treats when you reach a goal.
- Walk with a friend.
- Keep your perspective. Don't become obsessive about your walking or worry if you miss a day.
- Use your walking time to mentally relax and concentrate on nonstressful thoughts.

sistant to the pressures of stress. They suffer far fewer stress-related illnesses, and when they do get sick, they bounce back much more quickly.

Diet and Nutrition

The competitive bodybuilder's diet is bland and large—loads of complex carbohydrates, protein, and distilled water. He or she lives on mountains of steamed vegetables, baked potatoes and yams, steamed or broiled chicken and fish, hard-boiled eggs with the yolk discarded, plain white rice, rice cakes, and bunches of fresh fruit.

When a foreign country hosts an event, it tries to accommodate the athletes' food preferences, but the offerings are not always an exact match. So, worrying about whether they will have the right foods to stay on their training diet, at least until their event is over, creates a major source of stress for athletes at an international competition. Fortunately, most of them consume foods that help them ward off the fallout from stress.

I, too, closely watch what I eat during events like this, where the demands on me are more mental than physical. To keep my brain cells alert and clicking, I eat lots of protein and limit my carbohydrates to the complex sugars found in fruits and fruit juices. The extra amino acids I get from some proteins and supplements help repair cell damage brought on by stress. I also make sure that my toiletries bag contains a healthy supply of antistress vitamins and supplements. Keep reading to learn what these are.

Your eating habits can help on two fronts when battling stress:

TAKE ACTION

Low-Stress Foods

When you are under a lot of stress, or are about to enter a stressful time, eat carefully. Choose foods that are easy to digest and that do not create a buildup of toxic residues your body will have to wash out. You want your system free to handle the extra demands that stress puts on it. Here are my favorite low-stress foods.

Almonds	Chicken (skinless white meat, broiled)	Mushrooms	Raisins
Apples	Figs	Onions	Salmon
Bananas	Grapefruit	Oranges	String beans
Cabbage	Grapes	Pears	Tomatoes
Cantaloupe		Pineapple	Turkey
Carrots		Plums	
		Potatoes	

They can make you more stress resistant, protecting you from symptoms of stress, and they can also give you the fuel to meet the special demands put on your body and brain so that you're better equipped to harness and use stress to your advantage.

Food and drink can reduce your body's physiological reaction to stress. By watching what you consume, you can halt a stress response and help your body recover more quickly. Furthermore, the right diet can repair the damage from stress hormones, particularly cortisol; restore glucose levels to normal; nourish neurotransmitters; and protect against free radicals.

When emergency demands are made on your body and mind, you need an infusion of nutrients so that you have the energy and strength to handle the situation. In times of stress, your body gobbles up magnesium, vitamin C, vitamin E, proteins, and carbohydrates. One reason you might crave sweets or starchy foods when under stress, says Dr. Dharma Khalsa of the Alzheimer's Prevention Foundation in Tucson and the author of *Brain Longevity*, is that cortisol prompts the release of the brain chemical neuropeptide Y, which stimulates your hunger for carbs.

Stress also persuades the kidneys to conserve sodium, so sodium blood levels rise. This sodium draws water from tissues, thus increasing the volume of blood and so raising blood pressure. This reaction is called hypervolemia and, if chronic, can lead to hypertension. An obvious countermeasure to this chain reaction is to limit your salt intake during stressful times.

Researchers at the National Institute on Aging in Baltimore conducted studies of what salt did to people under stress. During a two-week period of high stress, medical students took either salt tablets or a placebo. The students who took the salt showed a rise in blood pressure, leading the scientists to surmise that salt and stress may work together on key hormones. Looking at these results, doctors recommend that, in times of stress, people limit their salt intake to about 3,000 mg a day—about a heaping teaspoon of salt.

Caffeine may do the same thing as salt. This time it is researchers at Duke University who gave students either caffeine tablets equal to two cups of coffee or a placebo, and then gave them a pressured test. While the blood pressure of the coffee group jumped twice as much as the noncoffee group, the adrenaline levels really told the story. The coffee group found that their stress hormones increased four times more than the placebo students. In concluding that caffeine clearly magnifies stress, the researchers also noted that it does so regardless of whether you drink one cup a day or five.

I have also found that crash dieting is extremely stressful. Skipping meals and drastically cutting back on vital nutrients deprives you of the very nutrients you need to combat stress.

A note of caution about eating and stress: Some people use eating as a way of coping with stress. When the pressure hits, they hit the refrigerator. This can create an unpleasant cycle of stress, overeating, worrying about gaining weight, and more stress. Eating as a coping mechanism is a kind of self-medication—either the act of consuming or the food itself makes a person feel better. But taken to its limit, self-medication can readily slip into addiction and self-abuse. In times of stress, you need to manage your diet more carefully, not relax your normal good eating habits.

Magnesium This essential mineral helps your body metabolize carbohydrates and fuels the efficient functioning of nerves and muscles. People whose diets do not contain enough magnesium are susceptible to heart attack, stroke, and high blood pressure. Stress as well as poor diet is an enemy of magnesium. Stress stimulates cells in the body to release magnesium, which is then lost in urine. This is why professionals in nutrition often recommend magnesium supplements for patients who are nervous, irritable, anxious, or depressed. Researchers in France found that it protects even better when combined with vitamin B_6.

Daily dose, depending on body weight, is 250–500 mg. Overdose side effect: diarrhea.

Vitamin A In times of chronic stress, vitamin A can keep the adrenal glands from swelling and spewing out too much cortisone, which will weaken your immune system. The best source of vitamin A is beta-carotene, which is found in carrots, squash, sweet potatoes, yams, cantaloupe, apricots, spinach, and citrus. (You can't go wrong if you stick with colorful foods, like orange, red, or yellow.)

As a supplement, the optimal daily dose is 5,000 IU. In high doses—one study looked at women who consumed 10,000 IU a day—vitamin A can be harmful, particularly for pregnant women. Consult your doctor before starting any new drug or vitamin regimen, especially if you are pregnant. Toxic side effects include headaches and an enlarged liver.

Vitamin C Vitamin C helps your body cut stress hormone production and so is a natural tranquilizer. It is also a powerful antioxidant, attacking the free radicals that are the toxic chemical by-product of stress. Some scientists believe that producing more free radicals is what makes stress so damaging, because they are so tough on a body. Free radicals damage blood vessels, DNA, and RNA; weaken the immune system; eat at neurotransmitters; and speed up physical aging.

The optimal daily dose is 1,500 mg, which should not be taken at one time, but parceled out three or four times a day, because the body cannot metabolize more than 500 mg at a time. Possible side effects from too much vitamin C are gas and diarrhea.

Vitamin E Vitamin E is another antioxidant that protects against the invasion of free radicals, boosts the immune system, and blocks the oxidation of bad cholesterol, which can damage cells. Food sources of vitamin E include leafy green vegetables, liver, whole grains, seed oils, nuts, and wheat germ.

As a supplement, the optimal daily dose is 400–800 IU. Vitamin E is fat soluble, meaning your body stores it, so it can reach toxic levels if too much is taken. Extremely high doses—over 800 IU per day—cause fatigue, nausea, headaches, raised blood pressure, and prolonged clotting time.

B Vitamins When you are under stress, your body chews up a lot of vitamin B. Because it is a water-soluble vitamin, it is not stored in body fat but is flushed through the system. As a result, you can quickly develop a deficiency during stress. Vitamin B_1, thiamine, helps you metabolize glucose, which provides needed energy. Optimal daily dose: 50–100 mg. Vitamin B_2, riboflavin, is also an energy producer and helps your adrenal glands produce antistress hormones. Optimal daily dose: 2 mg. Vitamin B_5 also nourishes your adrenal glands and helps prevent them from becoming enlarged and unable to produce stress-fighting hormones. Optimal daily dose: 100–200 mg. Vitamin B_6, pyridoxine, keeps your nervous system strong and resistant to stress. Optimal daily dose: 100 mg.

Amino Acid Supplements In times of stress, your body consumes amino acids (long strings of protein molecules). While you manufacture some amino acids, there are some you can get only through foods or supplements, and these are known as essential amino acids. When you're stressed, amino acids help the body cope—they beef up the immune system, provide energy to muscles and nerves, and convert amines into neurotransmitters. The amino acids that stress especially gobbles are lysine, tyrosine, and the branched-chain amino acids leucine, isoleucine, and valine. While you can beef up your amino acids by eating proteins, I find that taking an amino acid supplement once a day is more efficient and equally effective. Supplements are available at health food stores and some are specifically designed to meet the special needs of stress; follow their dosage recommendations.

Ginseng: The Root of Stress Protection Over the centuries, the herbal root ginseng has been credited with such miraculous powers as enhancing sexual performance and reviving comatose patients on the brink of death. Much of the evidence for its wondrous reputation is anecdotal, so I prefer to use it for what experts around the globe agree on—its potency as an antistress tonic. In fact, ginseng belongs to a category of medical substances called adaptogens, which means just what it sounds like—it helps your body adapt to various kinds of stress.

Ginseng, like any other plant, grows in many varieties. The most widely used are Asian ginseng and American ginseng, which are sometimes labeled with their Latin name, *Panax*. (What is called Siberian ginseng belongs to the same botanical family, and although it is not a true ginseng, it does help reduce stress.) Researchers believe that the ingredient in Panax ginseng responsible for its tonic properties is a chemical called a gensenoside. Studies have shown that ginseng has a pronounced effect on the adrenal glands, and possibly the other glands involved in the stress reaction, the hypothalamus and pituitary. Ginseng appears to help the adrenals pump out more hormones when under stress; smooth out hormone production in times of extended stress; and quicken the glands' return to normal once the stress reaction has ended.

Taking ginseng to fight stress is not like swallowing an aspirin when you have a headache. It usually takes at least a couple of weeks to show results. And it should not be taken all the time, but for brief periods when the stress is piling up or when you are entering a stressful time. Paul Bergner, an herbalist who has studied ginseng, recommends that people begin taking ginseng about three weeks before an expected onslaught.

Chinese herbalists also say that it may not relieve symptoms of stress like depression and headaches, which can arise from unhealthy lifestyles. On the other hand, ginseng readily defeats fatigue, anxiety, and insomnia.

Ginseng is commercially available in many forms, some of which have very little of the tonic root in them. As you are sorting through the extracts, teas, capsules, raw roots, tablets, and powders, look for an indication on Chinese or American products that the ingredients include gensenoside.

Take ginseng on an empty stomach and preferably with a food or drink that is easy to digest, such as in an herb tea. The dosage range for Asian ginseng is 1–6 grams; for American ginseng, 3–9 grams. Stop taking it if your blood pressure rises, you experience abdominal bloating, or if you overheat (with the Asian version) or become cold (a possible side effect from the American version).

ANTI-STRESS SUPPLEMENTS

Magnesium (250–500 mg/day)
Calcium (500–1,000 mg/day)
Selenium (100 mcg/day)
Zinc (30 mg/day)
Copper (2 mg/day)
Manganese (2 mg/day)
Vitamin A (5,000 IU/day)
Vitamin C (500 mg 3 times/day)
Vitamin E (400–800 IU/day)
Vitamin B complex
- B_1/thiamine (50–100 mg/day)
- B_2/riboflavin (50–100 mg/day)
- B_3/niacin (50–100 mg/day)
- B_6/pyridoxine (50–100 mg/day)
- B_{12}/cobalamin (50–100 mg/day)
- Folic acid (800 mcg/day)
- Pantothenic acid (100–500 mg/day)
- Biotin (200 mcg/day)

Inositol (50–100 mg/day)
Coenzyme Q10 (60–180 mg/day)
Phosphatidylcholine 95% (3–9 g/day)
Phosphatidylserine (300 mg/day)
Amino acids; especially:
- Lysine
- Tyrosine
- Glutamine
- Leucine
- Isoleucine
- Valine
- L-taurine

(Dose will vary with formulation; follow manufacturer's or physician's recommendations.)
Ginseng
- Asian (1–6 g/day)
- American (3–6 g/day)

Ginkgo biloba (30–60 mg/day)
Aspirin (80 mg/day or as directed by a physician)

Avoid:

- Salt
- Refined carbohydrates ("sweets")
- Alcohol
- Caffeine

Avoid:

Negative stress
Sleep deprivation
Skipping meals
Overeating

Note: Always consult your personal physician before beginning any nutritional or drug therapy program.

Relaxation and Breathing

Before each event at a bodybuilding competition, I like to watch the Asian athletes prepare for competition. I learn a lot from seeing how they integrate their meditation and breathing exercises into an atmosphere of controlled chaos. While other athletes are literally and mentally pumping themselves up with exercises and chatting with friends, the bodybuilders from Korea, Japan, and Southeast Asia are frequently off to the side by themselves. They seem to be watching the action, but their eyes are focused inward. Often, they are sitting ramrod-straight, their lower stomachs and shoulders gently rising and falling.

Perhaps the most effective way of handling stress is through relaxation. Relaxation, which is a little more complicated than reclining in your easy chair with a good book or a new video, can help you anticipate stress, reduce the intensity of its physiological effects, and recover more quickly once the situation has settled down.

Why does relaxation work? One big reason is that relaxation techniques are physical activities that trigger chemical actions in your body to counteract the chemistry of stress. Put another way, it's fighting fire with fire. Like stress, relaxation uses physiological responses to manipulate pivotal reactions—namely, metabolism, heart rate, blood pressure, breathing, and muscle tension.

For a long time, relaxation as treatment was considered a bit fringy—the province of New Age gurus and Eastern mystics. But modern science, in part led by Dr. Herbert Benson and his book *The Relaxation Response,* has changed all that. Recent research and clinical studies into the stress response and relaxation techniques have documented the medical reasons behind the success of various relaxation methods.

For instance, a study by scientists at La Trove University in Australia compared relaxation methods in ninety-six men and women and measured the effects on their stress reactions. People were randomly assigned to one of four groups to do either tai chi, brisk walking, meditation, or neutral reading. Each group participated in its specific relaxation treatment and then was measured for cortisol, heart rate, blood pressure, and stress hormones. All the treatments produced "significant" declines in cortisol levels, and for the other stress measurements, tai chi, which is considered moderate exercise, produced the most significant reductions.

In another study, researchers at the University of California Medical Center in Irvine found that transcendental meditation (TM) induced changes in pituitary hormones. The scientists concluded that TM may produce relaxation by pumping up the neurotransmitters that produce feelings similar to the endorphin high experienced by runners.

In learning how to use relaxation to combat stress, it helps to remember that relaxation is an end and that a number of roads will take you there. The best relaxation techniques involve the whole body. Spot reduction doesn't work. You can't focus just on your head or neck muscles when confronted by a tension headache—you need to engage your whole body.

Common techniques include yoga stretching, meditation, imagery, progressive muscle relaxation, and deep breathing. Scientists who have compared the relative benefits of these found that a single technique is not as effective as undertaking two or three methods within a single stress-reduction program.

Here's an overview of relaxation techniques and suggestions for using them for stress reduction.

Yoga Stretching Stretching exercises pull your mind away from troublesome thoughts and emotions, redirect your focus on simple movements, and so give your body a chance to recover from the physiological symptoms of stress, such as a racing heart or sweaty palms. I use tai chi movements, which combine proper posture; slow deliberate arm, leg, torso, and head exercises; and measured deep breathing. The exercises include stretching skyward, then dropping at the waist; torso and head twists; and floor exercises that involve bending toward knees and toes. The stretching is soothing, not difficult. I don't strain my muscles but gently elongate them.

I also like to combine the gentle movements of tai chi with the more ballistic, forceful movements of other Chinese gung fu styles and Shotokan karate. That way, I can switch from bursts of movement to calm, flowing movement during a single session, like combining the power of air, water, and fire.

Meditation Find a quiet place and a time of day when you are least likely to be distracted by "must do" thoughts or other people. Set aside fifteen to twenty minutes. Get into a comfortable position and try to relax your muscles, particularly those in your neck and shoulders. Close your eyes and draw your concentration inward to a

WORK THAT BRAIN

All relaxation techniques have common elements, namely:

- Repetition. You repeat a physical activity, image, word, or phrase throughout the exercise.
- Mental focus. You suppress daily thoughts and worries as your mind focuses on narrow and immediate sensations, such as the mechanics of breathing and the feelings of particular muscle groups.
- Mind-body perspective. Each technique has separate mental and physical elements that you practice, develop, and harmonize with one another.
- Discipline. You practice the technique virtually daily for at least a couple of months. When stress symptoms begin to subside, some type of relaxation technique is still part of your routine but not necessarily daily.

single, simple thought. You may choose to repeat a word or phrase, to think about your breathing, or to methodically contract and release individual muscle groups. Don't worry if your mind wanders, but become a passive observer of where it goes. Let your emotions wash through you, not grab you. Notice what makes you angry, pleased, or worried, and let it pass. Use your word or phrase to dislodge you from troubling thoughts or emotions and to center you as a passive observer.

Cognitive Strategies "Cognitive strategies" is a catch-all term for changing the way you automatically think in stressful situations. With thoughtful effort, you can replace the emotions of stress—anxiety, frustration, anger, fear, passivity, and self-doubt—with positive thinking and self-confidence. One way to do this is with Stress Inoculation Training, in which you learn to identify particular feelings and fears, to gradually expose yourself to them through imagery or role-playing, and to apply relaxation skills.

Psychological Skills Education is a strategy for people whose stress arises from their personal performance, not external sources. It is based on a two-pronged approach: mastering physical and psychological skills to succeed at a certain task, and developing mental skills for applying them, including making any necessary behavioral changes.

Goal-setting is another powerful strategy. While we're all familiar with long-term goals, such as wanting to be promoted to vice-president or to lose twenty pounds, more immediate and realistic goals are much better for attacking stress. Another characteristic of goal-setting is establishing short-term results that can be measured. And you must have a plan for reaching your goal.

Imagery "Imagery" is another word for concentrating your attention on mental images that are momentarily pleasant, inspiring, sensuous, or captivating. At stressful moments, use imagery to displace negative or fearful thoughts. Instead of becoming consumed by your stress, with panic and dread filling your mind, turn toward images that calm and reassure. For instance, when anticipating having to explain to your boss why something went wrong, push aside visions of arguments and anger and imagine a scenario in which the two of you have a friendly discussion about how you can improve the situation.

Successful imagery requires practice. To do this, find a quiet place, get comfortable, close your eyes, and visualize a shape such as a square, then visualize it a certain color, such as red. Do this a couple of times, each time making it a different color. Now imagine a three-dimensional shape, such as a bottle, and fill it with different-colored liquids. Add a label to the bottle or an object floating in it. Next, create a larger canvas—imagine a scene in a peaceful place and add as many details as you can. Put people in your scene, move them around, make them leave, and bring in newcomers. Lastly, imagine yourself as a star performer in a stressful situation—at the office, with family members, speaking before a group of people. You're cool, articulate, reasoned. Nothing ruffles you, and people listen to your thoughtful words. End this session with five deep breaths, then open your eyes and return to the world.

Progressive Muscle Relaxation (PMR) PMR is a technique bodybuilders use to relax after a strenuous workout, and I have found that while the goal is to relax the body, the mind also loses its tension. It is a systematic tensing and relaxing of specific muscle groups in a set order. Most PMR practitioners begin with their feet and work through calves, thighs, buttocks, abdomen, upper chest, fingers, arms, shoulders, neck, and face. PMR can relax the body within minutes, although when first learning the technique of contracting and relaxing certain muscles, you will have to devote at least thirty minutes a day to the exercise. Once your body knows how to tense and relax quickly, you will be able to apply the technique to stressful situations.

Breathing Everybody breathes, so what's so special about it? As serious athletes have known for decades, breathing *the right way* can make a measurable difference in performance and in how the body and brain handle stress from all directions. Some professional athletes even believe that correct breathing can help them find that elusive zone in which their minds and bodies effortlessly flow together.

When you get into an argument, or in any other stressful situation, your quickened heart rate and constricted blood vessels make you breathe faster and pull air from the chest in shallow gulps. This jolts the sympathetic nervous system into activating the flight-or-fight response. And, as hyperventilators and sufferers of panic reactions know, rapid shallow breathing feeds on itself, gets worse, and can produce dizziness, light-headedness, and strong feelings of fear. Breathing through the mouth and pulling air from the top of the lungs also activates stress hormones. This is why many people do not like to exercise. Panting—shallow breathing—is definitely unpleasant.

A much better way to breathe is a technique called yoga breathing, deep breathing, or nostril breathing. You inhale and exhale only through the nose. This delivers more oxygen to the lower lobes of the lungs and in turn better oxygenates the blood so it can deliver more energy to the muscles and brain. You draw air down through the heart of the solar plexus, diaphragm, stomach, and pelvic floor, to the base of your spine. As you exhale, focus your mind's eye on a point of light behind your eyes and place the tip of your tongue on the acupuncture point at the top of the mouth's soft palate.

Deep breathing quiets stressful reactions by stimulating the parasympathetic nerves, which work in just the opposite way from the sympathetic nerves. Parasympathetic nerves relax your muscles, slow your cardiovascular system, and do not set off your adrenal gland.

Deep breathing is now used by many professional athletes—runners, tennis players, even pro football players—and by medical professionals to treat stress-related illnesses. In one case, doctors at St. Bartholomew's Hospital in London taught deep-breathing techniques to twelve agoraphobia (fear of open spaces) patients. After two training sessions, the patients went through seven weekly exposures to fearful situations to which they applied their new breathing method. At the end of the study, and even six months later, the deep-breathers experienced a complete elimination of panic attacks.

Learning deep breathing is not difficult but does take practice. Here are some tips.

- Lie down flat, put your hand on your diaphragm (just below the belly button), and breathe through your nose. Your hand will gently rise and fall. Notice the feeling, and how it differs from chest breathing.
- Time your respiration rate. The normal range for chest breathers is between eight and seventeen breaths a minute; you want to aim for a steady eight to ten breaths a minute.
- As you exhale, contract your throat so that the air flowing out makes a rattling noise or a "Darth Vader" sound. This empties your lungs so that with your next breath, the air will travel lower to the abdomen.
- Slowly integrate your deep breathing into your daily routine, beginning with mildly stressful situations, like rush-hour driving. Consciously breathe through your nose, keeping your mouth closed.
- Practice deep breathing at least once a day. First thing in the morning when you're still in bed, and before going to sleep, are good times, because you're lying down, relaxed, and more aware of breathing sensations.
- Be patient, even though "learning to breathe" sounds like a snap. Professional athletes who use the technique say it took them anywhere from a week to three months before they were truly pulling air from their diaphragms.

MAKING STRESS WORK FOR YOU

The key to making stress work for you is distinguishing between the two types of stress, and cultivating the one while defusing the other. Acute stress generates those shots of adrenaline that are like brain juice, while chronic stress eats away at your body and brain cells. As you have just read, short bursts of stress can give you fuel and energy, but prolonged baths of stress chemicals not only slow you down mentally but speed up the aging process.

Harnessing Acute Stress

- Prepare yourself for the chemical rush by eating the right foods and vitamins, as well as amino acid supplements. One of my favorite meals during stressful times is a large grilled-chicken salad—skinless white-meat chicken on a bed of lettuce, cold cooked string beans, sweet onion, mushrooms, tomatoes, a small handful of nuts, and an olive oil and vinegar dressing—followed by a huge fruit salad for dessert (use orange juice for "dressing").
- Eliminate all forms of caffeine from your diet, as well as heavy salt and alcohol.
- Take ginseng daily before and during periods of acute stress. A reasonable starting dose if you're taking a liquid extract is 1,500 mg/day.
- Learn deep-breathing techniques and apply them in small, stressful situations so that this invaluable weapon is ready when you are hit with a large blast of stress.
- Do a combined breathing/muscle relaxation exercise: Lie on the floor with your lower legs on a chair and a rolled towel or pillow under your neck. Close your eyes and do nostril breathing, inhaling and exhaling very slowly. As your breathing allows you to relax, loosen your neck muscles so that your head is comfortably back. Take twenty-five deep breaths.

Harnessing Chronic Stress

- Monitor physical indicators of elevated stress, particularly poor sleeping, acid stomach, poor concentration, and bouts of irrational anger or depression.
- Review critical situations in your life from the retrospect/

A BRIEF REFRESHER

While severe, prolonged stress depletes our energy and jumbles our thinking, mild transitory stress can be harnessed to enable us to respond better and smarter to life's daily challenges. Each of us needs to be aware of our personal stress triggers and to develop a battery of ways to control stress. Here are some proven ways.

Exercise. Moderate exercise (forty minutes a day, three to five times a week) is just as good as heavy exercise. I do brisk walking.

Diet and nutrition. Particular foods help ease the effects of stress. These include fruits (e.g., apples, bananas), vegetables (e.g., string beans, carrots), poultry (white meat only), raisins, almonds, and salmon. Useful vitamins and minerals include magnesium, vitamin A, vitamin C, vitamin E, B vitamins, and amino acid supplements. Foods that aggravate stress include salt and caffeine.

Ginseng. This herbal root extract is a very effective stress beater for many people.

Relaxation. This helps counteract stress chemicals. Activities include meditation, yoga, stretching, tai chi, and progressive muscle relaxation.

Breathing exercises. Deep-breathing techniques help tap into chemicals that counteract stress chemicals.

Cognitive strategies. Learning new modes of thinking can reduce stress. These include Stress Inoculation Training and imagery.

prospect perspective. Remember, this is a type of reflection in which you compare a past, stressful situation that has completely blown over with a current situation that is bothering you.

- Incorporate regular exercise that is not necessarily physically demanding, but that allows your mind and body to focus on a repetitive action and so dissipate residual stress. This is what walking and light weights do for me. If you do nothing else, at least once a day walk the stairs of your office building rather than taking the elevator.

- Every day, grab a minivacation away from mundane concerns. This may be twenty minutes of meditation, a brief flight into imagery, or playing a computer game for a few minutes.

HOW DO YOU DEAL WITH STRESS?

This quiz tests how you react to the stress of daily living. By measuring your reactions to situations and people, you can identify which kinds of stress you find most difficult to handle. The scoring at the end will give you an idea of how your stress-coping skills affect your general health and longevity.

N=Never
R=Rarely
S=Sometimes
A=Always (or as much as possible)

	N	**R**	**S**	**A**
1. I feel generally happy.	−2	−1	+1	+2
2. I spend time with and enjoy family and friends.	−2	−1	+1	+2
3. I feel in control of my personal life and career.	−2	−1	+1	+2
4. I live within my financial means.	−2	−1	+1	+2
5. I set goals and look for new challenges.	−2	−1	+1	+2
6. I participate in a hobby or creative outlet.	−2	−1	+1	+2
7. I have and enjoy leisure time.	−2	−1	+1	+2
8. I express my feelings easily.	−2	−1	+1	+2
9. I laugh easily.	−2	−1	+1	+2

10. I expect good things to happen.	−2	−1	+1	+2
11. I get angry easily.	+2	+1	−1	−2
12. I am critical of myself.	+2	+1	−1	−2
13. I am critical of others.	+2	+1	−1	−2
14. I often feel lonely, even around others.	+2	+1	−1	−2
15. I worry about things out of my control.	+2	+1	−1	−2
16. I regret sacrifices I have made.	+2	+1	−1	−2

TOTAL: ____+____+____+_____=_____

Scoring:

−32 to −11: You are severely stressed and need relief immediately.

−10 to +6: You live with a lot of stress, but it's not overwhelming.

+7 to +18: Stress comes and goes in your life; it's very manageable.

+19 to +32: You're so unstressed you're almost euphoric.

SELECTED SOURCES

Benson, H., and Stuart, E. M. *The Wellness Book.* Simon and Schuster, New York, 1992.

Bergner, P. *The Healing Power of Ginseng and the Tonic Herbs.* Prima Publishing, Rocklin, Calif., 1996.

Brannon, L., and Feist, J. *Health Psychology, Second Edition.* Wadsworth Publishing Co., Belmont, Calif., 1992.

Braverman, E. R. *P.A.T.H. Wellness Manual.* Publications for Achieving Total Health, Princeton, N.J., 1995.

"Coffee worsens stressful situations." *Edell Health Letter,* Duke University Research, 9 (10), 6, November 1990.

Elias, A. N., and Wilson, A. F. "Serum hormonal concentrations following transcendental meditation—potential role of gamma aminobutyric acid." *Medical Hypotheses,* 44 (4), 287–91, April 1995.

Friedman, A., et al. "Pyridostigmine brain penetration under stress enhances neuronal excitability and induces early immediate transcriptional response." *Nature Medicine,* 2, 1382–85, December 1996.

Goldberg, L., and Breznitz, S., eds. *Handbook of Stress: Theoretical and Clinical Aspects.* Macmillan, New York, 1993.

Hoon, R., et al. "Acute effect of qiqong training on stress hormonal levels in man." *American Journal of Chinese Medicine,* 24 (2), 193–98, 1996.

Jaret, P. "You don't have to sweat to reduce stress." *Hippocrates,* April 1996.

Jin, P. "Efficacy of Tai Chi, brisk walking, meditation, and reading in reducing mental and emotional stress." *Journal of Psychosomatic Research,* 36 (4), 361–70, May 1992.

Khalsa, D. S. *Brain Longevity.* Warner Books, New York, 1997.

LeDoux, J. *The Emotional Brain.* Simon and Schuster, New York, 1996.

Miler, L. H., et al. *The Stress Solution.* Pocket Books, New York, 1993.

Monat, A., and Lazarus, R. S., eds. *Stress and Coping: An Anthology.* Columbia University Press, New York, 1991.

Proctor, S. P., et al. "Effect of overtime work on cognitive function in automotive workers." *Scandinavian Journal of Work Environment Health,* 22 (2), 124–32, April 1996.

Sapolsky, R. M. "Stress and neuroendocrine changes during aging." *Generations,* 16 (4), 35–39, Fall–Winter 1992.

Tate, A. K., and Petruzzello, S. J. "Varying the intensity of acute exercise: implications for changes in affect." *Journal of Sports Medicine and Physical Fitness,* 35 (4), 295–302, December 1995.

University of California, Berkeley, *Wellness Letter,* 9 (7), 7, April 1993.

[illegible]

[illegible] New York, [illegible]

[illegible]

[illegible]

[illegible]

[illegible]

[illegible]

[illegible] Press, New York, [illegible]

[illegible]

[illegible]

[illegible]

[illegible] University of California Press, [illegible]

Five

CEREBRAL SECURITY

HEADING OFF ALZHEIMER'S DEMENTIA

I regularly speak to groups of seniors about physical and mental fitness. A recent conference and health show in Las Vegas attracted about six thousand people, many of whom were over fifty-five and anxious to know how to protect themselves from Alzheimer's. The conference is a regular event sponsored by numerous organizations, such as the American Academy of Anti-Aging Medicine, and in years past, I have been peppered with questions about hormone replacement therapies and nutrition. But this year, Alzheimer's was on people's minds. I spoke at an afternoon session, and it was standing room only as a sea of folks insisted I talk about what they could do to fend off dementia.

Alzheimer's has grabbed people's attention with all the intensity of a nationwide manhunt for a serial killer. People want to know all about the "crime" and how to make sure they do not become a victim. Either they are afraid for themselves or they have watched the disease steal the personalities and lives of friends or relatives. Their fears are fueled partly by the assumption that Alzheimer's is unstoppable and cannot be prevented, postponed, or checked. For many years, this has been largely so.

However, discoveries about its genetic, biological, and possibly environmental causes, diagnosis, progression, and treatment are changing the landscape and starting to shift the odds in our favor. Alzheimer's is still the scourge of the senior years, but we have lots of say about when, how, and sometimes even whether the disease afflicts us.

FAMILY FEARS: WHO, WHEN, AND HOW IT HITS

Many of the people who crowded into the ballroom at Bally's Resort and Casino were women in their fifties and sixties. Their husbands were either long gone or more interested in a simultaneous session on human growth hormone. I enjoyed these women—they were blunt, practical, and hungry for information. Judging from their questions, I could tell they kept up with scientific advances but were impatient with research jargon that did not give them hard facts. One of the first questions was a version of "Who gets this disease?" and "What are my chances?"

I told them that there are three broad categories of people who are at risk: older people, women, and people with a family history of the disease. As most people know, Alzheimer's is a disease of aging, afflicting between 2 and 10 percent of people over sixty-four years old. As the years rise, the percentage increases: Among people over eighty-four years old, it grabs between 13 and 48 percent. But not only the aged are in jeopardy. Much to the chagrin of my audience, I had to tell them that women are more susceptible than men as they age, particularly as they reach sixty and beyond. One explanation is simply women's longevity: With more women than men surviving into their eighties, the incidence rate is going to be higher.

The risk level rises significantly if an immediate relative has had the disease. Alzheimer's in one first-degree relative (parent, sibling, grandparent) quadruples the odds of developing the disease *four times* and two first-degree relatives produces a forty-fold increase in likelihood. The family link in Alzheimer's is so strong that it has led researchers to uncover genetic origins.

Each cell in the body contains a nucleus, and inside the nucleus are chromosomes composed of genes. If you imagine Russian matrioshka dolls, those dolls within dolls within dolls, you get the picture. Genes are responsible for the body's chemistry—they manufacture every enzyme, protein, hormone, and growth factor. They also disseminate the body's master chemical plan: All physical features, from curly hair to skin color and some diseases are generated by genes. Genes come from parents—half from the mother, half from the father—and pass on information from generation to generation. Four different genes have been spotted as likely instigators in the development of Alzheimer's. One of these genes, called apoE4, is suspected of contributing to a variety of Alzheimer's that attacks late in life. Two other genes have been found among the much smaller group of patients (about 20 percent) who show signs of the illness as early as their fifties.

There are a couple of things to remember about the genetic influence on Alzheimer's. One is that having a certain gene or genes does not make the disease inevitable; it merely raises the odds. Second is that scientists are fairly certain this illness is not caused by one gene alone but involves a number of genes, plus a host of other influences. The disease has many different forms and causes, and more than genes are at work. For instance, poisons in foods, certain chemicals and metals in the environment, education, individual health and lifestyle habits have all been linked to Alzheimer's.

The genetic mysteries underlying the disease are, in truth, good news. It means that no one is absolutely doomed to contract this illness, and the individual has a significant degree of control over what happens.

AM I GETTING IT?

While the people listening to me talk were relieved to hear that no one's fate is sealed, at least half were convinced they were showing early signs of the disease. One woman described how she had lost her car keys and eventually found them in the freezer section of her refrigerator (the group surmised that when she got home, she immediately went for the ice cream and forgot what was in her hand). Another woman was sure that forgetting the names of her husband's business associates was proof of her creeping dementia. The group needed convincing that forgetfulness or a bad memory is probably *not* the dreaded disease. I shared with them these facts:

- It's normal for your spatial memory—remembering where you parked the car—to begin sliding in your twenties.
- It's normal after age thirty-five to forget the names of people you do not see often.
- A sign of early Alzheimer's (before sixty-five) is not memory loss but a change in emotional tenor—feelings of detachment, indifference, and loss of naturally affectionate mannerisms.
- Another sign of the early version is difficulty with language and verbal learning.

DIAGNOSIS DIFFICULTIES

The memory loss that comes with Alzheimer's is selective at first. You may remember events years past and not remember where you went this morning. Or you may have difficulty remembering how to do familiar tasks, like microwaving a frozen dinner. Neither of these signs is definitive. Diagnosing the disease requires a battery of cognitive and behavioral tests as well as a complete laboratory workup of blood and function tests. Only an autopsy can produce a definitive diagnosis, which is why the disease doesn't appear as a cause on

TAKE ACTION

Is It Alzheimer's?

While a firm diagnosis must be left to a medical professional, there are widely accepted markers and criteria that strongly suggest someone may be developing Alzheimer's. Take this quiz to see if your assumptions about Alzheimer's are close to true.

1. You forget how to program the VCR, which your son explained just last week.
2. You can't remember the name of someone you dated in college twenty years ago.
3. You can't remember the name of the kid who mows your lawn every week.
4. You can't remember why you opened a cupboard.
5. You can't remember how to operate your washing machine.
6. You regularly "lose" eyeglasses and keys.

1. No. 2. No. 3. Maybe. 4. No. 5. Yes. 6. No.

death certificates. Nevertheless, the tests doctors give patients are reliable 90 percent of the time.

A diagnosis can be elusive unless done by a medical professional, because mental or behavioral problems can point to other troubles. Memory and mood difficulties can be caused by stroke, tumor, clinical depression, thyroid malfunction, nutritional deficiency, infectious disease, or a side effect of medication. There is an entire other category of dementias that are not Alzheimer's: vascular or multi-infarct dementia, frontal lobe dementia, and dementia associated with Parkinson's.

So, what do doctors study to arrive at an Alzheimer's diagnosis? They begin with a complete history of symptoms (what is seen in someone else) and signs (what you see in yourself) from the patient as well as from family members. The cornerstone of the cognitive test is the Mini-Mental Status Examination, a series of questions about a person's sense of time and place; mood; thought processes; memory, attention, and concentration; ability to do practical tasks; and judgment and reasoning. The "Time and Change" test is frequently used with older patients. It's simple and considered fairly reliable: A person is asked the day and time, and to make a dollar's worth of change.

The behavioral and cognitive symptoms can be grouped into one of three stages, depending on how far the disease has advanced. On average, Alzheimer's takes about eight years to consume a victim, although some people live with the disease for twenty years or more. Medical experts may distinguish between five or even seven stages, but professionals and family members who take care of Alzheimer's patients separate the disease into three stages.

Early or Mild Symptoms

Confusion and memory loss
Disorientation and getting lost in familiar surroundings
Problems with routine tasks
Changes in personality and judgment

Moderate Symptoms

Difficulty with activities of daily living, such as feeding and bathing
Anxiety, suspiciousness, agitation
Sleep disturbances
Wandering, pacing
Difficulty recognizing family and friends

Severe, Advanced Symptoms

Loss of speech
Loss of appetite and weight

Loss of bladder and bowel control
Total dependence on caregivers

Laboratory tests hunt for underlying biological causes of memory difficulties and changes in behavior or personality. These can be problems with metabolism, infections, or inflammatory diseases. The tests include blood counts and function tests for electrolytes, liver, renal system, and thyroid, and screens for syphilis and deficiencies of vitamin B_{12} or folic acid. Studies have found that people with familial Alzheimer's frequently have low levels of vitamin B_{12}, but doctors do not know yet whether the deficiency somehow contributes to Alzheimer's or is the result of poor eating habits that accompany the disease. Brain scans such as magnetic resonance imaging (MRI) can also help identify the disease and distinguish it from vascular dementia.

SOLVING MYSTERIES ABOUT CAUSES

After describing the symptoms, I saw that my audience felt helpless. An older man at the back of the group, after hearing about signs of suspiciousness and sometimes paranoia, interjected, "They're suspicious for a good reason—people are trying to lock them up!" A sad chuckle ran through the group.

But there is a silver lining, I told them. While researchers are learning exactly what Alzheimer's looks like, they are also learning about how it attacks the brain and are unraveling the chemical mysteries surrounding the disease.

Scientists have a pretty good understanding of what happens with Alzheimer's. A brain with Alzheimer's has patches of dead neurons, particularly around the hippocampus and cerebral cortex, which are the areas involved in learning, memory, logical thinking, and language. These patches, also called plaques, are composed of fragments of protein, particularly beta-amyloid. The beta-amyloid protein kills the neurons, although scientists are just now learning that these errant proteins are focal points for inflammations and the production of free-radical damage within the brain.

A recent study conducted by Changis Geula, Ph.D., assistant professor of medicine at Beth Israel Deaconess Medical Center, Bruce A. Yankner at Children's Hospital, Boston, and coworkers shows

Parts of the Brain and Functions

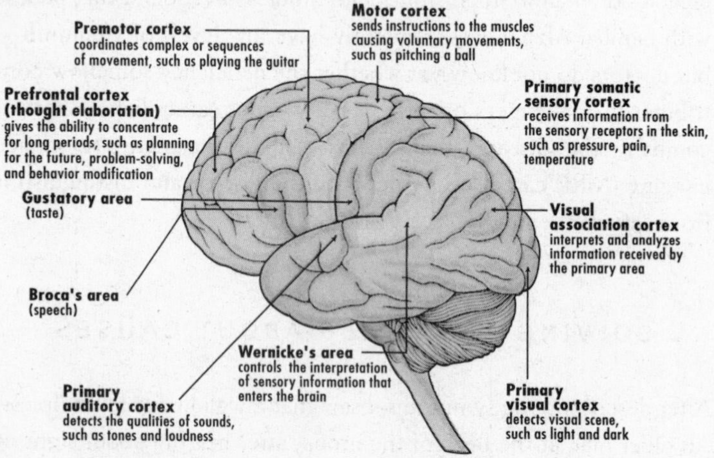

Premotor cortex
coordinates complex or sequences of movement, such as playing the guitar

Motor cortex
sends instructions to the muscles causing voluntary movements, such as pitching a ball

Prefrontal cortex (thought elaboration)
gives the ability to concentrate for long periods, such as planning for the future, problem-solving, and behavior modification

Primary somatic sensory cortex
receives information from the sensory receptors in the skin, such as pressure, pain, temperature

Gustatory area
(taste)

Visual association cortex
interprets and analyzes information received by the primary area

Broca's area
(speech)

Wernicke's area
controls the interpretation of sensory information that enters the brain

Primary auditory cortex
detects the qualities of sounds, such as tones and loudness

Primary visual cortex
detects visual scene, such as light and dark

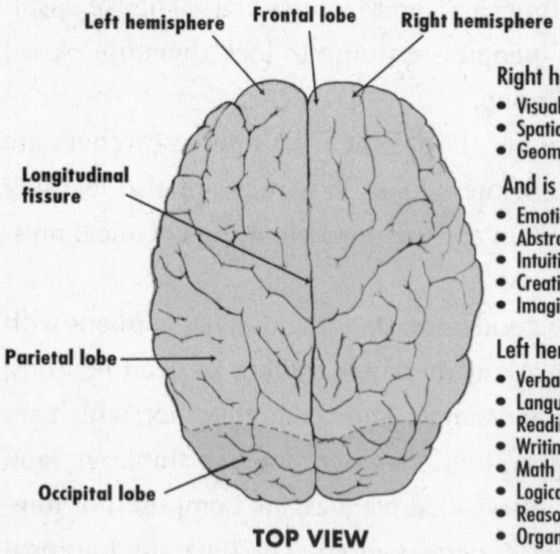

Left hemisphere
Frontal lobe
Right hemisphere
Longitudinal fissure
Parietal lobe
Occipital lobe
TOP VIEW

Right hemisphere controls perception of:
- Visual images
- Spatial relationships
- Geometric shapes

And is responsible for:
- Emotions
- Abstract ideas
- Intuition
- Creativity
- Imagination

Left hemisphere is responsible for:
- Verbal skills
- Language comprehension
- Reading ability
- Writing skills
- Math proficiency
- Logical thinking
- Reasoning
- Organizational skills

Adapted from *The Brain and Nervous System*, AMA Home Medical Library (1991)

that when beta-amyloid is introduced into the brains of aged animals at levels similar to those that occur in Alzheimer's disease, it causes profound brain cell death. In addition, the study implicates the aging process as an insidious partner in the disease. As Yankner says, "If we can learn why the aging brain, but not the young brain, is susceptible to the toxic effects of A-beta, we may be able to target the susceptibility factor with drugs."

Beta-amyloid is not the only villain here. Another protein called tau gets into the neurons and disrupts the long, fibrous tubules that carry nutrients and signals from one cell to another. The tau protein twists and turns around the tubules, creating tangles of neurofibers. These twisted fibers halt communication between cells and gradually starve the neurons.

While the exact chemistry of these plaques and tangles still mystifies scientists, they have found intriguing clues to their formation. For instance, both plaques and tangles contain a buildup of aluminum. This is a main reason that aluminum has been targeted as a possible contributor to the disease, and that some medical professionals suggest that people reduce their exposure to it.

The brain's metabolism—how its cells and molecules break down nutrients into energy—plays a role in the production of the proteins that cause plaques and tangles. Here's where some very useful discoveries have been made. For starters, one of the brain's vital chemicals, and a key component in forming memories, is acetylcholine. Brains with Alzheimer's lose their normal amounts of acetylcholine as well as other brain chemicals—serotonin, somatostatin (which inhibits the release of growth hormone), and noradrenaline. Thus, researchers are testing compounds, such as the drug selegiline, that block the enzymes that degrade these chemicals.

The precipitous drop in acetylcholine in an Alzheimer's patient has led researchers to promising new treatments for the disease—drugs that can increase or replace this chemical, or that can slow its disappearance. Called cholinesterase inhibitors, a number of these drugs are already in the clinical testing pipeline, and two, tacrine and donepezil, have been approved by the U.S. Food and Drug Administration as treatments for Alzheimer's. I'll tell you more about these drugs later.

Neuroscientists have also learned that a diseased brain cannot handle normal amounts of the chemical glutamate, and as a result, brain cells are flooded with calcium. Calcium is essential for neurons to receive and send messages, but too much calcium kills brain cells. One promising area of research is investigating whether antioxidants or the herb ginkgo biloba can slow the rate of brain cell death. Scientists have also found that the metabolism of glucose, the brain's only nutrient, slows down in an Alzheimer's brain. One intriguing theory suggests that the stress hormones, glucocorticoids, which usually enhance the production of glucose, might be killing brain cells through their effects on glucose metabolism in pathologic conditions. This theory is pointing researchers toward ways of reducing the stress hormones in the brain and so slowing brain cell death. Other researchers are investigating whether the naturally occurring compound ALC (acetyl-l-carnitine) can improve brain metabolism by reducing antioxidants and speeding up communication between brain cells.

Stressed-out Brain Cells

Some neuroscientists believe that stress is a major player in the Alzheimer's story. In the chapter on stress, I explained the glucocorticoid cascade, that chemical chain reaction triggered by stress and resulting in a flood of hormones that can damage brain cells. Dr. Robert Sapolsky, the originator of the cascade theory, has learned that people with Alzheimer's have a high level of hormone production. Their brains appear unable to stop production of stress hormones. Aging, among other things, seems to reduce the brain's ability to halt the stress response.

Alzheimer's disease is undoubtedly the result of a number of causes, and it is possible that one of the ingredients is the chemical onslaught that comes with the brain's reaction to stress.

A Virus Involved?

Yet another ingredient in the Alzheimer's stew may be a virus, which could point to an antiviral approach to prevention and treatment. A team of researchers examined the brains of ninety people, about half with Alzheimer's and half without, and looked at their genetic and viral history. The people whose brains were most likely to show signs of genetically triggered Alzheimer's were those who'd had a history of cold sores from the herpes simplex virus. In fact, the people with frequent cold sores were four times more likely to develop the genetic form of the disease.

The researchers explain in the authoritative medical journal *The Lancet* that the herpes virus is very common. Most of us are infected early in life, but not everyone shows symptoms. The virus stays dormant until, in some people, it is reactivated by environmental factors like stress or ultraviolet light and erupts into cold sores. The researchers found that the herpes virus and Alzheimer's disease are active in the same region of the brain, and they believe it is possible that people with cold sores may be more susceptible to developing Alzheimer's.

They also think that their findings may explain why anti-inflammatory drugs, which reduce virus activity, may prevent or delay the beginning of Alzheimer's symptoms. If their findings hold up in other studies, they suggest that early treatment for cold sores, such as applying a vaccine, could help protect against Alzheimer's dementia.

The American Way of Eating

A landmark study involving Japanese Americans and African Americans compared the prevalence of Alzheimer's among people with very different diets. Dr. William Grant did a side-by-side comparison of individuals living in the United States with those of the same ethnic background living in Japan or Africa. He found that Alzheimer's strikes 4.1 percent of Japanese living in the United States, while in Japan, the rate is just 1.8 percent. On average, 6.2 percent of African Americans in the United States get the disease, while 1.4 percent of Africans in Nigeria are victims.

What's so different in America? The answer seems to lie in the American lifestyle and environment. When Grant picked apart what these facets of American life might be, he found convincing evidence pointing toward diet and caloric intake. In particular, acid drinks, alcohol, fat, refined carbohydrates, and salt are believed to be the main culprits. These foods and minerals spawn free radicals in the blood, and when the free radicals reach the brain, they stress neurons to the point of inflammation, toxic poisoning, and cell death. The result is the plaques and tangles of Alzheimer's.

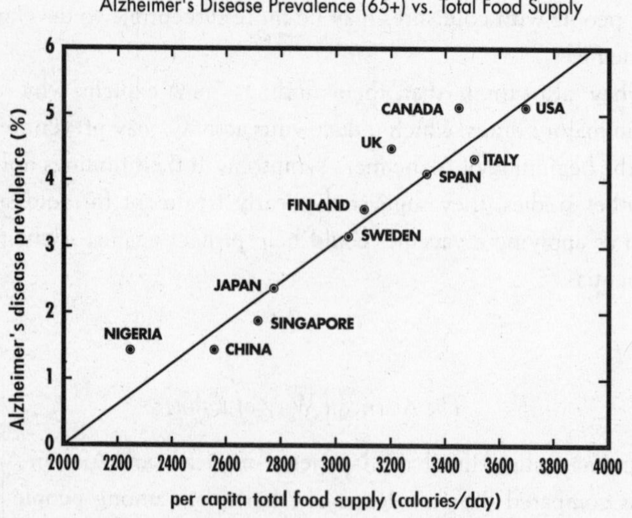

Adapted from *Alzheimer's Disease Review*, *http://www.coa.uky.edu/ADReview*

Poison Minerals

A prime suspect in the Alzheimer's investigation is aluminum, which people absorb through food, cooking utensils, personal care products, and medications. Doctors have found that people who have died with Alzheimer's have concentrations of the metal in their neurofibrous tangles.

Aluminum is the third most common element in the environment—it occurs naturally everywhere. You take in aluminum in spinach and berries, in acidic foods like tomatoes and cabbage, through foods cooked in aluminum pans, and in medications and health products, including antiperspirants, antacids, buffered aspirin, cosmetics, and some ointments. Water purification systems used by local municipalities and food preservation processes also may add aluminum. The human body does not absorb all aluminum compounds the same way. For example, the aluminum hydroxide in antacids does not easily dissolve, while the aluminum citrate found in milk of magnesia is quickly absorbed. The light metal seems to serve no purpose in the body and is toxic at high levels. The 10–15 milligrams you absorb a day through food and water is generally excreted by the kidneys.

There is no proof that aluminum causes Alzheimer's, but questions persist about whether it might be a cause or an effect. Studies in Canada, Australia, and Europe have linked aluminum sulfate, the form that is added to drinking water to remove bacteria, with increased incidence of Alzheimer's. Other research has shown that this man-made aluminum compound damages neurons in rat brains. There is other circumstantial evidence against aluminum, as well. Before the treatment was altered, renal patients were absorbing aluminum from dialysis fluid and equipment and showing symptoms of dementia. There are reports that residents of Guam, which has a high level of aluminum in its water, have a high rate of neurological diseases, especially tangles like those found in Alzheimer's. And some epidemiology studies have linked the disease with the metal, although the study methods have been questioned.

No one is accusing aluminum of sparking the disease, but some experts believe that it fans the flames. While the aluminum in cookware does not get into food, it may be possible to take in aluminum in other ways. So some experts advise against antacids containing the metal, aerosol antiperspirants (because the aluminum can enter the brain through the nasal passages), and tap water. For me, this is simply one more good reason not to drink tap water, which I believe is a slurry of brain poisons.

Another metal that is sometimes fingered is zinc, although the evidence for it is thin. A laboratory study of zinc and twenty-five other common metals found that it was the only one to bind to protein and produce a clump that resembled the infamous Alzheimer's plaques. Zinc is impossible to avoid, being an essential mineral that's everywhere. Nevertheless, it is probably a good idea to avoid taking in more than 50 milligrams a day. One Australian study reports that people given megadoses of zinc—90 mg a day—experienced mental deterioration.

An Electricity Connection?

Other environmental hazards may be harder to avoid. Joseph Sobel, a researcher at the University of Southern California, says there may be a connection between Alzheimer's and electromagnetic fields, the high-electricity areas around power lines and electrical machinery. Sobel points to three studies, two done in Finland and one in Los Angeles, which found that people who worked around power lines and electric machines were three times more likely to develop Alzheimer's than people who did not work around electric fields. The people in the studies who were most exposed encountered strong electrical fields from the electromagnetic radiation of machines and worked as seamstresses, dressmakers, and tailors.

TAKE ACTION

The Toxic Environment

These environmental elements are all possible suspects in the causes of neurological diseases including Alzheimer's, and some neurologists, as well as a report from the U.S. Office of Technology Assessment, recommend avoiding contact with them:

Aluminum (in antacids, aerosol antiperspirants, and tap water)
Zinc (limit intake to 50 mg/day)
Metals (cadmium, mercury, lead, iron, manganese)
Petrochemicals
Electromagnetic fields
Industrial chemicals and pesticides

WAYS TO PROTECT YOURSELF

The conference seniors leaned forward in rapt attention when I began talking about how they might protect themselves from the disease.

Solid Protection: Low Blood Pressure, Lowered Stroke Risk

Strong evidence is surfacing that the best protection against Alzheimer's and other dementias may be low blood pressure and stroke prevention. Why low blood pressure? Because people with high blood pressure are much more likely to suffer a stroke, and strokes and dementia have a long shared history. Recently, studies have probed further and found that strokes may trigger the symptoms of Alzheimer's.

Researchers have known for a while about a connection between hypertension and various kinds of dementia. Hypertension is a common cause of diseased blood vessels in the brain, which can bring on dementia. High blood pressure damages the body's arteries, including those that carry blood to the brain, and this damage can disrupt the steady flow of blood. Tiny clots may break loose and clog blood vessels, or arteries can narrow, either of which can kill brain tissue. Without sufficient blood, brain tissue dies. The death of brain tissue is called a cerebral infarct. Or a diseased blood vessel may cause bleeding in the brain and produce a cerebral hemorrhage. The end result of diseased blood vessels leading to the brain is some type of stroke. Depending on exactly where the damaged brain tissue lies, the stroke victim may experience mental confusion, memory loss, unconsciousness, paralysis of a limb, or loss of speech. While the fallout of many tiny strokes may seem to be temporary, neuroscientists have found that the effect is cumulative and dementia often follows.

Researchers in Göteborg, Sweden, followed 382 people, all aged seventy, for fifteen years and paid particular attention to their blood pressure and mental faculties. At the beginning of the study, none of the people showed any signs of dementia or Alzheimer's. As the study progressed, the researchers noticed that those people with high blood pressure, particularly the diastolic (lower) reading, were more likely to develop dementia five to ten years later. Even though the subjects' blood pressure declined as they grew older, the people with the higher readings when they were seventy-five years old were those who developed dementia beginning around age seventy-nine.

High blood pressure has also been associated with developing Alzheimer's late in life. Among the people in the Göteborg study, high diastolic blood pressure around age seventy was recorded in people who showed symptoms of Alzheimer's starting around age seventy-nine. This discovery about Alzheimer's seems to have been unexpected; the researchers reported, "Our finding that blood pressure was increased in subjects with Alzheimer's disease 10–15 years before dementia onset is significant."

Even more persuasive findings about the interaction of strokes

WHAT YOUR WRITING STYLE REVEALS

A fascinating finding from a study of almost seven hundred elderly nuns reveals that the way a young person writes—the number of ideas she expresses and the complexity of the grammar she uses—may indicate a susceptibility to developing Alzheimer's fifty years later. With access to the medical and personal records of the School Sisters of Notre Dame, Dr. David Snowdon and fellow researchers at the University of Kentucky Sanders-Brown Center on Aging read autobiographies written by ninety-three nuns when they first entered the religious order around age twenty. Their authors, now at least fifty years older, were given mental function tests and assessed for signs of dementia. The researchers found a strong correlation between "low idea density" and "low grammatical complexity" in an autobiography and poor cognitive function. Dr. Snowdon believes that "low linguistic ability in early life was a strong predictor of poor cognitive function and Alzheimer's disease in late life."

and Alzheimer's, and the possible protection provided by low blood pressure, have surfaced from another source, the School Sisters of Notre Dame.

The Nun Study

In 1990, David Snowdon, a professor of preventive medicine at the University of Kentucky Sanders-Brown Center on Aging, launched a longitudinal study involving an order of nuns, the School Sisters of Notre Dame. The study began tracking the lives and deaths of approximately 678 nuns aged 75 to 102, looking at how their minds and brains aged and the progression of any symptoms of dementia, particularly Alzheimer's. What makes this study extraordinary is that so many nuns agreed to participate fully, allowing access to their lifetime medical records, giving regular blood samples for genetic and nutritional testing, taking annual mental function tests, and donating their brains for study after they died.

For scientists investigating the aging brain, the Sisters of Notre Dame present a perfect petri dish. Their cloistered lives in convents in the midwestern, eastern, and southern United States helped to eliminate many of the variables that confuse other studies of aging individuals. They never married or had children, are college-educated, do not smoke, drink moderately if at all, live in similar environments, eat similar food, do similar activities, and have similar medical care. It is hard to imagine a more homogenous and pristine group of subjects. The nuns, who are mostly schoolteachers and dedicated to helping the sick and the poor, were eager to participate in the study. "A person with Alzheimer's disease is one of the poorest people I know," remarked one sister.

At the beginning of the Nun Study, Dr. Snowdon and his team collected detailed personal and family histories and gave each participant an extensive battery of memory, cognitive, and physical tests. All these have been updated at least every two years. As the nuns die and their brains are examined, Dr. Snowdon has been publishing his findings in a steady stream of studies on the possible origins, causes, and course of Alzheimer's.

One such study recently focused on the connection between brain infarctions caused by stroke and Alzheimer's. Dr. Snowdon and his team examined the brains of 102 deceased nuns and looked at their performance history on cognitive function tests and whether any had shown symptoms of dementia or Alzheimer's. What the scientists found has been called "exciting." The brains that had spots of dead tissue or infarcts, indicating a stroke, turned out to be those of the nuns with poor scores on the cognition tests and more likely to have had dementia. In contrast, nuns whose brains evidenced clear signs of Alzheimer's—numerous plaques and tangles—but no signs of stroke damage, had shown no signs of dementia and done well on cognition tests. Dr. Snowdon highlighted this startling finding: "Sig-

TAKE ACTION

Guard Against Strokes

To protect your brain against strokes, you need healthy cerebral arteries so that the blood supply is steady and constant. You have to guard against hardened arteries, gummed-up arteries that can throw off clots, and narrow arteries that can reduce blood flow. Entire medical books have been written about hypertension and stroke prevention. Here is what I have found to be useful.

- Maintain low-to-normal blood cholesterol levels—below 180 mg per deciliter of blood with HDLs (high-density lipoprotein) being at least 25 percent of total cholesterol. I have found that eating oatmeal regularly (three times a week) and taking niacin and aged garlic extract daily keep my cholesterol in this range.
- Consume a steady diet of fruits and vegetables. I eat one or two pieces of fruit with breakfast every day, regardless of what else I eat; and I always garnish lunch, whether it's a bowl of soup or leftovers, with fresh tomatoes, carrots, and/or green beans, or drink a glass of vegetable juice.
- Add an extra dose of potassium to your daily fare. An extra serving of potassium-rich food (about 400 mg of the mineral) every day can help prevent hypertension and so cut your risk of stroke by 40 percent. Potassium-rich foods include raw or cooked fresh spinach, fresh orange juice, cantaloupe, banana, baked potato, baked beans, and canned sardines.
- Take antioxidant supplements daily for healthy blood vessels. I take vitamin A (2,500 IU), vitamin C (2,000–4,800 mg), and vitamin E (200–400 IU).

nificant numbers of individuals with abundant neuropathologic lesions of Alzheimer's disease do not become demented."

While Dr. Snowdon also stated that he could not explain why someone with Alzheimer's damage in the brain was not demented, he hinted that the answer might lie in stroke damage. "These findings suggest that cerebrovascular disease may play an important role in determining the presence and severity of the clinical symptoms of Alzheimer's disease."

Dr. Snowdon thinks that a number of small strokes may produce the poor thinking of dementia and ultimately Alzheimer's. Put another way, you may ward off what Alzheimer's can do to your memory and thought processes by taking measures to prevent high blood pressure and strokes. Stroke prevention may be Alzheimer's prevention.

Caution: Be careful about letting your blood pressure drop too low, which can happen if you are on hypertension medication and

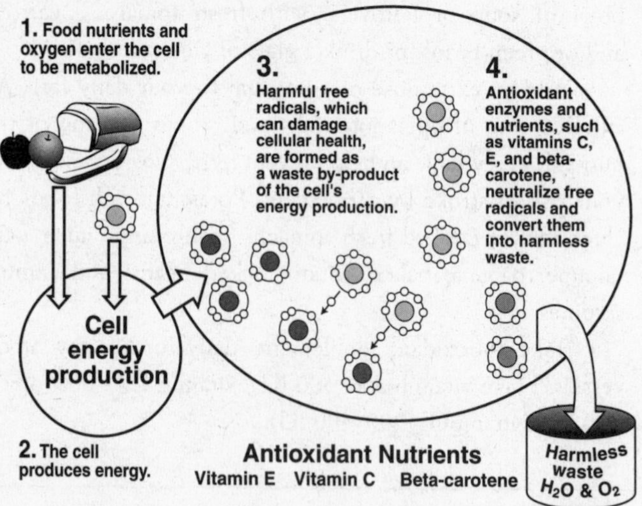

Adapted from *Stopping the Clock* (1996)

overmedicating. If your blood pressure drops way below normal (90/50 or lower), the blood supply to the brain can be disrupted, and this can alter your thinking and memory, as well as damage neurons.

More Protection: Antioxidants

Neuropathologists (scientists who study diseased brains) are discovering that antioxidants may do as much for retarding the signs of Alzheimer's as for fending off strokes. Antioxidants, as the name implies, fight against the tissue damage caused by oxidation. As the brain goes through its usual business of turning glucose and oxygen into energy, it throws off renegade oxygen molecules called free radicals, which trip chemical chain reactions that destroy tissue through oxidation. Oxidation is what makes apples turn brown, iron rust, and brain cells die. Many scientists believe that free radicals are at least partly responsible for the body's aging as well as for many diseases, including cancer, heart disease, and Alzheimer's.

Even though the production of free radicals may be unavoidable, it is possible to combat and even repair the damage they do. By consuming foods and vitamins that contain antioxidants, you put into play molecules that can neutralize the damage that free radicals are wreaking on the body and the brain.

Scientists in England investigating the effects of antioxidants have found that Alzheimer's patients have high levels of two enzymes that play an active role in oxidation and low levels of the antioxidants vitamin A (beta-carotene) and vitamin E. A study at Central Middlesex Hospital in London involved forty people, half with Alzheimer's or dementia, and half nondemented people, and concluded that not enough antioxidants in the blood may accelerate a brain's degeneration and the onslaught of dementia. More to the point, it also suggested that antioxidant vitamin supplements may slow the symptoms of dementia.

Research at the University of South Florida College of Medicine adds weight to the idea that Alzheimer's may be caused in part by the damage from free radicals. Dr. Michael Mullan, a professor of biological psychiatry, has found that the beta-amyloid protein, the leading suspect in the search for causes of Alzheimer's, generates the release of toxic free radicals.

The theory that antioxidants may be effective weapons against Alzheimer's was put to the test by a team of scientists at twenty-three medical centers working with the U.S. government–sponsored effort called the Alzheimer's Disease Cooperative Study. For two years or more, 341 patients with moderately severe Alzheimer's took 2,000 IU per day of vitamin E or 10 mg per day of selegiline (a drug used for Parkinson's disease that may operate like an antioxidant), or both the vitamin and selegiline, or a placebo. At the end of the study, both the powerful antioxidant, vitamin E, and the selegiline had effectively reduced the normal progression of the disease. While earlier studies with selegiline (also known as Deprenyl and prescribed as eldepryl) have indicated that it helps slow Alzheimer's dementia, this study was the first large-scale test of vitamin E. Mysteriously, patients taking both selegiline and vitamin E did not outperform those taking one or the other. The researchers suggested that the benefits of antioxidants may have limits.

Anti-Inflammatories: NSAIDs

Evidence has been mounting that people who regularly take nonsteroidal anti-inflammatory drugs (NSAIDs), which include ibuprofen medications like Motrin and Advil, are less susceptible to Alzheimer's.

One survey, for instance, tracked older people who regularly took NSAIDs for arthritis and found that their risk of developing this dementia was cut in half. A six-year survey of more than 7,600 older people by the National Institute on Aging, which included a test of thinking ability, found that those taking aspirin or NSAIDs regularly were mentally sharper. Yet another study followed more than 1,600 people for over fifteen years and discovered that people taking NSAIDs were half as likely to develop Alzheimer's as those who were not.

Researchers at Duke University Medical Center looked at fifteen studies involving anti-inflammatories and Alzheimer's and concluded that "fourteen of these studies suggest that such treatments (especially nonsteroidal agents) prevent or ameliorate symptoms of Alzheimer's disease."

Scientists think that inflammation and the body's immune system play a pivotal role in the destruction of brain tissue by Alzheimer's. They have found that areas of a brain with Alzheimer's are frequently inflamed, and so conclude that NSAIDs may help reduce the swelling.

While the medical community is encouraged about anti-inflammatories as possible neuroprotective drugs, experts point out that so far the evidence has come from surveys, not blind, placebo-controlled studies. This means that there are not yet any rigorous, scientific findings confirming the drugs' benefits, or guidelines for doses. Experts also remind people that NSAIDs were not designed to be taken over long periods and can produce dangerous side effects, including ulcers, intestinal bleeding, and kidney damage.

Nevertheless, the signs so far are very promising, and, like people at risk for heart disease who began taking aspirin regularly before all the scientific evidence of its benefits was known, people worried about Alzheimer's may well begin adding a low-dose NSAID to their daily handful of vitamins.

A Lifesaving Hormone?

Many of the people in my audience at the conference were personally familiar with the wonders of another possible neuroprotective drug for Alzheimer's—estrogen. In a showing of hands, almost half the women in the ballroom said they were on hormone replacement therapy to counteract the symptoms of menopause and protect themselves against osteoporosis and heart disease. None were taking hormone supplements to boost their flagging mental functions. But that's just what the female hormone appears to do.

The first widespread inkling that estrogen may do more than combat the signs of menopause came around 1990 when two scientists from the University of Southern California School of Medicine began examining data from almost nine thousand women living in a retirement community. They followed the group for eleven years, then noted how many had died, what percentage had had Alzheimer's disease, and what percentage had been taking estrogen replacement therapy. They discovered that the women on estrogen were 40 percent less likely to develop Alzheimer's. Furthermore, the longer a woman took the hormone, the better her chances. Although earlier studies had shown that estrogen helps people who have Alzheimer's, this study pointed to its power to protect against the disease.

An explanation of why estrogen deflects Alzheimer's revolves around how the hormone acts in the brain. It appears most active in the hippocampus and cerebral cortex, the memory and learning centers, and multiplies the amount of nerve growth factor, thus protecting neurons and enhancing cell health. Growth factor, particularly insulin-like growth factor 1 (IGF-1), seems to play an active role in an Alzheimer's brain. Explains Dr. Thierry Hertoghe, an international expert in brain chemistry, "The IGF-1 level in the cerebrospinal fluid of Alzheimer's patients seems similar to that of normal people but in the forgetful patients, there is an excess of IGF-1 binding proteins. A high concentration of these proteins may mean the binding is too tight or even literally sequesters the molecules, which virtually inactivates them and prevents sufficient amounts of valuable IGF-1 from entering the brain. This decreased availability of IGF-1 for brain cells might be one of the factors that predisposes to Alzheimer's."

Estrogen also stimulates growth of the synapses that carry signals between cells and helps the brain maintain its output of acetylcholine, the neurochemical essential to learning and memory. Furthermore, the hormone stimulates blood flow in the brain so that it gets more oxygen and glucose. "The brain just lights up with this stuff," said Dr. Galen Buckwalter at a symposium on estrogen and Alzheimer's disease at the University of Southern California in Los Angeles.

A study in the works right now, the Women's Health Initiative (WHI), sponsored by the U.S. National Institute on Aging, is looking at the health and aging of thousands of women. The estrogen replacement portion of the WHI study began in 1989 and will ultimately involve 27,000 women. Both doctors and women are eagerly waiting for early results. But even without the government study, estrogen is accumulating accolades. Here are some recent findings.

- A five-year study lead by Dr. Richard Mayeux at Columbia University involved 1,124 women over seventy years old and found that the women who had been taking estrogen for at least ten years reduced their chances of developing Alzheimer's by 30 to 40 percent. However, taking the supplement for just one year also lowered their odds. Dr. Mayeux also found that the hormone lowered the risk for women who had inherited the gene ApoE4, which is known to quadruple a person's likelihood of having dementia.

- The first controlled study of the effects of estrogen also generated promising results. Unlike other studies, which have been surveys of women's health and drug-taking regimens, this study compared two groups of subjects, one wearing a hormone patch and the other unknowingly wearing a placebo patch. Mental function tests found that the memory of those women soaking up estrogen was two and one-half times better, and their attention 150 percent better. While the study, conducted by Dr. Sanjay Asthana at the Veterans Medical Center in Tacoma, Washington, involved only a dozen women, larger tests are planned.

- Doctors Claudia Kawas and Ann Morrison, researchers at Johns Hopkins Bayview Medical Center in Baltimore, followed

472 women for sixteen years and concluded that those who had never taken estrogen were 2.3 times more likely to have Alzheimer's.

Unfortunately, the case for estrogen as a miracle brain drug is not airtight. One study has shown that estrogen replacement therapy did *not* improve the subjects' mental functions. Like the study mentioned earlier, this one examined a group of women living in a retirement community in Southern California. Eight hundred women aged sixty-five to ninety-five took cognitive function tests and reported whether they were taking estrogen replacement therapy. Over the fifteen-year study, the researchers detected no difference in the thinking skills between the women taking and not taking estrogen.

Naturally, as I read the steady stream of news about estrogen and Alzheimer's, I have this nagging question in the back of my mind. What about men? Should they be taking estrogen? So far, the answer is no. For starters, men have a much lower risk than women of developing Alzheimer's or other dementias. About 4 million Americans have Alzheimer's and three-quarters of them are women. Neuroscientists say that men's brains contain an enzyme that converts testosterone to estrogen and, unlike women, their basic hormone levels do not plummet in middle age. However, much older men with declining testosterone levels may benefit from testosterone replacement therapy.

Help from DHEA

As scientists have been trying to unravel the chemical mystery of what Alzheimer's does to the brain, they have made some intriguing findings. A number of studies have discovered that the brains of people with Alzheimer's have markedly less DHEA than healthy brains. The difference in some cases is almost half. Consequently, scientists believe that DHEA may act as a kind of neuroprotector by enriching brain tissue cells.

A study of sixty-one men in nursing homes, aged 57 to 104, found a correlation between plasma DHEA-S levels and the men's daily activities. The men with more of the hormone pumping through their veins were more independent and more able to participate in normal activities.

Less Fat, More Fish

Here's one more reason, and for me it's the most persuasive, not to eat a lot of fat. Most dietary fat and high-calorie diets can destroy your brain. As Dr. Grant discovered when he examined the diets of Japanese Americans and African Americans, fat molecules oxidize into neuron-killing toxins. The killer fats appear to be those found

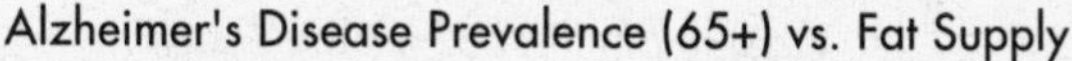

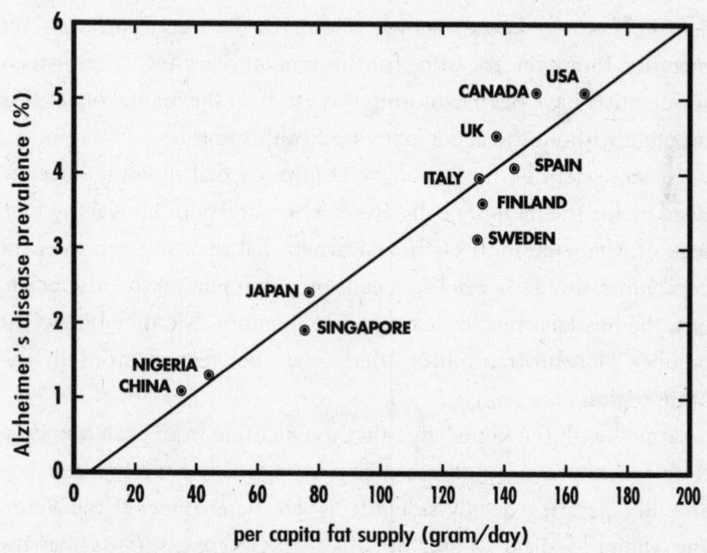

Adapted from *Alzheimer's Disease Review, http://www.coa.uky.edu/ADReview*

in protein (e.g., animal fat), refined carbohydrates (e.g., pastries and pies), and saturated fats (e.g., fried food). Another feature of the high-fat diet is consuming large numbers of calories. Dr. Grant found that the threshold for moving into a risky high-calorie, high-fat diet was eating more than 2,000 calories a day.

People who have much less risk of getting Alzheimer's do not live on diets loaded with these fats but rather eat largely whole grains, fresh fruits, and vegetables. Europeans, however, take in almost as much fat as Americans, but a different kind of fat. They eat much more fish than we do. Figures about eating patterns in England, Sweden, and Spain, as well as Japan and Singapore, point to a direct link between more fish for dinner and less Alzheimer's. Dr. Grant offers this unequivocal conclusion: ". . . increased fish consumption can lower the incidence of dementia."

A Long Shot: The Nicotine Patch

As smokers may know, nicotine improves their concentration and memory. However, the price for this mental sharpness is very steep, so scientists have been exploring ways to reap the mental benefits of nicotine without the accompanying health hazards.

Recent scientific findings have confirmed that nicotine does, indeed, tickle the memory cells. Researchers at Baylor University College of Medicine in Texas have learned that nicotine improves the communication between brain cells by zeroing in on the hippocampus, the headquarters for learning and memory. Nicotine boosts the number of neurotransmitters that travel between neurons in this brain region.

Armed with the knowledge that the nicotine from even one cigarette can improve a person's memory, scientists have found a way around cigarettes' deadly side effects. Dr. Peter Engel at the Veterans Affairs Medical Center in Albany, New York, reports that the steady drip from a nicotine patch raises learning test scores in

Alzheimer's patients. However, I am not suggesting seniors start smoking for a nicotine mind pump.

A substance inspired by a marine worm may work even better than a nicotine patch. Scientists at the University of Florida have found that a synthetic form of a poison found in certain marine worms helps relieve some Alzheimer's symptoms by stimulating a piece of the brain called the alpha 7-type nicotine receptor. (The brain has a variety of nicotine receptors.) By juicing just this brain cell receptor, the scientists were able to spur thinking without causing the other side effects that come with stimulating other nicotine receptors. The synthetic chemical, called GTS-21, has also helped slow the onset of Alzheimer's symptoms, and it is being tested at the University of Florida.

Use It or Lose It: Education

One of the sturdiest defenses against Alzheimer's involves a decision relatively early in life to develop and use your mind. Study after study shows that a person's level of education and the mental demands of an occupation or daily activities can guard against dementia. As a person obtains more education and/or engages in mentally challenging activities, the odds drop as to when and even whether he or she will show signs of Alzheimer's.

For instance, a study in the Netherlands involving 7,528 patients aged 55 to 106 came to this conclusion: "People with only primary education or low-level vocational training were significantly more likely to develop dementia than those with medium-level vocational training or university-level education."

Another study had similar results and framed its findings in positive terms. The 593 people involved lived in New York City. Following standard neurological tests, 106 were found to be demented. The researchers, led by Yaakov Stern, concluded, after collecting information about their education and work history, "The data suggest

TAKE ACTION

Brain Exercises

One reason better-educated people seem protected from Alzheimer's is that the learning process has increased and strengthened the connections between brain cells. This brain tissue surplus keeps them alert and sharp as their brains age, brain cells shrink, or Alzheimer's begins to encroach. Here are some "brain exercises" that, like education, will stimulate your neurons.

- Keep a daily journal, writing at least a paragraph about your thoughts or interesting events. Or try writing poetry.
- Do regular puzzles. If you don't like crossword puzzles, try jigsaw puzzles. While crosswords help maintain your vocabulary, jigsaws will help your spatial memory skills.
- Participate in TV quiz shows. Shout out that *Jeopardy!* answer or that *Wheel of Fortune* phrase.
- Tackle small fix-it jobs in which you have to think through a problem, like replacing a faucet washer or changing your car's oil.
- Take lessons on any musical instrument. The mechanics of learning finger movements and how to recognize notes require extraordinary and novel brain coordination. If you feel totally incapable of learning to play an instrument, take singing lessons.
- Create something. For instance, draw, knit, paint, or make up a story for your children or grandchildren.
- Learn something new: attend a class, listen to a seminar, read a book or magazine article on a subject you know nothing about.

that increased educational and occupational attainment may reduce the risk of incident AD [Alzheimer's disease], either by decreasing ease of clinical detection of Alzheimer's or by imparting a reserve that delays the onset of clinical manifestations."

There is a downside to the "more education equals less Alzheimer's" equation. Scientists have found that while educated people (those with high school diplomas and some higher education) are less at risk, if they ultimately do show symptoms of the illness, their thinking ability declines very quickly. One possible explanation is that while the disease may hit people at more or less the same age, the educated person does not show signs of it until years later. When it does surface, the damage that had been hidden looks much worse in the clever person who had been successfully covering up the symptoms, than in someone else whose very gradual decline has been apparent from the beginning.

SLOWING IT DOWN

Even when someone begins to show signs of Alzheimer's, it may be many years before he or she is incapacitated. The progress of the disease varies from person to person, and neuroscientists are discovering that individuals have some control over the rate of deterioration. You can take steps to keep your mental faculties longer.

Today, there are only two U.S. government–approved drugs on the market designed specifically to treat Alzheimer's. They are tacrine (trade name Cognex) and donepezil (trade name Aricept), and both work the same way. These drugs pump up the brain's supply of the chemical messenger acetylcholine by disrupting the activity of cholinesterase, the enzyme that breaks down acetylcholine. Thus, the drugs are called cholinesterase inhibitors, and are part of a large class of drugs that can improve the memory, judgment, reasoning ability, and daily functioning of patients with mild to moderate symptoms.

These drugs are available only by prescription and can produce gastrointestinal side effects, namely diarrhea and nausea. Generally, they are prescribed when a doctor is reasonably certain that a patient is showing signs of dementia.

A number of pharmaceutical companies and drug developers are working on finding other medications that can boost the amount of acetylcholine in circulation. One obvious approach, eating foods or taking supplements that are precursors to acetylcholine, like choline or lecithin, has, unfortunately, not shown promising results.

Other medications operating in the brain's cholingeric system that have shown promise include physostigmine (by Forest Laboratories, New York) and huperzine A, a compound formed from the Chinese herbal medicine *qian ceng ta.* The *Journal of the American Medical Association* reports that huperzine has been used for centuries in China to treat fever and inflammation and, more recently, for dementia. In the United States, clinical trials for huperzine are in the planning stages.

The herb horse balm contains a substance, carvacrol, that also seems to halt the breakdown of acetylcholine in the brain. So, it may be a promising treatment for Alzheimer's. Another herb that may help is rosemary, which seems to be a powerful antioxidant and attacker of free radicals.

The Calcium Route

Another theory about what Alzheimer's does to the brain involves calcium levels in diseased brain cells. Too much calcium, which cells use for communication and which is carefully regulated, destroys neurons, and researchers are tinkering with a category of drugs called calcium channel blockers. These are an established, medically proven class of drugs that are already prescribed for high blood pressure. The National Institute on Aging reports that at least one calcium blocker drug for Alzheimer's is being tested and another is under consideration for human tests.

Going After Free Radicals

Armed with strong suspicions that free radicals may be implicated in Alzheimer's, scientists are investigating and testing a number of compounds aimed at combating the formation of free radicals or diminishing their damage.

I've already told you about the exciting findings of a test with the antioxidants vitamin E and selegiline. Selegiline has a checkered test history: In some tests it has improved patients' thinking and in others it has had no effect. However, doctors at the Veterans Affairs Medical Center in Cleveland analyzed the test data from eleven controlled tests of selegiline and found that eight produced improvements on such thought processes as word fluency, delayed recall, and total recall. In one study, done in Czechoslovakia, the researchers noted that 10 mg per day was an effective dose. It improved patients' thinking without producing hypertensive side effects, which it can do at high doses.

Another drug in testing for fighting free radicals in the compound acetyl-l-carnitine (ALC), which has been shown to improve thinking by juicing up the brain's energy exchange and metabolism. Researchers also believe that it reduces production of free radicals. ALC has already produced positive results in improving people's age-associated memory impairment and is now in advanced clinical trial testing by Sigma-Tau Pharmaceuticals Company.

Scientists are also exploring what the herbal tonic ginkgo biloba, which is extracted from the leaves of the maidenhair tree, can do for Alzheimer's. Ginkgo has a long history of helping to improve thinking. In repeated controlled studies, this herb has sharpened people's fuzzy memory, concentration, and thinking. As with so many other cognitive remedies, ginkgo prevents damage from free radicals and the cell oxidation that restricts the flow of nutrients in the brain.

Studies aimed solely at Alzheimer's symptoms have also generated persuasive numbers. For instance, when half of forty Alz-

WATCH OUT

These drugs or compounds are currently being tested for their effects on the symptoms of Alzheimer's. The Pharmaceutical Research and Manufacturers of America, which compiled this list, notes that these new medicines are mostly in phase II or phase III clinical trials, meaning that they are nearing the end of their experimental tests.

Drug	Company	Development Status
AIT-082	NeoTherapeutics	Phase I
ALCAR (acetyl-L-carnitine)	Sigma-Tau Pharmaceuticals	Phase III
Ampalex	Cortex Pharmaceuticals	Phase I
celecoxib	Searle	Phase II
eptastigmine	Mediolanum Pharmaceuticals	Phase III
Exelon	Novartis Pharmaceuticals	app submitted
idebenone	Takeda America	Phase II/III
lazabemide	Hoffmann-La Roche	Phase III
Memric	SmithKline Beecham	Phase III
metrifonate	Bayer Pharmaceuticals	Phase III
milameline	Hoechst Marion Roussel	Phase III
propentofylline	Hoechst-Roussel	Phase III
Reminyl	Janssen Pharmaceutica	Phase III

SR 46559	Sanofi Pharmaceuticals	Phase II
SR 57746	Sanofi Pharmaceuticals	Phase II
Synapton	Forest Laboratories	Phase III
xanomeline	Eli Lilly	Phase II

Note: The drug development information refers to a stage of clinical testing. Phase I testing involves about 20 to 80 normal, healthy volunteers and is designed to test a drug's safety. Phase II testing involves 100 to 300 volunteers, some with the target illness and some healthy, and is designed to test a drug's effectiveness. Phase III testing involves 1,000 to 3,000 patients in clinics and hospitals and is designed to test the drug's effectiveness and side effects. After a drug successfully completes all three phases, the manufacturer applies for a new-drug application. If the U.S. Food and Drug Administration approves this application, the drug can then be prescribed by doctors.

By permission, New Medicines in Development for Older Americans, Pharmaceutical Research and Manufacturers of America, August 1997.

heimer's patients unknowingly took 80 mg of ginkgo extract three times a day for three months, their memory and concentration improved "significantly" in just the first month of taking ginkgo.

Other research projects have looked at various doses. According to a report in the English medical journal *The Lancet,* European doctors have been using daily doses between 120 and 200 mg. Ginkgo has been tested in forty controlled tests, mostly in France and Germany, and doctors have noticed that it begins to show effects only after four to six weeks. The herbal extract produced no serious side effects except for mild stomach problems.

Another possible neuroprotectant is the amino acid DL-phenylalanine (DLPA), which is a contributor to the chemical production of the neurotransmitter norepinephrine. DLPA is essential to healthy

TAKE ACTION

Drugs That Can Impair Your Thinking

These widely used medications can slow or confuse thought processes, somewhat mimicking symptoms of Alzheimer's. Medications that consume the brain's store of acetylcholine, like tranquilizers, painkillers, antihistamines, and sleeping pills, need to be especially avoided by anyone at risk for dementia.

Analgesics (e.g., codeine)
Antiarrhythmic drugs (e.g., quinidine)
Antibiotics (e.g., metronidazole)
Anticonvulsants (e.g., carbamazepine)
Antidepressants (e.g., imipramine)
Antihistamines and decongestants (e.g., diphenhydramine)
Antihypertensive drugs (e.g., propranolol)
Antiparkinsonian drugs (e.g., levodopa)
Corticosteroids (e.g., hydrocortisone, prednisone)
Muscle relaxants (e.g., methocarbamol)
Sedatives (e.g., phenobarbital, diazepam)

memory, and while most people probably get enough through the proteins they eat, some people supplement their intake.

NEW COMPOUNDS

One of the most exciting new medications about to become available is the drug ampakine. Discovered in 1991 by Dr. Gary Lynch, ampakine improves communication between brain cells by keeping the lines of communication, the synapses, open a few seconds longer than normal. In a test using a mild dose of the drug, it sharpened the memory of men aged sixty-five to seventy to that similar to the memory of students in their twenties. Ampakines (Ampalex) are be-

A BRIEF REFRESHER

Alzheimer's is a disease of aging that more often afflicts women and people with a family history of the disease. Yet no one is completely fated to become demented, and there is much you can do to protect yourself against the onset of Alzheimer's or, should it strike, to slow its progression. Here are some strategies.

Improve brain metabolism. Increasing blood circulation and oxygen delivery retards the buildup of toxins and damaging plaques and tangles, and increases the circulation of vital neurochemicals. Reducing stress and the production of stress hormones is a way to do this.

Consume antioxidants. These combat free radicals, the harmful by-products of the natural oxidation process in the body that may well be a cause of the brain damage that comes with Alzheimer's. Powerful antioxidants include vitamin E, vitamin A and foods that contain beta-carotene, selegiline, and the herb ginkgo biloba.

Watch what you eat. High-fat, high-salt diets have been linked to Alzheimer's, so reduce consumption of fats, especially saturated fats, refined carbohydrates, and salt. On the other hand, the oils in fish found in deep, cold waters, like tuna, mackerel, and salmon, may help ward off the disease.

Take anti-inflammatory medication. Over-the-counter anti-inflammatories like aspirin and ibuprofen have shown promising results as neuroprotectants.

Lower risk of stroke. Strokes can do an enormous amount of brain damage and may well be a leading contributor to dementia. You can lower your risk by controlling your blood pressure, not smoking, and watching your cholesterol.

Take estrogen. Hormone replacement therapy in women is probably one of the surest ways to protect against Alzheimer's.

Exercise your brain. Mental activity builds neural connections that act as buffers against the dementia that follows brain cell death.

Slow it down. Two prescription drugs, tacrine and donepezil, help slow the progression of the disease.

ing developed by Cortex Pharmaceuticals and are currently being tested in clinical trials as a drug to treat Alzheimer's.

On the Horizon

• Molecules from the Caucasian snowdrop plant have been found to slow the breakdown of acetylcholine. Scientists have molded the plant's molecules into a compound called galanthamine, which is in clinical trials.

• A study of a large population group in South Carolina pinpointed a possible link between high fluoride and reduced risk of Alzheimer's. Taking sodium fluoride, the study suggested, may slow the progress of the disease.

• Scientists in Romania have been testing a new Alzheimer's drug formula that affects brain metabolism. Called Antagonic Stress, the drug is a combination of antioxidants, nootropic medications, antistress compounds, and minerals. In a study involving 343 people aged sixty to seventy-six and with a history of organic mental disorders, Antagonic Stress was pitted in double-blind, placebo-controlled tests against a placebo, a nootropic drug, a free-radical scavenger, and cerebral vasodilators. The experiment extended over three months, and at the end, people taking the Antagonic Stress capsule showed improvements on depression and anxiety tests, memory and intelligence scales, and exhibited slower mental deterioration. Another study in Romania came up with similar results, and the drug has been clinically tested and approved for use in that country.

• Scientists believe they have finally found a drug compound similar to nerve growth factor, which helps brain cells regrow, but without its fatal flaw, which is an inability to pass from the bloodstream into the brain. Researchers at Guilford Pharmaceuticals, whose founders include Solomon Synder, a preeminent neuroscientist, are developing a new class of drugs that can stimulate brain cells damaged by Alzheimer's. The drug class, named GPI-1046, may soon be tested in clinical trials.

SELECTED SOURCES

"Aluminum, fluoride and Alzheimers' disease: a review." *Nutrition Research Newsletter,* 11 (7–8), 90–92, July–August 1992.

American Family Physician. "Early identification of Alzheimer's disease and related dementias." *Clinical Practice Guidelines,* March 1997, 1303–14.

Barrett-Connor, E. "Estrogen replacement therapy and cognitive function in older women." *Journal of the American Medical Society,* 269 (20), 2637–42, May 26, 1993.

Branch, D. R. "Slow-release physostigmine improves cognition." *Family Practice News,* February 1, 1997.

Breitner, J. C. "The role of anti-inflammatory drugs in the prevention and treatment of Alzheimer's disease." *Annual Review of Medicine,* 47, 401–11, 1996.

Brody, J. E. "Alzheimer studies thwarted." *New York Times,* March 5, 1997.

Carper, J. *Food: Your Miracle Medicine.* HarperPerennial, New York, 1993.

Easley, L. P. "Alzheimer's disease: is it aluminum? (aluminum in the body may play a role)." *Harvard Health Letter,* 15 (12), 1–3, October 1990.

Elias, M. "When to worry about forgetting." *Harvard Health Letter,* 17 (9), 1–4, July 1992.

"Estrogen eases Alzheimer's symptoms." *Science News,* 150, 399, December 21, 1996.

Fackelmann, K. "Forever smart: does estrogen enhance memory?" *Science News,* 147 (5), 72, February 4, 1995.

Fricker, J. "From mechanisms to drugs in Alzheimer's disease." *Lancet,* 349 (9050), 480, February 15, 1997.

Gatz, M., et al. "Dementia: not just a search for the gene." *Gerontologist,* 34 (2), 251–55, 1994.

Grant, W. B. "Dietary links to Alzheimer's disease." *Alzheimer's Disease Review* (University of Kentucky), June 19, 1997.

Itzhaki, R. F., et al. "Herpes simplex virus type 1 in brain and risk of Alzheimer's disease (early reports)." *Lancet*, 349 (9047), 241–45, January 25, 1997.

Khalsa, D. S. *Brain Longevity*. Warner Books, New York, 1997.

Langreth, R. "Nerve-regenerating drugs may help in Alzheimer's, Parkinson's disease." *Wall Street Journal*, April 16, 1997.

Lipkin, R. "Sea worms and plants spur new drugs (Alzheimer's disease medications)." *Science News*, 147 (14), 212–13, April 8, 1995.

McCaddon, A. and Kelly, C. L. "Familial Alzheimer's disease and vitamin B12 deficiency." *Age and Aging*, 23 (4), 334–37, July 1994.

National Institute on Aging. *Alzheimer's Disease: Unraveling the Mystery*. National Institutes of Health, October 1995.

———*Progress Report on Alzheimer's Disease 1996*. U.S. Department of Health and Human Services, National Institutes of Health, Silver Spring, Md.

Nidecker, A. "Memory-enhancing drug may benefit Alzheimer's." *Family Practice News*. February 15, 1997.

Orrell, M. W., and O'Dwyer, A. "Dementia, aging and the stress control system." *Lancet*, 345 (8951), 666–68, March 18, 1995.

Ott, A., et al. "Prevalence of Alzheimer's disease and vascular dementia: association with education. The Rotterdam study." *British Medical Journal*, 310 (6985), 970–74, April 15, 1995.

Pharmaceutical Research and Manufacturers of America. *New Medicines in Development for Older Americans*. Washington, D.C., 1995.

Predescu, V., et al. "Antagonic-stress: a new treatment in gerontopsychiatry and for a healthy productive life." *Annals of the New York Academy of Science*, 30 (717), 315–30, June 1994.

Rozzini, R., et al. "Protective effect of chronic NSAID use on cognitive decline in older persons." *Journal of the American Geriatric Society*, 44 (9), 1025–29, September 1996.

Sano, M., et al. "A controlled trial of selegiline, alpha-tocopherol, or both as treatment for Alzheimer's disease." *New England Journal of Medicine*, 336, 1216–22, April 24, 1997.

Skolnick, A. A. "Old Chinese herbal medicine used for fever yields possible new Alzheimer disease therapy." *Journal of the American Medical Association*, 277 (10), 776, March 12, 1997.

Skoog, I., et al. "15-year longitudinal study of blood pressure and dementia." *Lancet*, 347 (9009), 1141–46, April 27, 1996.

Snowdon, D. A., et al. "Linguistic ability in early life and cognitive function and Alzheimer's disease in late life: findings from the Nun Study." *Journal of the American Medical Association*, 275, 528–532, 1996.

Snowdon, D. A., et al. "Brain infarction and the clinical expression of Alzheimer disease." *Journal of the American Medical Association*, 277 (10), 813–17, March 12, 1997.

Sobel, E., et al. "Elevated risk of Alzheimer's disease among workers with likely electromagnetic field exposure." *Neurology*, 47 (6), 1477–81, December 1996.

Stenson, J. "Protein damages blood vessels in Alzheimer's." *Medical Tribune*, April 4, 1996, 12.

Stern, Y., et al. "Influence of education and occupation on the incidence of Alzheimer's disease." *Journal of the American Medical Association*, 271 (13), 1004–11, April 6, 1994.

Tang, M. "Effect of oestrogen during menopause on risk and age at onset of Alzheimer's disease." *Lancet*, 348 (9025), 429–33, August 17, 1996.

Tolbert, S. R., and Fuller, M. A. "Selegiline in treatment of behavioral and cognitive symptoms of Alzheimer's disease." *Annals of Pharmacotherapy*, 30 (10), 1122–29, October 1996.

Tucker, M. "Nicotine patch may help cognition in Alzheimer's." *Family Practice News*, July 1, 1996, 36.

"Vitamin levels in Alzheimer's disease." *Nutrition Research Newsletter*, 11 (6), 77, June 1992.

Weiner, M. F. "Alzheimer's disease: what we now know, and what you can now do." *Consultant*, 35 (3), 313–17, March 1995.

White, L., et al. "Prevalence of dementia in older Japanese-American men in Hawaii." *Journal of the American Medical Association*, 276 (12), 955–60, September 25, 1996.

"The zinc link to Alzheimer's: is there a reason to worry?" *Environmental Nutrition*, 18 (5), 7, May 1995.

Six

THE EMOTIONAL BRAIN

SEXUAL STIM

As you have probably guessed by now, I'm a mind-body guy. I firmly believe, and have lots of scientific evidence to back me up, that thought processes affect our bodies, and that the health of our bodies affects our brains and thinking. But, as we all know, our lives consist of more than thoughts. There is whole other side to each of us: our emotions. The sharpest, most knowledgeable mind is useless if it shares space with undeveloped or destructive emotions. By tending to our relationships with others, by giving and getting the smorgasbord of feelings that makes us vital human beings, we add muscle and staying power to our mental wealth.

Emotional healthiness is not as elusive as it may sound. There are ways to cultivate our emotional and sensual selves. To do this, we must look at the chemical stew that courses through the brain and body, especially our hormones.

A vivid demonstration of how hormones steer our emotional lives occurred at an international conference on Anti-Aging Medicine and Biomedical Technology in Las Vegas attended by more than

1,500 health care professionals from around the world. As chairman of the sponsoring organization, the American Academy of Anti-Aging Medicine, I was a participant in the doings, including some of the lively relationships that developed and changed. While avoiding any description that might warrant an "R" rating for this book, let me tell you about some of my emotional encounters and what I did to make them healthy and productive.

Given the locale and the people attending the conference, it is understandable that personal relationships were an unwritten agenda item. Huge conferences that push together active, curious people into an intense couple of days always throw off some sparks. I was a speaker at the three-day conference, and although each day was packed with symposia and presentations, there was ample time for catching up with old friends and meeting new ones.

Regardless of where you are or what you are doing, your sex hormones are always going to influence some facet of your behavior or thinking. They certainly did with me. Between lectures, I found myself intrigued by a woman I had just met but knew by reputation. Her nutritional supplement company was an exhibitor at the conference and she seemed to be everywhere. What turned my head were not only her obvious physical assets but more elusive qualities, too. Like the way she laughed with her eyes (okay, that's a physical asset, too) and seemed to share my opinions of people. For instance, we found ourselves both rolling our eyes at long-winded academic answers to simple questions. Like me, she was intense and at times became so focused on reading or listening that she was oblivious to her surroundings.

In looking back at that conference, I think my behavior, and maybe hers, too, was driven largely by hormones. And if we had realized and understood what was happening to us, the outcome might have been different.

This quiz illustrates what scientists know about the differences in men's and women's brains, and how these variations influence specific abilities and skills. For instance, women have more sensitive hearing, better short-term memory, are verbal and good with words,

DO YOU HAVE A MALE OR A FEMALE BRAIN?

The "gender" of your brain is determined by the amount of female or male hormones you were exposed to in utero. Men can be born with feminine traits and brains, and women with masculine traits and brains. Take this quiz for a general idea as to whether your brain, and your thinking habits, are more male or female.

1. When you were in elementary school, how did you do in spelling bees and writing stories? a) Excelled at both; b) Excelled at one; c) Excelled at neither.

2. You're a tourist in a foreign city, walking around and exploring the sites. How readily do you know which way is north? a) You have no idea; b) If you think for a minute, you can find it; c) You know intuitively and immediately.

3. You're working late and the only discernible noise in your office is the soft hum of a computer printer. Your reaction to it is: a) You hear it and try to block it out; b) It's only mildly irritating; c) You hardly hear it at all.

4. You are walking through a parking lot and a car alarm goes off. How readily can you identify which car is making the noise (without looking for any flashing lights)? a) After a moment's thinking, you can place it; b) You can immediately pinpoint it; c) You can't identify the source at all.

5. While driving you hear a new tune on the radio. The next time it comes on, how much of the tune and lyrics do you remember? a) You're singing along to most of it; b) You can hum the chorus but that's all; c) It sounds familiar but you don't remember any of the music or words.

6. You are interviewing for a new job, and the recruiter gives you a tour of the company offices and introduces you to half a dozen people. A few days later, when you learn that you've got the job, the recruiter mentions that you will be working with four of the people you met. Do you remember what they

looked like? a) You can picture each of them; b) You remember a couple; c) You can't give a face to any of them.

7. You stop by a neighborhood yard sale and are introduced to a neighbor you've seen around and said hello to in passing. A couple days later, that neighbor telephones you. a) You know who she is immediately; b) You know who she is only after she gives her name; c) Even after she gives her name, it takes you a couple of seconds to place her.

8. You've decided to see a movie on your own, and as you enter the theater, you see that there are clusters of people sitting in the middle and near the aisles. Where do you sit? a) Right next to other people so you can see better; b) Near the clusters but a couple of seats away; c) Off by yourself with lots of empty seats around you.

9. You're checking out from the grocery store and bagging your groceries. Given different-size containers and bags of produce, a) You quickly give up making things fit and put just a couple of items in each bag; b) You bag items as they are rung up; c) You neatly fit everything into one or two bags.

10. You are at a company party and know a coworker is having an affair with someone in the department. Can you tell who? a) You easily detect the relationship; b) You have a good idea but aren't sure; c) You see no clues and cannot tell.

Scoring:

Men: For each a) answer add 8 points, for each b) answer add 4 points, for each c) answer subtract 4 points. Most will score between 0 and 48. A score below 0 indicates a strong male brain. A score above 48 indicates female brain traits.

Women: For each a) answer, add 12 points, for each b) answer add 4 points, for each c) answer, subtract 4 points. Most will score between 40 and 80. A score above 80 indicates a strong female brain. A score below 40 indicates male brain traits.

and are more perceptive and intuitive about other people. Men are more adept with objects, shapes, and geometrical problems, are better with geography and at reading maps, and are more sensitive to personal space around them.

SEX HORMONES

Long before any of us see the light of day, sex hormones are washing through our fetal brains, shaping the arrangements of certain neurons, adjusting the chemistry, and orchestrating our sexuality. Hormones are brain chemicals, setting off a chemical chain reaction that alters our physical selves, our emotional selves, and our thinking selves.

At the beginning, everyone is bathed in testosterone and estrogen. Even after gender is set, both these sex hormones are present in our bodies. After the chromosomes have set in motion the chemistry that makes a person male or female, the developing gonads produce more testosterone or estrogen and the brain grows more or less susceptible to certain sex hormones. As we all can attest, the sex hormones are fairly quiet until adolescence, when their production kicks into high gear. After that, their activity varies. Some hormones stay at the same level in the body for many years and decline in the middle years, while others rise and fall in cycles or steadily decrease.

Up to a point, men's and women's brains and bodies travel the same sexual path. We all have a hypothalamus that produces pituitary hormones and directs the sexual response and mating behavior. Our hormones are especially busy in a spot of the brain called the sexually dimorphic nucleus (SDN), which is very sensitive to estrogen and testosterone. It's here that guys and gals part ways. Researchers studying the SDN have found that in men it is much larger than in women. In one hundred autopsies of normal brains, the men's SDN was two and a half times larger than the women's. While not sure exactly what the SDN does, many scientists suspect that it participates in establishing gender identity and mounting behavior.

Given the differences in brain structure and chemistry, it is not surprising to find that men and women do not behave the same way. By and large, men are naturally promiscuous and seek out many sex partners. Their brains are wired that way. However, men are not in a constant state of sexual arousal. The sense that stimulates them first, and most, is visual—what they see. They like sex with the lights on, they like watching sex, they like pornography, they are turned on by sexual pictures of women. (I know these are generalizations, guys, so don't be offended if they don't apply to you.)

The sensory experiences that turn women's heads stem from their sense of touch, smell, and sound. They like foreplay and intimate talk, and are more aroused by the idea of a relationship than by pictures of penises. (Ditto for you, gals—I know this doesn't describe all of you!)

Sexual gratification is much more important to men than to women, and it is more of a certainty. Virtually every man is capable of climax, while fewer women—maybe only one in five—experience consistent rapidly induced orgasms.

Daily Fluctuations in Serum Levels of Testosterone in Elderly (69–80 yrs.) and Young (26–36 yrs.)

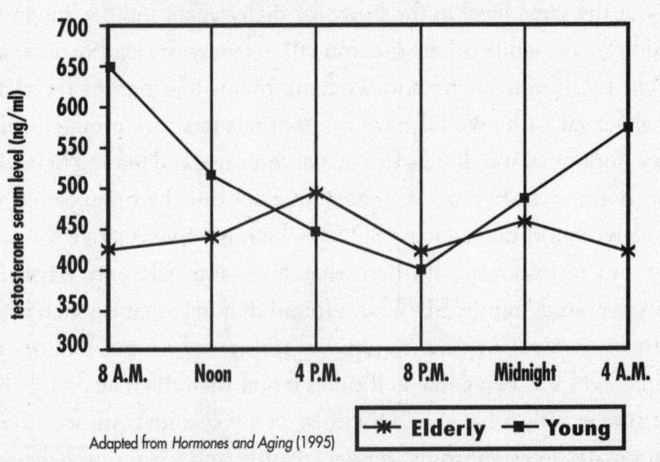

Adapted from *Hormones and Aging* (1995)

Over time, our hormone levels change, and aging alone is not the only influence. Physical activity as well as diet, nutrition, and lifestyle can also affect them. Contrary to what you might feel at times, our hormones are not always in charge. We can manipulate them, even the two most abundant and powerful, testosterone and estrogen. Here's a rundown of their marquee features, and it's important to keep in mind that none of the sex hormones functions alone. They are constantly interacting in a ballet of balance, counterbalance, and feedback loops. Thus, in concert, they engage in a chemical dance that stimulates our emotions, thoughts, and behavior.

The Take-Charge Hormone: Testosterone

This hormone pushes all of us around, men and women. It's in charge of the sex drive—not the desire for intimacy or a relationship, but simple, uncomplicated intercourse. It's also what makes us aggressive and competitive, even violent. It shapes the body, too, stimulating the growth of certain organs and hair, and helping the body convert protein into muscle. Of course, men have much more than women—ten times more—and it cycles differently in men. In a single day, a man's testosterone rises and falls six or seven times, which can whipsaw his emotions and thoughts. It climbs during the night so that in the early morning, it's double what it is in the late afternoon. There's a reason men think a lot about sex, especially first thing in the morning! Men's testosterone is also higher in the autumn than at other times of the year. A woman's testosterone moves in a monthly cycle, rising just before or during menstruation and making her feel sexy.

Outside forces also influence testosterone production. An arousing situation can pump it up, while a stressful situation can dampen it. Certain foods and activities also shove it around.

Testosterone also seems to have a strong influence on personal relationships. Sociologist Alan Booth at Penn State University and psychologist James Dabbs at Georgia State University have looked

TAKE ACTION

Get a Grip on Your Testosterone

These foods, activities, and seasons affect testosterone levels:

Sexual intercourse. Researchers believe that sex affects testosterone levels, not vice versa.

December surge. Measurements of testosterone levels in more than four thousand military veterans aged thirty-two to forty-four found that the hormone peaked in December. Among men in their early thirties, testosterone peaked in November.

Fights or arguments. Confrontations or physical threats can increase testosterone.

Red meat. This food has been linked to higher testosterone levels.

Vegetarian diet. Red meat may increase testosterone.

Zinc. A deficiency of this nutritional mineral, which you consume either in foods like fish and oysters or in supplements, has been linked with subpar testosterone. A recommended daily dose is 30–50 mg.

Vigorous exercise. Exercise, especially weight training involving large muscle groups like the quadriceps, boosts testosterone.

Aerobic exercise. Excessive stamina activities, like jogging and cycling, lower testosterone.

Stress. Worry, tension, and other kinds of psychological stress generate chemicals that suppress testosterone.

at the interplay between men's testosterone levels and their marital relationships. They discovered that married men with higher levels of this hormone had less stable unions. They were more apt to be abusive, to have affairs, or to seek divorces.

Women's relationships, too, may be colored by testosterone. Dr.

Patricia Schreiner-Engel, a professor of obstetrics and gynecology at Mount Sinai School of Medicine in New York, measured testosterone levels in thirty working women and found that those with higher hormone levels were not only the most success-oriented but, more telling, none was married or in a long-term relationship. By comparison, the women with less testosterone had either been married for many years or were in lasting relationships.

Women with high testosterone levels are not only more sexually active but have more muscle and weigh less. Signs in women that the hormone level has gone too far are lots of facial hair, a rise in bad cholesterol, weight gain, and lowered voice.

Too little testosterone in either men or women dampens the libido. Men feel listless, irritable, and depressed when this vital hormone dips below normal. For women, no testosterone means no orgasm.

Slowly, as we get older, much of the testosterone turmoil quiets down. With men, the slide becomes detectable in their forties, fifties, or sixties, as the sexual fires and hard-driving personality traits mellow. Women also lose some of this juice around the middle years. Although their ovaries continue to generate testosterone even after menopause, other sources of it—the adrenal glands, body fat, and brain—slow down production.

In relationships, testosterone is often a hidden troublemaker. It can make people behave irrationally and fan bursts of temper or combativeness. Especially in men, considering that it's rising and falling throughout a single day, this pugnacious hormone can make them seemingly moody or so focused or single-minded that they block out other people's feelings or opinions. I've seen this happen to my friends—they get pumped up and determined, then annoyed, if not outright angry, when someone tries to take them off-course. Sometimes their hormones can jerk them around to the point of ridiculousness.

On the second morning of the anti-aging conference in Las Vegas, I noticed a colleague steam into the hotel restaurant looking for a quiet corner table. He had a sheaf of papers, and he obviously wanted to prepare his talk uninterrupted over breakfast. His expression was grim and determined, and I knew he felt under the gun to get his work done before his 10 A.M. session. I glanced around the room and saw Gale, a woman he had been chatting up at the cocktail party the evening before. She was watching him, waiting for him to look around so she could catch his eye. He did look up as he poured his coffee, and she gave him a big smile and gestured for him to join her. He didn't stir, but gave her a grim smile, frowned at his pen and paper, and went back to writing. She looked a little hurt, so when she caught me watching her, I smiled, picked up my juice, and joined her.

About twenty minutes later, we had both finished a pleasant breakfast and were talking casually when our grouchy colleague appeared beside the table. He was giving me a very dirty look. I knew exactly what he was thinking—that I was moving in on Gale. I gestured at an empty chair, but he just growled.

"Isn't it a little early in the day for you?" he snapped at me. I shrugged helplessly, knowing he would not hear any explanation I offered.

"You've no call to say that," Gale declared. She pushed back her chair, stood up, gave me a sweet "Thanks for breakfast," and strode away without a word to him.

"Nice going, yo-yo," I said. "For your information, I was talking about you, telling her what a great guy you are."

All of a sudden, the piss and vinegar drained out of him. He looked crestfallen. "Oops" was all he could say.

The Sap of Life: Estrogen

Women are really fortunate to have this hormone that does so much not just for sexuality but also for personal relationships, mental functioning, and even as protection against Alzheimer's. Men do have a dusting of estrogen—about one-twentieth of a woman's—so they, too, experience a sampling of its wondrous effects.

As the biological sap of a woman's reproductive life, estrogen prepares her body and organs for sex and children. Physiologically, it makes her eager for and receptive to intercourse, and it nourishes and lubricates tissues and organs. This is the hormone that can make a woman want to wear sexy, high-heeled shoes (they accentuate instinctive "display" behavior) and makes her skin more sensitive to touch. Estrogen is more subtle in the mating dance than testosterone. It makes a woman eager for a mate, but not pushy. It does not compel her to initiate sexual activity (if she does, it's the testosterone at work) but instead makes her definitely interested and available.

A woman's estrogen rises and falls in a twenty-eight-day cycle, and while it peaks twice, just before ovulation and about a week before menstruation, it can swing enormously. Human cell tissue has at least three hundred receptors for estrogen, so it influences many organs. The upshot is that this female hormone may be constantly whispering in a woman's ear and affecting her moods, behavior, thought processes, even how well she does at math.

(A study led by Barbara Sherwin, a leading hormone researcher at McGill University, suggests that men's memories are enhanced by estrogen. She looked at thirty-three young men, measured their free testosterone and estradiol—the most potent form of estrogen—levels, and gave them a number of memory and attention tests. The men with the highest estradiol outshone their fellow test-takers in visual memory skills.)

But estrogen is not the only sex hormone being produced. Progesterone, another reproductive chemical, is also surging and ebbing, and this tide of hormones can tamper with a woman's moods and actions. In the first part of the cycle, a woman's estrogen makes her brain more lively—she's more alert, sharper and quicker with math problems, more buoyant and upbeat, more positive, and more confident. Toward the end of the cycle, progesterone spikes, which reduces blood flow and oxygen consumption in the brain. The effect is like that of a sedative, and a woman may feel sluggish and even depressed.

TAKE ACTION

Manage Your Estrogen

These activities and foods will raise or lower your estrogen production, although there is no natural way of reversing the hormonal shutdown of menopause:

Regular, strenuous physical activity lowers estrogen.
Sexual intercourse raises estrogen.
Sexual abstinence lowers estrogen.
Significant weight gain or obesity raises estrogen.
Severe weight loss or calorie restriction lowers estrogen.
High-fat, low-fiber diet raises estrogen.
Fiber diet of wheat bran supplementation lowers estrogen.
Low-fat diet lowers estrogen.
Phytoestrogens (estrogens from plants) in soy products and whole-wheat products raise estrogen.
Alcoholism raises estrogen.

Sometime in her forties, a woman's production of estrogen and progesterone starts to slow down and become erratic. This pre-menopause stage, or perimenopause, can wreak havoc in a woman's life as her hormones take her on an emotional tsunami. In a single day, she may feel buoyant and positive, achy and sluggish, irritable and out-of-sorts. Around age fifty, at menopause, all this hormonal activity ceases. A woman's estrogen and progesterone production plummets. Again, her moods and behavior can span entire oceans. Some women find themselves going through the stereotypical feelings of depression and lethargy, and living with an emotional hair trigger, quick to cry or laugh. Others discover that menopause brings a certain liberation, with feelings of confidence, energy, and well-being.

While certain foods and activities, as well as hormone replacement therapy, can affect and smooth out a women's hormonal production, it is useful for both men and women to realize that their relationships may be at least partly at the mercy of hormonal fluctuations.

HIS AND HERS

An essential ingredient in any successful heterosexual romance or relationship is an understanding of how differently men and women think and feel. The reason lies in what Woody Allen once called his "second favorite organ"—the brain. From almost the time of conception, even before gender is determined, men's and women's brains develop into slightly but profoundly different structures. The mixture of hormones circulating through the fetal brain helps shape its physical layout and determine whether its construction will be primarily male or female. Since the early 1970s, with the publication of the first study to show the structural difference between male and female brains, numerous studies have shown that they part ways synaptically, anatomically, and in terms of cellular organization. Autopsies plus scans of an active brain as it tackles a problem or task confirm the existence of His and Her models.

Here's a rundown of where our brains part ways and theories about how these two routes influence our abilities and behavior.

- Men's brains are about 15 percent larger than women's. Specific regions that are bigger include an area within the hypothalamus that is in charge of mating and sexual behavior: It is two and one half times larger in men. However, before my male readers

RIGHT AND LEFT HEMISPHERES

Right: visual, spatial, geometric shapes, emotions, abstract ideas

Left: verbal skills, language, reading and writing, logical thinking and reason

begin to feel superior, keep in mind that bigger does not necessarily translate into smarter. If you doubt this, consider the elephant's eleven-pound brain (ours weighs about three pounds) and its mental abilities.

- The cerebral cortex, the brain's outer layer, is thicker on the right hemisphere in men. In women, it is thicker on the left side. Thus, men tend to be more visually oriented and women tend to be more adept with verbal skills. This may be why, say researchers Anne Moir and David Jessel, authors of *Brain Sex*, men are excited by pornography and women's sexual fantasies run to gentle foreplay and pillow talk.
- When faced with an abstract problem, men tap mainly into the right hemisphere, while women utilize both halves of the brain. As a result, men have an easier time thinking about and solving mathematical and geometric problems, from how to find something to catching a high-arcing baseball. Another illustration of this difference was developed by neuroscientist Cecile Naylor, who used brain scans to find that men and women use different parts of their brains when spelling. In a different study, researchers at Yale University scanned men's and women's brains while they were reading and saw that men's left side was activated, while both sides of the women's brains were active.
- A man's brain has specific regions on the left or right side responsible for certain skills. In contrast, a woman's brain pulls from regions in both halves to accomplish certain skills. For example, men's emotional responses are rooted in the right side, and women's emanate from both right and left. This organization also means that men's emotional responses are distinctly separate from their verbal abilities in the left hemisphere, and so they are less able to express their feelings. On the other hand, women's thoughts (left side) always have an emotional component (right side). Men's cerebral compartmentalization makes it easier for them to concentrate and be single-minded. The emotional underpinnings of women's thought processes may explain why more women than men suffer from depression.

• In women, there seem to be more or better-developed fibers in the corpus callosum, the tissue connecting the two halves of the brain. Although this structure starts out larger in men, it shrinks as they age, while a women's does not. Perhaps this is why women are more able to integrate words and thoughts and tend to be more articulate and fluent. This connection also makes women more sensitive to and sharper at detecting clues about other people. The combination of thought and emotion gives her the power of empathy and an ability to intuitively extract meaning from gestures, facial expressions, and body language. As we noted earlier, when testosterone therapy is given to transsexual women (women undergoing medical treatment to make their bodies more male), the masculinized women become better at spatial tasks but lose their language fluency.

• Subtle wiring differences probably account for men's and women's sensual variations. Namely:

- Women have better hearing and can duplicate a tune more easily.
- Men are better at handling acute pain, while women are better at tolerating chronic pain.
- Men's and women's sense of smell is the same.
- Men have a stronger sweet tooth than women.
- Men see distances better; women see better at night.

MORE HORMONES TO MUDDY YOUR RELATIONSHIPS

Estrogen, progesterone, and testosterone are not the only confections complicating and confusing your relationships. Our bodies and brains process a pharmacopoeia of hormones, which are simply chemicals that regulate organs and affect tissues. Dozens of these chemicals are constantly tinkering with all we do, think, and feel. So, it is not surprising that they can also manipulate our relation-

WHERE OUR BRAINS PART WAYS

These are the differences between men's and women's mental skills:

Men's Strengths	Women's Strengths
Math calculations	Verbal communication
Spatial reasoning, e.g., geometry, hand-eye coordination	Linguistic learning, e.g., vocabulary
Reading a map	Fine motor and hand skills
Seeing in bright light	Seeing at night
Sensitivity to salty taste	Sensitivity to bitter and sweet tastes
Interest in objects	Interest in faces and people
Hearing memory	Visual memory
Concentration, single-minded focus	Integrating thought and emotion

ships and sex lives. Here are the main chemical characters that can alter everything from whom we find attractive to the intensity of orgasms.

Luteinizing Hormone Releasing Hormone (LHRH)

LHRH is vital to the rise and fall of testosterone and estrogen. It's a chemical traffic cop, regulating the stop and go patterns of other hormones. It sets the tempo of hormonal cycles. In women it is affected by stress, and in men by emotional or sexual situations. LHRH in a nasal spray has been used somewhat successfully as a treatment for male impotence and in women as a fertility drug.

Progesterone

This is a gestational hormone that prepares the uterus and body for pregnancy, a precursor hormone that the body converts into other steroid hormones. It lowers testosterone levels and so dampens the sex drive. A synthetic form is used as a contraceptive.

Prolactin

A woman produces prolactin when she nurses, and one of its effects is to reduce the sex drive and lower testosterone. In short, it serves as a sexual inhibitor so a new mother can devote herself to the infant. However, should a woman produce too much, it can cause impotence and depression. In both men and women, it is stimulated by physical activity, during sleep, and at times of stress.

Oxytocin

Circulating in the reproductive systems of both men and women, oxytocin is the bonding and parenting hormone, and is stimulated by touch. While it can cloud your thinking and reasoning ability, it also creates strong feelings of attachment. It is a "surging" hormone, meaning you produce it in splurges rather than in steady rising and falling doses, and it can generate an immediate response.

Surging powerfully when people are constantly touching each other, oxytocin can create a strong bond. You have more control over oxytocin than other hormones through the decisions you make about whom to touch. It mixes with estrogen for its best effect, so women tend to be more swayed by it than men. Without estrogen, it doesn't arise. The production of oxytocin may thus be a consideration for a woman thinking about estrogen replacement therapy.

Vasopressin

Vasopressin is an androgen, or male hormone, that moderates the sex drive and general temperament. It helps men think and concentrate and improves their memory. Vasopressin is not produced in a steady drip but fluctuates through days, weeks, and months. It is especially active during REM sleep, and some scientists think it may contribute to the emotional intensity of dreams. Vasopressin in men can do what oxytocin does for women—cement a relationship and create a bond between two people who have intimate physical contact. It also makes men more sensitive to the inviting sexual behavior of women.

Vasopressin works in concert with testosterone and so stirs up men's aggressive behavior as well as their confidence and ordered thinking. It's also the hormone behind animal grooming behavior—in apes or men—heightens sex appeal, and launches mating rituals.

Vasopressin is available in a nasal spray (trade name Diapid). If you are tempted to try it, however, bear in mind that it is a powerful chemical that can alter your body's other hormones. And, according to Dr. Michael Colgan in *Hormonal Health,* the long-term consequences of taking regular doses of vasopressin are unknown and potentially hazardous.

DHEA (Dehydroepiandrosterone)

Both men and women have more DHEA in their bodies than any other hormone, and more or less the same amount. DHEA is called the mother of hormones because the body uses it to churn out other steroid hormones, including estrogen and testosterone. It also metabolizes into pheromones and so worms its way into our sex lives. It's with us every step of the day, influencing whom we find attractive, making us eager and ready for sex, and rushing through the brain during orgasm. It's especially powerful in its effect on our skin—how it looks, how it feels, how it smells, and by giving off erotic odors. Its production rises during our twenties and thirties, then begins to taper off and hits its trough around age sixty.

In women, DHEA does not fade away at menopause and continues to stir sexual desire. This may be why a woman's interest in sex does not disappear with her midlife change. Men are probably less influenced by DHEA, perhaps because of the powerful tides of testosterone. In men, DHEA has more say over muscle mass, energy level, and feelings of attractiveness than sexual behavior. Although available over-the-counter in capsules, DHEA as a supplement to boost your sex life is not a clear winner. However, you can sway your natural production of it.

Pheromones

Pheromones, one of DHEA's offspring, are secreted in men's and women's sweat and send out subtle sexual scents that enhance sexual attractiveness. Other people's pheromones affect you, and yours affect them. Among animals, pheromones are definitely a sexual

TAKE ACTION

Ways to Increase Your Natural Production of DHEA

Practice meditation.
Exercise.
Reduce stress and lower cortisol level.
Get pregnant.

Ways to Lower Your DHEA

Drink alcohol.
Stay stressed
Be overweight.
Manifest type A behavior: aggressiveness, anger, impatience.

come-hither. Scientists suspect that the sense of smell and the sex drive are connected in humans, but they are not positive.

Pheromones appear to affect your sensuality more than your sexuality; that is, they heighten your desire for touch and closeness, more than they do for sex. While undetectable to the naked nose, they may play a potent role in your behavior and feelings.

The Erox Corporation, a pharmaceutical company in Utah founded by David Berliner, is currently developing commercial pheromones for perfumes. Erox has introduced "Realm Men" and "Realm Women," which contain synthetic human pheromones.

PEA (Phenylethylamine)

PEA circulates through men and women and stimulates emotions and feelings of attachment. It is a natural stimulant that is sometimes called the love hormone, because it gives you that wonderful floating, euphoric feeling when you are smitten by someone. Your PEA production especially revs up during orgasm.

MASTERING YOUR EMOTIONS

While our hormones boss us around like a drill sergeant, we do have some say in how we respond and behave. Although we can only tinker with our hormones, we can master our emotions. One powerful emotion we can harness is that bunch of positive feelings some people call happiness, and others call contentment, satisfaction, or joie de vivre.

How to Find Happiness

To find happiness, psychologists and geneticists agree, a person need look no further than his or her own temperament and life.

ARNOLD'S RELATIONSHIPS

For Arnold Schwarzenegger, the secret to successful relationships may lie in his attitude. Here's how a close friend of his, Jim Lorimer, describes that attitude: "Here is a guy who defines himself in terms of joy, and I think that enables him to handle much more effectively all of his relationships and all of his dealings. He is always enjoying himself, and when you are enjoying yourself and involved and committed, you are likely to be more alert and likely to retain information better. I think his basic philosophy is, 'I love my life.' "

Studies and research into people's reactions to dramatic events in their lives, like crippling accidents or getting married, reveal that each of us has a "happiness set point." This set point is our predetermined genetic disposition. Like the notion of a set point in individual weight—that our bodies are programmed to be a certain size and actively resist any attempts to lose or gain weight—the happiness set point is the innate feeling of well-being that we are born with. Our temperament or outlook on life, which ranges from sunny and enthusiastic to grim and depressed, is determined by our genetic makeup.

A proponent of this theory is Dr. David Lykken, a behavioral geneticist, who compared the feelings of well-being in fifteen hundred pairs of twins. He discovered that identical twins raised apart had the same outlook on life, regardless of their family situations, professional accomplishments, or financial status. Such achievements as advanced degrees or high salaries or successful marriages produced only a 2 percent difference in the twins' mental outlook.

Even more remarkable, researchers have found that even the most traumatic events in people's lives do not alter their outlook for any length of time. People who have been divorced, widowed, or crippled by spinal-cord injuries mourn their loss, but within a year resume their natural outlook. Grieving and depression for more than a year are signs of a serious illness, not a change in temperament or personality.

There is another half of this equation, however, one that has direct relevance to our lives. Our happiness set point is accountable for probably about half our emotional temperament. The other half, say psychologists, comes from the small pleasures and joys we seize. Given that we emotionally shrug off monumental events, we should seize the small delights that brighten our day.

Dr. Lykken says we have a range of happiness, and should find ways to live at the top of that range: "Be an experimental epicure. A steady diet of simple pleasures will keep you above your set point. Find the small things that you know give you a little high—a good meal, working in the garden, time with friends—and sprinkle your life with them. In the long run, that will leave you happier than some grand achievement that gives you a big lift for a while."

Eating for a Better Sex Life

The idea that food can affect your emotions and even your sexual reactions is not as far-fetched as it may sound. It's only logical that some foods will put a bounce in your step and others will turn you off. We know that the body breaks down food into molecules that travel to the brain. Here they are converted into chemicals that behave just like sex hormones. It's not unheard-of to eat a great meal and discover afterward, over dessert so to speak, that your mind is dwelling on amorous thoughts. More than the candlelight and soft fragrances may be at work.

> The greatest discovery of my generation is that a human being can alter his life by changing his attitude.
>
> —William James

It is possible that your steak and red wine perked up your brain's dopamine, the ultimate pleasure chemical. While widely known as a natural stimulant—it's considered the mastermind that drives addictive behavior—dopamine is also thought to be behind men's and women's sex drive. Male rats with high levels of dopamine not only have a heightened sex drive but ejaculate quickly. In females, it makes reaching orgasm easier. On the other hand, too little dopamine has been blamed for a nonexistent sex drive or sexual aversion. An almost nonexistent sex drive is one of the complications of Parkinson's disease, which is tripped by a shortfall of dopamine.

Foods that contain the precursors or ingredients tyrosine and choline are converted into neurotransmitters, including dopamine. You can find tyrosine (an amino acid) in protein-rich meals and choline in meals that contain lecithin. However, scientists are unsure about the precise chemistry that is needed to put more dopamine in circulation and how it reacts with other molecules to affect the sex drive. The more accepted ways of boosting its production fall to taking certain drugs, namely Deprenyl (also called Eldepryl) and certain types of antidepressants like Wellbutrin.

Perhaps your dinner included a chocolate dessert. That could have sparked romance. Chocolate contains amine compounds, including the molecules of the "love hormone" I mentioned earlier, phenylethylamine (PEA). People theorize that this may be one reason behind the passion of "chocoholics" and for giving chocolate to loved ones. However, scientists are quick to note that other foods, such as pickled herring and cheddar cheese, contain more amine compounds than chocolate. I leave it to you to decide whether it's a love potion.

A much stronger connection has been found between vitamin C (ascorbic acid) and men's sexual potency. Vitamin C is a powerful antioxidant, and studies have shown that free radicals, those damaging molecules that antioxidants beat up on, can damage sperm cells. (This is why men grow infertile with age—it's from years of exposure to pollutants that spawn free radicals.) At the University of California, Berkeley, researchers compared two groups of men, those with low levels of ascorbic acid and those on a controlled diet with their ascorbic acid intake adjusted up or down. When the vitamin C intake dropped from 250 mg a day to 5 mg, the men's sperm counts fell by half, and when it was bumped up to 60 mg or 250 mg a day, the sperm counts doubled. When researchers at the University of Texas Medical Branch in Galveston gave 1,000 mg a day of vitamin C to men unable to conceive because of low sperm counts, everything started moving. After a month of taking ascorbic acid supplements, the men's sperm counts rose by 60 percent and, even more noteworthy, all their wives conceived. Guys should also be aware that smoking can hammer their sperm counts. The University of Texas researchers also gave vitamin C supplements for a month to a group of heavy smokers. At the end, the sperm counts of the men taking placebos did not change, while the sperm counts of those taking either 200 mg or 1,000 mg markedly improved.

Women who eat certain plant foods may find themselves feeling the effects of ebbing or flowing estrogen levels. There is a category of plants called phytoestrogens that help regulate a woman's production of the hormone, pepping it up when it's low or suppressing activity when it's high. Plants rich in these natural estrogen regulators include beans, peas, soybean products, and leafy vegetables like cabbage.

Fat appears to be a real turnoff, in more ways than one. Besides the other obvious physical consequences, fat also gums up the sex hormones. A fatty diet can alter the amount of estrogen in a woman's body. Women with a high-fat, low-fiber diet have higher estrogen levels than women who eat vegetarian. In normal amounts, estrogen is wonderful for a woman's body and helps nourish her sex drive. But wide swings in estrogen production can play havoc with her moods and temperament, and a high-fat diet may contribute to this.

A comparison between women in Boston on a 40 percent fat diet and Asian women in Hawaii on a 21 percent fat diet found the former had 30 to 75 percent higher estrogen levels. The postmenopausal women in the Boston group had 300 percent more estrogen than the postmenopausal Asian women. Women who used

THE GOOD, THE BAD, AND THE UGLY FOR GREAT SEX!

Good	Bad & Ugly
Increases testosterone: Red meat Zinc (30–50 mg/per day) Vigorous anaerobic exercise	Lowers testosterone: Vegetarian or high-fat diet Zinc deficiency Stress Regular, exhaustive aerobic exercise
Increases estrogen: Sexual intercourse Significant weight gain (recommended only if severely underweight Alcohol (moderate amounts) Beans, peas, leafy vegetables, soybeans and whole wheat products	Lowers estrogen: Sexual abstinence Extreme weight loss Severe caloric restriction Excessively low fat diet Overly strenuous physical activity on a regular basis
Increases neurotransmitters: Tyrosine (protein-rich meals) Choline (lecithin) Deprenyl Antidepressants Chocolate Pickled herring Cheddar cheese	Overstimulates serotonin: High glycemic index carbohydrates: bread, rice, pasta, potatoes, corn, carrots, sweets
Increases sperm count: Antioxidants, especially Vitamin C	Reduces sperm count: Free radicals Pollutants Smoking

a low-fat diet to lower their fat intake from 69 grams of fat a day to 32 grams of fat a day significantly dropped their serum estrone and estradiol. A high-fiber diet—two months of eating wheat bran supplements—also markedly lowered their estrogen mixture (oat bran or corn bran had no effect).

Men on fatty diets may encounter difficulties in their love lives. A group of men at the University of Utah School of Medicine were asked to fast on two separate nights. After the first night, they were given either a high-fat drink or a low-fat drink. Blood tests of sex steroid levels before and after revealed that the fatty drink lowered their free testosterone (but not their estrogen or LHRH). The researchers surmise that fatty foods may inhibit a man's testosterone production.

Fat may also ruin a guy's performance. Erections depend on blood flow, and a high-fat diet can lead to atherosclerosis and so gum up the plumbing needed to achieve and maintain an erection. One of the main causes of impotence is clogged arteries.

Other foods can squash your sexual hankerings. Foods that act as ingredients of the brain chemical serotonin can increase its production, and over stimulation of this chemical has been shown to dampen sexual reactions in animals. Carbohydrates are one such food. Starchy or sweet foods like rice, corn, potatoes, pasta, and sugary dishes increase the brain's demand for tryptophan and this boosts serotonin production.

CULTIVATING EMOTIONAL SMARTS

Personal relationships are such a vital part of my life, as they are of everyone's, that I often think about how to improve them. Here's what I try to keep in mind and apply to my life.

Hormonal Heads-Up

Everyone is subject to hormone changes. A man may become needlessly combative, aggressive, argumentative, or stubborn. A woman may become teary, moody, or needy. I watch for behavior that is out of the ordinary, and if I detect a hormonal shift, I accommodate. This may mean backing off and avoiding a confrontation with a man or letting a woman vent her feelings. At these times, I am careful about what I say, not wanting my hormones to grab my tongue or to overreact to someone else's outburst. I am always ready to apologize if my temperament has made me say something inappropriate. And I don't take to heart anything said to me in anger, frustration, or out of impetuousness.

Acknowledge Strengths

In personal as well as professional relationships, I often defer to a person's strengths. Typically, women are geared toward verbalizing, communicating, and talking out a problem. Men lean toward action, looking for immediate results and forging ahead.

Sexual Savvy

A lack of interest in sex is not normal and can indicate a physical problem. In men, it can signal low testosterone production. It may stem from impotence, which can be caused by blocked arteries, too little DHEA, or any number of diseases including heart disease, hypertension, and alcoholism. Smoking and stress can aggravate impotence. A man may be taking medications that limit his abilities.

A woman's aversion to sex can be hormonal. A woman who is nursing produces the hormone prolactin, which shuts off the sexual feelers. It is possible that a woman's testosterone production is far

A BRIEF REFRESHER

Personal relationships and emotional well-being frequently turn on the rise and fall of our hormones and our ability to recognize other people's strengths. Here's what I keep in mind about men and women.

Testosterone rising. Men's testosterone rises during fights or confrontations, vigorous muscle-building exercise, in the fall and winter, in the early morning, and with the consumption of red meat.

Testosterone falling. Men's testosterone declines when they're under stress, eat solely vegetarian, have a zinc deficiency, and during exhausting aerobic exercise.

Estrogen rising. Women's estrogen rises with weight gain or obesity, with alcohol consumption, with a high-fat, low-fiber diet, and from consuming plant-derived estrogens like those found in soy products.

Estrogen falling. Women's estrogen falls during regular, strenuous physical activity, when she's cutting calories, losing weight, on a low-fat diet, and when she abstains from sex.

Men's strengths: manipulating objects, math calculations, coordination, spatial orientation, geometry problems, bright-light vision, concentration, reading maps and geography, and sensitivity to personal space.

Women's strengths: sensitive hearing, short-term memory, verbal ability, linguistic ability, fine motor skills, night vision, perception, visual memory, and intuition.

below normal, signaling the need for replacement therapy. She may be going through perimenopause or menopause, times when some women report a loss of interest. Certain antidepressants and dieting are also known to dampen a woman's sex drive.

SELECTED SOURCES

Colgan, M. *Hormonal Health.* Apple Publishing, Vancouver, B.C., 1996.

Crenshaw, T. L. *The Alchemy of Love and Lust.* G. P. Putnam's Sons, New York, 1996.

Dabbs, J. M., Jr. "Age and seasonal variation in serum testosterone concentration among men." *Chronobiology International,* 7 (3), 245–49, 1990.

Dabbs, J. M., Jr., and Mohammed, S. "Male and female salivary testosterone concentrations before and after sexual activity." *Physiology and Behavior,* 52 (1), 195–97, July 1992.

Dawson, E. B. "Effect of ascorbic acid supplementation on the sperm quality of smokers." *Fertility and Sterility,* 58 (5), 1034–39, November 1992.

Frags, C. G. "Ascorbic acid protects against endogenous oxidative DNA damage in human sperm." *Proceedings of the National Academy of Sciences, U.S.A.,* 88 (24), 11003–6, December 15, 1991.

Gallamine, D. "Forget money: nothing can buy happiness, some researchers say." *New York Times,* July 16, 1996.

Gibbons, A. "The brain as 'sexual organ.'" *Science,* 253 (5023), 957–60, August 30, 1991.

Gorbach, S. L. "Dietary modification of hormone levels." *Cancer Researcher Weekly,* May 24, 1993, 25–27.

Kampden, D. L., and Sherwin, B. B., "Estradiol is related to visual memory in healthy young men." *Behavioral Neuroscience,* 110 (3), 613–17, June 1996.

Khalsa, D. S. *Brain Longevity.* Warner Books, New York, 1997.

Konner, M. *The Tangled Wing: Biological Constraints on the Human Spirit.* Henry Holt and Co., New York, 1982.

Krantz, M. "Two scents' worth: a new fragrance company takes advantage of pheromones." *Omni,* 16 (4), 24, January 1994.

Lazarus, R. S., and Lazarus, B. N. *Passion and Reason: Making Sense of Our Emotions.* Oxford University Press, New York, 1994.

McNaughton, N. *Biology and Emotion.* Cambridge University Press, Cambridge, England, 1989.

Meikle, A. W., et al. "Effects of a fat-containing meal on sex hormones in men." *Metabolism,* 39 (9), 943–46, September 1990.

Moir, A., and Jessel, D. *Brain Sex.* Dell Publishing, New York, 1991.

Spring, B., et al. "Effects of protein and carbohydrate meals on mood and performance: interactions with sex and age." *Journal of Psychiatric Research,* 17 (2), 155–67, 1982–83.

Van Goozen, S. H., et al. "Activating effects of androgens on cognitive performance: casual evidence in a group of female-to-male transsexuals." *Neuropsychologia,* 32 (10), 1153–57, October 1994.

Seven

MIND CALM

HOPE FOR THE WORRIED WELL

I have been fortunate never to have needed the help of a psychiatrist, but this does not mean that I am unfamiliar with the mental and emotional wounds that can skew thinking and jangle feelings. My art-collecting activities have introduced me to people who are brilliant sculptors and painters but who suffer from subclinical and clinical mood disorders like manic-depression and depression.

One particular friend is an art-restoration specialist whose erratic behavior and skewed thinking have sabotaged what might have been a brilliant career. John is a manic-depressive who, despite years of medical treatment, persists in self-destructive habits. Although he knows he must keep regular sleeping hours, he not infrequently becomes so absorbed in projects that he goes for days without sleep. During this time, he is enormously productive but on a very selective level. He will throw himself into a project and ignore everything else. Promises, commitments, meetings, schedules—he shrugs them off when he is in a manic frenzy. During these times, much that he has built up in terms of working relationships and prospective business collapses. Adding to his difficulties during these times is his explosive temper. He becomes irrational and either lashes out at people for no reason or becomes totally uncommunicative.

At times, we are all subject to jumbled emotions. Yet, no matter how overwhelming, all of us, even someone like John, can get a better grip on the mental storms that blow through. John chooses to go off his medication and opt for the energy of his mania over the steady, stable feelings he gets from psychotropic drugs. What he is sacrificing is mental acuity—his ability to think quickly and coherently.

It's hard to be mentally sharp when brain chemicals are messing with your emotions. Of course, mental illness can put you in the hospital and even threaten your life, but even mild, subclinical bouts can ruin memory, logic, concentration, and intellectual functioning. It is essential for brain fitness that you recognize in yourself signs of mental glitches that are disrupting your thinking life. This may not be as easy as it sounds.

While some mental illnesses are unmistakable, like the psychosis of schizophrenia or the feverish energy of mania, others may insinuate themselves into your mind more subtly. They may well be disguised, or so ingrained into your thinking patterns that you do not realize how much they are draining your mental resources. Mental illness is as much a medical disease as epilepsy and can require concentrated medical attention. However, we have a little more control over certain varieties in their nonclinical forms (that is, not so bad as to demand constant medical care). These are the ones I want to talk about—depression, attention deficit disorder, and anxiety.

SHADES OF BLUE

When you hear that someone is depressed, you probably conjure up a picture of someone who is morose, listless, and sad to the point of tears. In truth, depression has many expressions. A person who is depressed may be restless with a very short attention span. She (I say

TAKE ACTION

Are You Depressed?

Answer yes or no to these questions:

1. Do you feel sad a lot?
2. Do you often feel guilty or unworthy?
3. Does your life seem meaningless?
4. Do you feel that nothing good is ever going to happen to you?
5. Have you lost interest in what you once enjoyed, like sports, music, movies, dining out?
6. Do you find it hard to make up your mind about things?
7. Do you often forget things and find it hard to concentrate?
8. Do you get angry and irritated often? Are you so touchy that you lose control for no reason? Do you frequently overreact?
9. Have your sleeping habits changed lately?
10. Do you feel restless or tired much of the time?
11. Do you think about death often or do thoughts of suicide come into your mind?
12. Have you lost or gained weight lately without trying to?

If you answered yes to four or more of these questions, and the feeling has persisted for longer than two weeks, you are probably depressed and need to see a doctor now.

"she" because women are twice as likely to suffer depression) may appear bored and blasé, or unusually cheerful and erratic.

The outward signs of major depression are well known. They include clear feelings of sadness or emptiness, lack of interest or pleasure in anything, insomnia, major weight loss or gain, agitation, fatigue, inability to concentrate, feelings of worthlessness and thoughts of suicide, *and* most of these feelings have to persist daily over at least two weeks. If this is what is going through your mind, you should see a doctor immediately.

Mild or moderate depression, however, lets a person get through the day but takes the excitement out of new ideas and the satisfaction out of small victories. Depression can make it difficult for you to remember trivial as well as important things, to concentrate on your work, to read for any length of time, and even to think logically. Among the elderly, loss of memory and changes in behavior that are typically labeled Alzheimer's are, in actuality, very often caused by depression.

The roots of depression are tangled in a person's biochemistry and neurochemistry. Hormones, particularly estrogen, are probably a powerful influence, one likely reason women suffer more. Neurotransmitters, particularly serotonin, are surely partly to blame. The biological basis of the disorder is why antidepressants can be so effective.

However, certain experiences can trip the outbreak of a mental disorder. For instance, taking psychedelic drugs can make a susceptible person psychotic, and erratic sleep habits, especially going without sleep for days, is a common trigger for manic-depressive episodes. There is much in your daily routine that could push you toward depression. Food, medication, exposure to sunlight, and the amount of exercise you get may play a role in whether a person suffers from a mood disorder.

The following connections between depression and what you eat are cited by Dr. Gary Null in the *Townsend Letter for Doctors and Patients.*

- Among Indian patients suffering from depression, doctors found that the amount of zinc in their bodies dropped remarkably after they recovered.
- An article in the *Southern Medical Journal* noted that a lack of vitamin B_{12} in one's diet can cause depression.
- A deficiency in folic acid is common among patients with depression.
- High levels of heavy metals like aluminum, lead, and mercury

in the air and water have been associated with depression and anxiety.

Depression has also been traced to nutritional deficiencies in vitamin B_6 (pyridoxine) and riboflavin and to excesses in sugar and caffeine. For some women, birth control pills blacken their outlook. In addition, depression has been linked to a lack of exposure to sunlight, prompting research into the depressive syndrome, seasonal affective disorder (SAD).

My first line of defense against depression, especially when I feel vulnerable (during long dark winter days), is the right diet. I make sure I eat foods rich in the nutrients that combat depression.

Eating spinach is a tasty way to ensure that I get enough folic acid (part of the B complex). About two cups of spinach a week, whether tucked into lasagna or as part of a salad, give me enough protection. Doctors studying chronic depression and folic acid have found that 200–500 micrograms a day show results.

Folic acid is wrapped up with depression because it affects the balance of the neurochemical serotonin. Brain researchers have been making startling discoveries about how this neurotransmitter affects your moods and thoughts.

Secrets of Serotonin

Serotonin made a big splash a few years ago as the secret behind the blockbuster antidepression drug Prozac. Prozac belongs to a family of drugs called serotonin selective reuptake inhibitors. These drugs increase the amount of serotonin coursing through the brain. A steady supply of serotonin improves a person's mood, and vice versa. When a person has low levels of serotonin, whether from drugs, diet, or natural chemistry, depression and mood swings follow. If the imbalance is extreme, thoughts of suicide are not uncommon.

The federal government approved using Prozac (the generic

name is fluvoxamine) for depression in 1987, and since then scientists have found that serotonin does more than manage depression. People in the grips of obsessive-compulsive disorder and bulimia also get better when their serotonin levels are pumped up. The new diet drug Redux, which was recently recalled by the FDA, quiets a person's appetite by raising the level of serotonin. And scientists suspect that boosting a person's serotonin may also relieve migraine headaches, anxiety, and premenstrual syndrome.

Given the discoveries about serotonin, it is not surprising that scientists have been delving into which foods and nutrients the body converts into it. Clinical researchers have been concentrating on foods rich in tryptophan, an amino acid that the body converts into serotonin. Their attention has been on foods, not supplements, because supplements are not as effective, possibly because they have difficulty crossing the blood-brain barrier.

Experiments with foods heavy in tryptophan have dramatically changed people's moods and lifted their depression. British scientists put a group of fifteen women with histories of depression (although they were not on antidepressants and had eating disorders as well) on a diet of foods either lacking tryptophan or packed with it. To the scientists' surprise, ten of the women developed symptoms of depression immediately after lowering their tryptophan levels by 75 percent. "The mood change was quite dramatic for those women. It was very quick—within hours, really," said Dr. Katy Smith, a psychiatrist at Oxford University. "They were the typical symptoms of depression—low mood but also the other symptoms such as a change in amount of activity, an increase in guilty thinking, particularly," she added. Other reports from doctors have said the same thing: The amount of tryptophan in foods and drinks can alter a person's feelings of depression.

You find tryptophan in complex carbohydrates and some proteins. According to Drs. Judith and Richard Wurtman at the Massachusetts Institute of Technology, people prone to depression may be inadvertently trying to self-medicate themselves when they crave starchy foods. Their body chemistry is driving them to replenish their depleted serotonin.

For most people, the recommended daily intake of tryptophan is 500 milligrams, and people susceptible to depression may consume up to 1,500 milligrams. Dr. Andrew Weil suggests a daily supplement of 1,500 milligrams of the amino acid DL-phenylalanine (also known as DLPA), which, in studies using doses of 150–200 milligrams a day, has eased some people's depression. To ward off depression, I make sure that I eat healthy portions of carbohydrates and select proteins at least twice a day. These are the foods I am sure to have on my menu: pumpkin seeds, turkey, peas, beans or pasta, and any rice-based food, such as rice crackers or sushi.

As every carbohydrate-craver knows, you can satisfy your nagging desire to nosh and raise your tryptophan by eating sweet, starchy snacks. But I stay away from sugar when I sense depression lurking on the horizon. A shot of glucose will certainly pump you up, but it can also drop you into a funk. A chunk of chocolate or a handful of cookies will raise your serotonin, but when the effect wears off, your chemical levels may have plummeted to below where they started, and you will feel even more in the dumps. (The section on anxiety coming up offers more about what sugar can do to you.) Doctors have found that about a third of the people prone to depression are especially sensitive to sugar. To learn whether you are one of these unfortunates, cut sugar from your diet completely for two weeks (artificial sweeteners are okay) and watch what happens to your mood.

An Essential Lubricant

Serotonin is not the only brain chemical behind depression. Scientists have found a road connecting a type of fatty acid and the incidence of depression. This polyunsaturated, essential fatty acid ("essential" means that it's vital to your immune and nervous system but available only through diet) is omega-3, found in fish. This fat, along with others, circulates through the brain to make chemicals more fluid and to sharpen communication between neurons. Think of omega-3 and other fatty acids as lubricants for the brain. For years, doctors have known that eating fish reduces a person's risk of heart disease. Just recently, the power of fish oil has been discovered for treating mental diseases. Omega-3 fatty acids are so vital to the diet that some national governments, notably those of Canada and Denmark, recommend that people consume them regularly.

According to scientists at the Laboratory of Membrane Biophysics and Biochemistry at the National Institutes of Health (NIH), population studies in the United States and other countries have found a correlation between people consuming fewer omega-3 fatty acids and rising rates of depression. It also seems that people in countries where fish is a dietary staple, like Taiwan, China, and Japan, suffer much less depression. For instance, the Taiwanese have only one-tenth the incidence of depression than Americans.

Omega-3 fatty acids contain substances called eicosanoids, which exert a powerful effect on body functions. Some eicosanoids help your body, others hurt it. For instance, omega-6, which is found in corn oil and soybean oil, has a reputation for gumming up your works. Perhaps not surprisingly, the NIH researchers looking into fatty acids and depression found that people with severe symptoms of depression had high levels of omega-6 in their blood.

The best source of omega-3 fatty acids is fish, particularly cold-water fish like trout, sardines, salmon, tuna, herring, and anchovies. The simplest way to get enough omega-3 is to eat this type of fish at least once a week, remembering, of course, not to cook the fish in vegetable oil and so reduce the benefits. Omega-3 supplements are also available, generally in 300-mg capsules, which deliver much more than does eating. You can also take supplements of DHA (docosahexaenoic acid), which is a form of omega-3 fatty acid. Doses that have helped the mental outlook of students ranged from 1 to 2 grams a day. However, scientists have not yet looked at exactly how much omega-3 is needed for depression relief, so megadoses may

TAKE ACTION

Perk Up: Eat Something

Here's what I eat when I feel depression could get the better of me.

Toasted pumpkin seeds
Turkey sandwich
Grilled tuna
Spinach and pasta
Vitamin B complex supplement

not be called for. For me, it is enough to know about the strong tie between the fatty acids and my state of mind, so I include fish in my weekly diet.

Herbal Relief

Scientists have been getting remarkable results with an herbal treatment for mild depression. Doctors in England and Germany watching depressed patients who were taking either a placebo or an herbal remedy found that the plant extract was "significantly superior."

TESTIMONIAL TO AN HERB

Neurologist Ron Lawrence sometimes prefers an herbal approach to treating depression. "I've been impressed with St.-John's-wort hypericum. It does work and I encourage it rather than using Prozac or selective reuptake inhibitors. If you give St.-John's-wort a chance, which usually takes about three weeks, I found it to be very good in alleviating depression and very safe."

Equally exciting, very few of the people taking the herb experienced any side effects. The evidence for this miraculous herb has been mounting, and recently, researchers in Munich reviewed twenty-three studies of the herb, involving almost eighteen hundred patients and found that the remedy was just as effective as antidepressant medication.

This herb is an extract of a bushy shrub with yellow flowers called St.-John's-wort and is also known as hypericum. (Don't let the word "wort" throw you off—it means "plant" or "root" in Middle English.) It is available over-the-counter in capsules and tablets under the names Hypericum Verbatim, St. John's Wort, and Kira. Regardless of the producer, each dose should contain 0.3 percent hypericum. Experts say that it takes a couple of weeks to produce a noticeable effect. The suggested daily dose is 300 milligrams at least once a day and up to three times a day, depending on your doctor's recommendation. If you are taking antidepressant medication, do not switch to St.-John's-wort until you have talked to your doctor.

Sweat Out the Sadness

When it comes to dueling with depression, exercise is as piercing as a drug. It requires a heftier commitment than does swallowing a tablet, but then its side effects—stronger heart, better muscle tone, increased energy—make you even healthier.

You need to raise your heart rate and breathe hard, but not to the point of pain or exhaustion. Nevertheless, the activity deserves all your attention. If you can read a newspaper while pedaling a stationary bicycle or carry on a conversation while jogging, you're not exercising, you are engaged in a relaxing pastime.

A single workout will not fend off the blues. You have to lace up your Reeboks at least three times a week for thirty minutes, for a month or more. It took six weeks for sports doctors to notice results from an exercise experiment with one hundred male college professors. The profs were first tested for symptoms of depression, then put on an exercise program and monitored. After a month and a half, those who were most depressed showed the biggest improvement. In a study involving moderately depressed men, it was ten weeks of aerobic exercise before doctors saw a difference in outlook. And the guys who did stretching instead of aerobic workouts, and for two weeks instead of ten, did not get better.

A study of forty women with a depressive disorder at the University of Rochester Sports Center found that an aerobic activity—running or walking—or working out on weight machines almost completely erased signs of depression. The women exercised about three times a week. Each workout consisted of a five- to ten-minute warm-up, a main session of either progressing through a ten-station weight circuit or walking or jogging around an indoor track until they sustained an 80 percent of capacity heart rate, and ten minutes of cooldown. A control group of women with similar signs of depression did no exercise. After eight weeks, the active women's scores on standard depression tests had improved dramatically, while their sedentary peers registered no improvement in their mental health. Moreover, the women were again tested for signs of depression a year later, and the exercising group maintained their rosier outlook.

The psychological reasons why exercise makes people feel better are clear. When people exercise regularly, they feel a sense of accomplishment, and more in control of themselves and their lives. The physiological reasons that moving and sweating lift depression stem from bursts of chemical activity and improved cardiovascular function. Strong lungs and a strong heart help your body to better grapple with the pressures of stress and make you less vulnerable to depression. Flexing your muscles and constant motion also increase the flow of adrenaline, another possible explanation for why exercise acts as an antidepressant.

And exercise stimulates your natural opioid system—those endorphins that raise your pain threshold and lower blood pressure. Scientists at the University of Göteborg in Sweden think that the endorphin "high" of exercise may be an effective treatment not only for depression but also for alcoholism, drug addiction, and anorexia nervosa.

For exercise to kick in as an effective antidepressant, you have to stick with it. So pick an activity you find fun and relatively convenient. We all know that if something is a lot of trouble, costly, time-consuming, or full of hassles, we won't do it. There are lots of choices. I prefer brisk walking, but you may prefer jogging, climbing a stair machine, running on a treadmill, swimming, or riding a stationary bike. If you are new to regular exercise, start light and easy. Begin with fifteen-minute workouts at a relatively low resistance and only gradually increase the duration and difficulty. Your first goal should be to establish a routine you can live with. If you finish your workout with some energy and motivation left over, you'll be back the next day.

IT'S NOT ALWAYS DEPRESSION: ATTENTION DEFICIT DISORDER

Sometimes a person may act depressed, irritable, unmotivated, and glum, but the demon may be not a mood disorder but adult attention deficit disorder (ADD).

Many believe that ADD afflicts only children and then burns out in the teen years, but experts now estimate that about one-third of the cases of childhood ADD stretch into adulthood. While ADD in children strikes boys ten times more often than girls, it tends to linger with girls longer. So, by the time its sufferers reach adulthood, the gender split is fairly even.

Like depression and other mental illnesses, ADD floats through families and generations. And, like depression at times, adult (sometimes referred to as residual) ADD is a thinking disease. It can make concentrating, remembering, solving problems, even listening excruciatingly difficult. Here are the kinds of mental blunders ADD can cause.

TAKE ACTION

Beating Depression

- Fill in nutritional deficiencies. Boost your intake of folic acid, vitamins B_6 and B_{12}, and riboflavin.
- Eliminate nutritional aggravators, particularly sugar and caffeine.
- Expose yourself to at least thirty minutes of sunlight or two hours of high-intensity artificial light every day.
- Eat foods rich in tryptophan, particularly complex carbohydrates.
- Consider taking supplements of DLPA.
- Load up on foods with omega-3 fatty acids.
- Try St.-John's-wort.
- Make time for at least thirty minutes of vigorous exercise three times a week and keep it up for at least a month.

- Spelling errors
- Mistakes in simple arithmetic
- Misunderstanding or missing important points in reading material
- Inattention while driving—missing turnoffs, running signals
- Mind-wandering during conversation
- Constant and major memory lapses—forgetting simple things, from where you put something to important meetings
- Impetuous behavior, e.g., dangerous lane switching when driving
- Intolerable impatience, e.g., inability to wait in line
- Inability to finish projects
- Repeated procrastination

Hyperactivity is sometimes, but not always, part of the condition. Someone who is constantly in motion—pacing, gesturing, shifting position, scratching, tapping—may be in the grips of the hyperactive version. Doctors distinguish someone with ADD from someone who is simply fidgety by watching whether the perpetual motion becomes more pronounced over the course of an interview. If a person calms down after the initial novelty of an encounter or experience wears off, hyperactivity is probably not behind the restlessness. For instance, if someone finds it impossible to sit through a two-hour movie without getting up and down or repeatedly shifting in her seat, hyperactivity may be the fuel. But if this person settles down as she becomes engrossed in the movie, she probably isn't hyperactive.

Diagnosing ADD is tricky. All of us at one time or another feel impulsive, disorganized, or unable to follow a conversation or understand a piece of reading material. For a doctor to make a firm diagnosis, the long list of possible symptoms and glitches in thinking must be accompanied by other features. For one, ADD does not first crop up in adulthood; a person must have had it as a child. Adults who were undiagnosed as children are told to dig out old school records and family histories to identify early symptoms that were ignored. The symptoms have to be chronic—that is, persist for years—not just flare up and disappear on occasion. And the muddled thinking has to invade every part of a person's life—work, family life, personal relationships.

A person with ADD can be very successful, having unconsciously devised ways to get around his or her handicaps. Rather than treat the disease, someone with ADD may deftly compensate. She may be always keeping lists of things to do, dutifully recording every event to remember in an elaborate calendar, and letting other people do those tasks, like lengthy reading, that she cannot manage.

> The ability to concentrate and use your time well is everything if you want to succeed in business—or almost anywhere else for that matter.
>
> —Lee Iacocca

The very smart person can be especially adept at configuring her life and work so that ADD does not interfere.

Getting Control

The standard treatment for ADD, as most people know, is the drug Ritalin (methylphenidate), an amphetamine that helps people settle down and focus. (In people who do not have the disorder, amphetamines—speed—and all their cousins rev them up. Another one of their uses is as a diet pill.) Ritalin is so effective in combating the disorder that it is even used to diagnose it. Doctors unsure of whether a child or adult has the disease prescribe Ritalin and watch the patient's reactions. If it sharpens behavior and thinking, and is not abused as an upper, the doctors confirm the diagnosis. Other effective amphetamines are Dexedrine (dextroamphetamine) and Cylert (pemoline). Antidepressants like imipramine, amitriptyline, and desipramine are also prescribed for ADD. But many people do not like taking these drugs because of the disturbing side effects in some who take them: insomnia, weight loss, nausea, dizziness, and headaches. Antidepressants may also tamper with your blood pressure or heart rate, and should not be taken by anyone with heart disease.

Any medication you use for ADD should be buttressed by nonmedical strategies. Dr. Edward Hallowell, a leading expert on the illness and author of *Driven to Distraction,* recommends a three-pronged treatment program: structure, motivation, and novelty. By inserting structure or systems for organizing your life, you eliminate many of the holes that ADD punches into your memory, attention span, concentration, and patience. For instance, the following organizational aids can help you to remember appointments and finish projects.

- A home filing system for unpaid and paid bills, receipts, notices
- Write-on, reminder calendars everywhere: kitchen, home office, purse, office, car

- For doing quick arithmetic, inexpensive hand calculators in the kitchen, on your desk, in the television room
- Notepads and pens everywhere for notes to yourself and lists
- Bulletin boards on which you tack up every slip of paper listing something you must do or remember
- Central appointment book such as a Day Runner or Filofax to keep track of appointments, meetings, etc.

Developing motivation requires more subtle steps. It means making manageable changes in destructive or futile ways of behaving. It goes hand in hand with educating yourself and those close to you about ADD and how it affects your actions and thinking. For instance, people with ADD are notorious for apparently not listening when someone is speaking to them and for appearing to be indifferent to the requests and needs of others. Once this trait is recognized and talked about, it can be relieved of its emotional baggage. Not listening can be understood as an attention problem, not a sign of self-centeredness or lack of caring. When a characteristic of ADD is understood to be a symptom and not a psychological problem, it is easier for a person to confront it and try to change.

Novelty is important to people with ADD. Boredom and impatience come easily to them, so tasks and activities need to be planned to include opportunities for spontaneity, creativity, and bursts of excitement. A person with ADD cannot be expected to sit in front of a computer screen for hours on end doing on-line research, for example. If such a job is necessary, the assignment should include lots of breaks to walk around and talk to others, and enough flexibility to briefly pursue interesting diversions.

Studies have been examining children to learn whether certain foods aggravate or ease the symptoms of attention deficit disorder. Scientists in at least three studies watched what happened when children ate either a high-carbohydrate meal or a high-protein meal. In each study, the kids consuming mostly protein did much better on tests of attention and listening, and were less physically restless.

For some people, caffeine works as a stimulant similar to Ritalin.

When ADD hyperactive children were given caffeine tablets in doses up to 600 milligrams a day, some calmed down and shed their impulsive, restless behavior. Of course, so large a dose of caffeine can also produce stomachaches, nausea, and insomnia.

A deficiency of essential fatty acids may play a role in the disorder. Scientists from Purdue University reported that among almost one hundred hyperactive ADD boys, more than half had much lower than normal concentrations of fatty acids in their bodies. Other researchers looking into this have noticed that more boys than girls have ADD, and boys in general have higher essential fatty acid needs. ADD youngsters often show signs of essential fatty acid deficiency, namely excessive thirst, eczema, allergies, and asthma. The Purdue researchers noticed that the boys were especially lacking in omega-3 fatty acids, which come mainly from deep-water fish.

ALWAYS ON EDGE

The psychiatrists' handbook for diagnosing mental disorders, *DSM-IV,* bunches a number of thinking problems under "Anxiety Disorders." These include panic attack, phobias, obsessive-compulsive disorder, post-traumatic stress, and degrees of anxiety.

The kind of anxiety I guard against, and the most common, is called generalized anxiety. When you find yourself always on edge; constantly, uncontrollably worrying; easily tired; unable to concentrate; irritable; and unable to sleep, you've got this bug. However, for a formal medical diagnosis, these feelings have to last for at least six months. And if your mental distress undermines your family life, work, or relationships, you need to seek professional help. While milder bouts of apprehension may not put you in the doctor's office, they also demand attention.

Your mind's reaction to anxiety, like its reaction to stress, gushes from physiological as well as psychological springs. Flawed chemistry on top of fixed, nagging ideas can make logical, crisp thinking virtually impossible. Scientists believe that a sputtering supply of the amino acid GABA (gamma-aminobutyric acid) fans the fire of anxiety. The brain uses GABA to manufacture neurotransmitters, which are needed for nerve cell function.

A number of studies have delved into the connection between anxiety and foods that contain nutrients like amino acids. Although it is still not clear whether a shortage or surplus contributes to the anxiety, or whether anxiety has produced the imbalance, there is definitely a relationship between what you put in your mouth and the extreme discomfort of general anxiety. Here's a sampling of recent findings:

- A study of patients anxious about impending surgery found that the most nervous had low levels of potassium in their blood.
- A study in England of fifty people given selenium showed that this nutrient improved their mood and decreased anxiety.
- German doctors gave a group of very anxious people either a kava extract or a placebo over four weeks and found that the extract slowly reduced anxiety.

To protect myself from anxiety, my first line of defense is to guard against a physiological assault. Psychotherapy can also be effective, but I cannot help you with that. I *can* explain how I try to shield myself from anxiety through diet and nutrition.

Particular foods, drinks, and minerals fuel anxiety. Caffeine in any form can perk you up to the point of discomfort; alcoholic drinks can raise the level of toxic chemicals in the body and make you anxious; and food additives like artificial sweeteners and monosodium glutamate can put you on edge. Allergies to specific foods can also tip the scale. Reactions to the gluten in wheat and other grains, dairy products, and chemicals in ham or bacon can readily make you anxious. You should consider how each of these may be stoking your uneasiness. One relatively easy dietary change you can make to arrest anxiety is to reduce the amount of sugar you consume.

Here's what goes on in your body and brain after you've polished off a sugary snack.

- Simple sugar is quickly converted by the body into glucose, which floods the bloodstream. In response, your pancreas releases a stream of insulin to remove the glucose. At this point, your blood sugar level sinks and you feel nervous, twitchy, and light-headed.
- When your blood sugar level is low, your adrenal glands step in to help out with an injection of cortisol. This, then, may make you feel somewhat panicky, ready to "fight or flight."
- Sugar robs your body of vitamin B complex, which your brain uses for memory and reasoning, to fight antioxidants, and to enhance circulation.
- Sugar can stimulate your appetite, tempting you to eat even more unhealthful food.

Americans consume an enormous amount of sugar. On average, each of us takes in sixty-five pounds of the sweet stuff a year. Sugar is a carbohydrate and comes in three varieties. Simple sugars are fructose and glucose; complex sugars are lactose, maltose, and sucrose. A third type is found in sugar beets. The sugar you want to cull from your diet is the kind that immediately converts into glucose, or blood sugar. This is the sweetener that whipsaws your chemistry. Of course, glucose is vital to brain function, but many people eat too much and the wrong kind, like refined sugars and artificial sweeteners. They snack on sugars that the body quickly reduces to glucose, instead of food with sugars that are broken down gradually and so offer a steadier source of energy. The sugar in complex carbohydrates is the preferred type. Fructose, or fruit sugar, provides the kind of brain fuel that will not make you anxious and jittery.

Here are some foods listed according to how quickly the body converts them into glucose. Those at the top of the list are the slowest to transform and so are preferred for a strict antianxiety diet.

Fructose
Grapefruit
Milk
Yogurt
Apple
Orange juice
Spaghetti
Table sugar (sucrose)
Banana
Brown rice
White bread
Wheat bread
White rice
Honey
Carrot
Potato
Glucose

HEADACHES AND MIGRAINES

One of the hallmarks of anxiety is a dull headache that is like a nagging relative. Almost everyone gets headaches—70 percent of us, according to surveys. And, listening to people talk about their headaches, it's easy to get the idea that almost anything can bring them on. On the list of headache stimulants are caffeine, red wine, champagne, chocolate, cured meat, aged cheese, milk, and monosodium glutamate. Other candidates for the headache hit parade include bananas, figs, onions, lima beans, potato chips, yogurt, and nuts. And then there are all the nonfood, environmental aggravations: smoking, smog, strong perfume, the smell of gasoline, loud noises, bright lights, a change in the weather, and high altitudes. Some people find that even sex and orgasm unleash a throbbing head pain. Scientists studying the possible causes of headaches believe that no single trigger is universal and that emotions, diet, physical environment, and hormones can all bring on the sledgehammer.

At the Princess Margaret Migraine Clinic in London, doctors found that people who get migraines are most sensitive to alcohol, red wine more than white wine, and most of all, to beer. Cheese or chocolate, often both, started headaches in about one-sixth of the sufferers. People with tension headaches, however, were not sensitive to food, and only one of the forty tension types reacted to alcohol.

A cascade of chemical and neural reactions brings on a headache attack. With a migraine, the blood vessels on the surface of the brain first contract, which produces the strange lighting of an aura, then dilate. As the blood vessels dilate or become inflamed, they press on nearby nerves. Scientists are uncertain, however, about whether this dilation is a cause of the pain or the result of some other chemical activity. Your brain itself does not feel pain; pain is "felt" in pain sensors in the nerves around the arteries. Scientists are pretty sure that serotonin is mixed up in headache chemistry and know that a person's serotonin level swings up and down during a migraine. This neurotransmitter is an inhibitory chemical, meaning that it shuts down nerve cell communication. Rising and falling levels of serotonin can set off a chemical seesaw of blood vessel expansion and contraction, the result being a pounding pain in your head.

The Hangover Headache

Excessive drinking causes a headache because alcohol dehydrates you, temporarily robbing the brain of a plentiful supply of cerebrospinal fluid and so disrupting nerve cell action. Most alcohol also contains congeners, which are flavoring and coloring chemicals that are known headache triggers.

The Harvard Medical School measures to prevent hangover headaches include 400–800 milligrams of vitamin E and 1,000 milligrams of vitamin C before drinking. These vitamins help prevent free-radical injury to the brain from the toxic by-products of alcohol. Also drink lots of water before, during, and after drinking alcohol in order to prevent dehydration and to speed the elimination of alcohol from the bloodstream. Over-the-counter ibuprofen taken with a snack before drinking can also save you from a pounding head the next morning. The anti-inflammatory helps prevent inflammation of the nerves of the menages, the connective tissue covering the brain, which is where you feel head pain.

Lighten Up: Fighting Tension Headaches

Tension headaches are the crabgrass of headaches, the most common kind of throbbing pain. This headache comes from all directions. It may be prompted by tight head and neck muscles caused by poor posture or straining over the wheel of your car for hours. Or it may be brought about by anxiety or stress over work or an argument with your spouse. Danish scientists looking at headache patterns among four thousand people found that tension headaches were usually set off by stress, mental tension, and tiredness. A tension headache frequently begins after you have been looking down or bending your neck for a long time, and doctors have found that people with relatively heavy heads and unstable neck bones are more likely to get tension headaches.

Hitting Back: Treatment

Of course, there are many headache medications available. For years, the standard medication for migraines has been ergotamine, which helps contract blood vessels. Antidepressants, and beta-blocker and calcium channel blocker drugs, which are normally used to treat high blood pressure and coronary artery disease, also work for some headache victims. The newest drug, sumitriptan (trade name Imitrex), adjusts the balance of serotonin in the brain. Available in tablet form and by injection, it is remarkably effective with migraines, even once the pain has set in. However, it's not recommended for people with high blood pressure or heart disease.

Sometimes caffeine helps because it constricts blood vessels that may be swollen. A cup of coffee, a Coke, or another soft drink containing caffeine may be just the thing to wash away a headache. For some people, caffeine withdrawal can generate a mean migraine. People who consume a certain amount of caffeine every day can suffer a blistering headache if they suddenly halt their caffeine consumption for even a few days. This kind of headache is combated by evening out your caffeine intake.

Some people swear by the herb feverfew. A feathery plant that belongs to the daisy family, feverfew is used by migraine sufferers as a headache preventative. Its active ingredient is thought to act like an anti-inflammatory and to adjust serotonin levels. In a couple of studies in England, migraine victims taking capsules filled with freeze-dried feverfew daily experienced fewer and much less painful headaches than study members who took a placebo.

Lots of people, myself included, use herbal or over-the-counter pain medications sparingly. One practical reason is the rebound phenomenon, which happens to people who regularly use headache painkillers. If you take pain pills more than three times a week, your body loses its ability to respond, and the headaches get increasingly worse. Aspirin, anti-inflammatories, acetaminophen, antihistamines, and muscle relaxants work well for lots of people, but if your headaches are a regular firestorm, you need to counterattack. Here's what I do to head off brain-draining pain:

- Temperature adjustment. My first reaction to creeping headache pain is either to chill, numb, and reduce swollen nerves or to warm and relax spastic muscles. A tension headache usually gets the cold treatment—a small, homemade ice pack held around the painful area, usually my upper neck, top or side of my head, or my eyes. Eye masks (plastic, gel-filled masks available in drugstores) can be frozen and worn when you get a killer tension headache. I apply ice for up to twenty minutes and reapply it once an hour if the pain persists. I seek out heat when I can feel that the pain is coming from taut, strained muscles in my upper back, neck, or eyes. A heating pad is my first choice, but if none is available, I use a warm washcloth. If the tension feels like it's enveloping me, I will try to find a steam room or take a warm shower, positioning my head so that the soothing water massages the trouble spots.
- Muscle shake-out. The strain of concentrating on paperwork or maintaining a forced posture for a long period of time may

push me toward a headache. This type of pain is so common that I routinely stretch throughout the day, even without prompting from head pain. I stretch my head and neck by rotating my head in a 360-degree motion five or six times, and then gently use my hand to stretch my head first over my left shoulder, then over my right shoulder. I may try to stretch my chin far down on my chest or lay my head back as far as it will go. When I return to whatever I was doing, I am careful about my posture and consciously use my abdominal muscles to sit up straight. No slouching or tilting or crooked spine allowed!

- Ease the eyes. Some days, I feel like my eyes are constantly straining. Part of the problem is creeping farsightedness, which

TAKE ACTION

Finding Your Headache Triggers

Doctors ask these questions about recent behavior to help headache sufferers pinpoint what started their pain and learn what to avoid:

1. Have you skipped a meal?
2. Have you eaten a meal with nitrites (cured meat, hot dogs), tyramine (aged cheese), monosodium glutamate (processed foods, Chinese food), or phenylethylamine (chocolate)?
3. Have you spent a lot of time in the sun or exposed to bright light?
4. If a woman, are you going through hormonal changes from your period, pregnancy, menopause, or birth control pills?
5. Are you missing sleep or sleeping too much?
6. Have you just completed a stressful experience and feel some letdown?
7. Have you physically strained lately; for instance, put in a long day of gardening or driven nonstop for many hours?
8. Have you spent time in a closed room with strong odors, like heavy perfume or gasoline fumes?

happens to everyone sometime after age forty, and can be aggravated by poor lighting, staring at a computer screen, and hard-to-read print. To prevent my eyes from tiring, I have invested in good lighting. Around the computer screen, the light is bright and diffused with no glare. In reading areas, I use strong halogens. My final line of defense is darkness. If I feel eyestrain coming on, I'll find a dark room, sit quietly for five or ten minutes with my eyes closed, and gently massage the orbicularis muscle that encircles my eyes.

- Exercise for relief. Aerobic activity helps me defeat a headache. It delivers more oxygen to the brain, pumps up the amount of pain-fighting endorphins in circulation, and takes my mind away from stressful thoughts. Twenty minutes of sit-ups, StairMaster, brisk walking, or vigorous stretching exercises turn my mind toward moving my muscles and away from headache pain.

When to See a Doctor

When migraines become chronic, attacking at least twice a month and disrupting your daily life, you should seek professional help. Another sign of a serious condition is headache pain that gets worse over time with accompanying changes in your memory, behavior, or vision. Your general practitioner may well send you to a neurologist

TUMOR WORRY

In my first year of medical school, I worried that the smallest headache twinge signaled a tumor. I could have saved myself some anxiety if I had known that brain tumors are rare and the first signs are usually not headaches but dizziness, blackouts, vomiting, problems with vision, and/or seizures. Only a very advanced tumor causes a headache, which can feel like a head squeeze or a sharp pain in one area.

for a battery of tests to rule out brain disease. Once this has been eliminated, treatment may consist of medication and/or some type of behavioral modification aimed at your headache triggers. Your doctor may also ask you to keep a "headache diary" in which you record the time, duration, severity, possible dietary or environmental triggers, sleep patterns, physical health and activity at the time, and medications you are taking.

Headache Facts

- More women than men get them.
- Menstrual migraines, which attack before, during, or after a period, afflict more than half the women who get headaches.
- Migraines run in families and are probably genetic.
- Migraines tend to weaken as you get older.
- About 20 percent of headaches are caused by what you eat.
- Drugs that ease tension headaches also work with migraines, and vice versa.
- About a third of the people who have tension headaches also experience the nausea and light sensitivity typical of migraines.
- Skipping a meal can cause a headache because low blood sugar can dilate the blood vessels in the head. Sleeping late can also alter blood sugar and produce a headache.

DON'T IGNORE THAT HEAD BANG

A somewhat hidden danger to the brain is trauma from a fall, an inadvertent head bang, or an accidental blow. A child hitting you with a toy, a hard fall while doing sports, or a fender-bender on the highway can produce a mild traumatic brain injury (TBI) that alters your thought processes and emotions and endangers your physical health. What's scary about TBI is that you may not know it's happened. You may not have lost consciousness, or if you did, only

TAKE ACTION

Guide to Your Headaches

Kind: Allergy
Triggers and symptoms: Pollen, molds, and some foods. Watery eyes and sinus congestion.
Treatment: Antihistamines. If chronic, you may need desensitization shots.

Kind: Arthritis
Triggers and symptoms: Like arthritis in general, it isn't clear what triggers this headache. Pain at back of head and in the neck, which gets worse with movement.
Treatment: Anti-inflammatory drugs and muscle relaxants

Kind: Cluster
Triggers and symptoms: Alcohol or smoking can cause severe pain around or behind an eye. The pain frequently starts during sleep and can cycle on and off for days or weeks. These headaches can occur regularly, even weekly or daily. Most sufferers are twenty-to-thirty-year-old men.

Treatment: Migraine medication (ergotamine), nasal inhalant of anesthetic, oxygen inhaling, lithium

Kind: Common and classic migraine (also called vascular headaches)
Triggers and symptoms: The common migraine strikes quickly with intense throbbing on one side of the head. The classic attacks gradually, sometimes beginning with sensitivity to light. Both can bring nausea, even vomiting. Although thought to have a genetic basis, migraines can be triggered by food, drink, environment, and stress.

Treatment: Over-the-counter and prescription painkillers, feverfew, ice, biofeedback, diet modification

Kind: Hypertension
Triggers and symptoms: Feels like a tight metal band around the head. Caused by high blood pressure (at least 200/100).
Treatment: Medication for blood pressure, diet modification

Kind: Temporomandibular joint (TMJ) headache
Triggers and symptoms: Caused by teeth grinding, jaw clenching, and poorly aligned teeth. The jaw may click when eating or yawning.
Treatment: Biofeedback, relaxation, professional dental attention to correct the bite

Kind: Tension
Triggers and symptoms: The most common type of headache, it comes from straining muscles in the neck, scalp, and head. Usually triggered by daily hassles. Also considered a "muscle contraction" headache. May also be triggered by vascular constriction.
Treatment: Over-the-counter painkillers, relaxation therapy, biofeedback

briefly, and neurological tests and scans after the accident may register normal. However, you may start to behave and feel odd. Your thinking and memory may be fuzzy. You may get headaches more often. Or your personality may show subtle changes; for example, new moodiness or angry outbursts. For some people with TBI, it is years between a "harmless" head jarring and diagnosis and help.

When I was competing in karate tournaments, one of the great concerns was getting hit with a backhand to the temporal area of the

BRAIN INJURIES TURN HEADS

Brain injuries are getting more attention these days, in part because of a new federal law, the Traumatic Brain Injury Act, which officially recognizes traumatic brain injury and authorizes money for research and state grants. One reason behind the act is that more than fifty thousand people die every year in the United States from brain injuries.

head. There are delicate, somewhat weak bones in the temporal region, and a blow to that area could lead to a hemorrhage and fatal bleeding. This is why strikes to the face are banned in many tournaments, or protective headgear is required.

What happens with brain trauma is that neurons on the brain surface that connect each other are stretched or torn and areas of the frontal and temporal lobes are bruised. The effects of the blow or fall depend on exactly which nerves are damaged and later scarred.

Symptoms may show up in the form of headaches, dizziness, double vision, or ringing in the ears. Nausea and a weakened sense of smell, taste, or hearing are also signs. A person's thinking may suffer, especially memory, concentration, attention span, judgment, and abstract logic. Or the injury may damage a person's emotions, and he may become irritable, depressed, or lose his social skills and inhibitions.

To make a firm diagnosis of TBI, a doctor asks whether there was loss of consciousness for as long as thirty minutes, loss of memory of events surrounding a head trauma, or any change in mental condition. The person may be tested according to the Glasgow Coma Scale, which measures the degree of injury.

Treatment for TBI usually focuses on cognitive and psychological therapy. While little may be done for the brain damage, which time has perhaps reduced to scarring, patients need help understanding and learning to cope with mental or emotional impairments. For in-

A BRIEF REFRESHER

I am always on guard against mild mental disturbances that can slow or sidetrack my thinking. Depression, attention deficit disorder, generalized anxiety, and headaches are relatively common ailments that disrupt a person's mental sharpness. Here are ways to protect yourself.

Fight depression. Eat right by taking in more folic acid, vitamin B_6, riboflavin, foods rich in tryptophan, especially complex carbohydrates, and foods rich in omega-3 fatty acids. Eliminate foods that might bring on depression, such as caffeine and sugar. Get at least thirty minutes of sunlight or two hours of bright artifical light a day. Consider taking DLPA or St.-John's-wort.

Counteract attention deficit disorder. To avoid the pitfalls of a short attention span and forgetfulness, create a home filing system for bills and receipts, use write-on calendars for every facet of your daily life, keep notepads around the house and in the car, hang a bulletin board to post reminders and important papers, and maintain a comprehensive appointment book.

Ward off anxiety. Avoid foods that fuel anxiety, especially caffeine, alcohol, some additives, and refined sugar.

Protect against headache. I try to eliminate the causes of most headaches by using heat and cold to reduce swollen nerves or to warm tense muscles, regularly relaxing tense head and neck muscles, giving relief to strained eyes, and doing regular aerobic exercise.

stance, increased irritability is considered the most common personality change in someone with TBI, and unless a patient and his loved ones understand this, relationships may suffer. If a brain trauma is diagnosed, treatment may include medication for migraines, controlling seizures, fever, and brain inflammation; antidepressants; and drugs like methylphenidate (Ritalin) to help concentration.

SELECTED SOURCES

American Psychiatric Association. *Diagnostic and Statistical Manual of Mental Disorders, Fourth Edition (DSM-IV).* Washington, D.C., 1994.

"Depression may have nutritional link." Reuters, March 28, 1997.

Doyne, E. J. "Running versus weight lifting in the treatment of depression." *Journal of Consulting and Clinical Psychology,* 55 (5), 748–54, 1987.

Feifel, D. "Attention-deficit hyperactivity disorder in adults." *Postgraduate Medicine,* 100 (3), 207–18, September 1996.

Gruskin, S. "The trials in surviving brain injury." *USA Today,* January 9, 1997.

Hibbeln, J. R., and Salem, N., Jr. "Dietary polyunsaturated fatty acids and depression: when cholesterol does not satisfy." *American Journal of Clinical Nutrition,* 62, 1–9, 1995.

Johnson, E. S., et al. "Efficacy of feverfew as prophylactic treatment of migraine." *British Medical Journal,* 291 (6495), 569–73, August 31, 1985.

Kiester, E., Jr. "Doctors close in on the mechanisms behind headache." *Smithsonian,* 18 (9), 175, December 1987.

Lark, S. M. *Anxiety and Stress.* Celestial Arts, Berkeley, Calif., 1996.

McDowell, B. "Homeopathic treatment of mild traumatic brain injury." *Alternative and Complementary Therapies,* April–May 1995.

National Institute of Neurological Disorders and Stroke. "Headache: hope through research." National Institutes of Health, Bethesda, Md., May 1997.

Nicoloff, G., and Schwenk, T. "Using exercise to ward off depression." *Physician and Sports Medicine,* 23 (9), September 1995.

Null G., and Feldman, M. "Nutrition and mental illness: sampling of the current scientific literature." *Townsend Letter for Doctors and Patients,* November 1995.

Peatfiled, R. C. "Relationships between food, wine, and beer-precipitated migrainous headaches." *Headache,* 35 (6), 355–57, June 1995.

Prigatano, G. P. "Personality disturbances associated with traumatic brain injury." *Journal of Consulting and Clinical Psychology,* 60 (3), 360–68, 1992.

Sayegy, R., et al. "The effect of a carbohydrate-rich beverage on mood, appetite, and cognitive function in women with premenstrual syndrome." *Obstetrics and Gynecology,* 86, 520–28, 1995.

Thoren, P., et al. "Endorphins and exercise: physiological mechanisms and clinical implications." *Medicine and Science in Sports and Exercise,* 22 (4), 417–28, 1990.

"A type of fat we may need more of." *Tufts University Health & Nutrition Letter,* 15 (1), 4–6, March 1997.

Ulrich, V., et al. "A comparison of tension-type headache in migraineurs and in non-migraineurs: a population-based study." *Pain,* 67 (2–3), 501–6, October 1996.

Werbach, M. R. *Nutritional Influences on Mental Illness: A Sourcebook of Clinical Research.* Third Line Press, Tarzana, Calif., 1991.

Appendix A

GLOSSARY

Acetylcholine is a neurochemical circulating at all nerve-muscle junctions and is the primary carrier of memory. Phosphatidylcholine is the most important nutrient to support production of acetylcholine, along with B vitamins and vitamin C.

Acetyl-l-carnitine enhances energy metabolism, brain function, and the immune system.

ACTH **(adrenocorticotrophic hormone)** is produced in the pituitary gland. It stimulates the outer layer of the adrenal glands to produce cortisol and androgen hormones. Levels of ACTH increase in response to stress, emotion, injury, and infection.

Adrenal cortex is the outer layer of the adrenal gland.

Adrenal extract boosts the body's ability to deal with stresses such as infection, physical challenge, allergens, and sexual stimulation.

Adrenal glands are located at the top of each kidney. The outer part or cortex produces corticosteroids, which regulate blood sugar levels and pH balance, and metabolism. The inner part, the medulla, produces epinephrine, which prepares the body for stress.

Adrenaline (epinephrine) is a hormone that prepares the body for danger or stress.

Aerobic exercise includes swimming, jogging, and cycling, activities during which the rate at which oxygen reaches the muscles keeps pace with the rate at which it is used up.

Allicin is a pungent sulfur-containing compound that becomes beneficial when garlic is minced, crushed, swallowed, or digested. It has been shown to lower cholesterol, blood pressure, and the risk of cancer.

Aluminum is a light metallic element, harmful to the body, that enters the body through ingestion or absorption of antacids, cooking utensils, antiperspirants, and food additives such as potassium alum, which is used to whiten flour.

Alzheimer's disease is a progressive degenerative condition in which the nerve cells of the brain degenerate and the brain substance shrinks. The exact cause is unknown, but it may be linked to heredity or aluminum poisoning.

Amino acids are the building blocks of proteins. The value in eating protein is that it is broken down into its amino acids by hydrochloric acid in the stomach and then by digestive enzymes in the small intestine. There are twenty amino acids that make up the protein in humans: twelve made by the body (nonessential) and eight that must be obtained by diet (essential).

Anaerobic exercise is a brief, high-intensity workout such as sprinting that relies on a series of biochemical reactions to obtain energy from the stores of sugar and fat in muscle.

Androgens are a group of hormones that cause the development of male secondary sex characteristics, including facial hair, deep voice, and increase in muscle mass.

Aneurysms are caused by the ballooning of an artery due to the pressure of blood flowing through a weak area. They can occur anywhere in the body, but most often occur in the brain and aorta.

Antioxidants are substances in vitamins that prevent cellular damage due to oxidation and exposure to unstable molecules called free radicals.

ApoE4 (apolipoproteinE4) is a protein gene that occurs more often in people with Alzheimer's disease than in the general population. The other two forms of the gene, apoE2 and apoE3, may protect against the disease.

Arginine and **ornithine** are amino acids usually prepared and sold in combination. Arginine is the building block needed by the anterior pituitary gland in the production of human growth hormone. Ornithine serves as a reserve supply because it is easily converted to arginine.

Ascorbic acid (vitamin C) is a potent water-soluble antioxidant that appears to be effective in preventing diseases caused by cellular damage from free radicals, e.g., heart disease, cancer, and cataracts. It may be an important factor in strengthening and maintaining the immune system.

Atherosclerosis is a disease of the artery walls in which the inner layer thickens and thus impairs blood flow. It is responsible for more deaths in the United States than any other condition.

Atrophic gastritis is a chronic inflammation of the stomach with atrophy of the mucous membrane.

Axon, or nerve fiber, is the part of a nerve cell that carries electrical impulses between cells.

Basal ganglia are paired nerve cell clusters in the cerebrum that play a vital part in movement, specifically the smoothness of actions and stopping and starting. Degeneration of the basal ganglia is present in those with Parkinson's disease.

Beta-amyloid is a protein found in dense deposits at the center of the neuron plaques that are one of the distinctive tissue formations of Alzheimer's disease.

Beta-carotene is the precursor to vitamin A. It is an antioxidant that functions in neutralizing free radicals. It may help prevent cervical cancer and atherosclerosis. It is an immune system booster and appears to protect against respiratory diseases and environmental pollutants.

Blue-green algae are single-cell aquatic plants that contain trace minerals; may have neurostimulatory effects.

Borage oil contains a linoleic acid that reduces the risk of atherosclerotic heart disease.

Boron is a trace mineral that aids in the synthesis of steroids, particularly estrogens and testosterone. It may help prevent osteoporosis, maintain strong bones, and prevent memory loss.

Branched-chain amino acids (leucine, isoleucine, valine) aid in reversing liver damage due to alcoholism, restore muscle mass to a body recovering from muscle tissue breakdown and fatigue, and may be used as a possible treatment for neurologic disorders.

Calcitonin is a hormone that slows the rate at which bone is broken down, thus decreasing the amount of calcium that is dissolved in the blood.

Calcium is the most plentiful mineral in the body. All but a small percent is found in the bones and teeth and helps maintain their strength. Vitamin D is required for the absorption of calcium. Calcium also functions with magnesium to keep the heart healthy and the electrical rhythm of the heart pulsing regularly. It is also important in the transmission of impulses between nerves throughout the body. Nonanimal, healthy sources of calcium are soybeans, peanuts, walnuts, sunflower seeds, dried beans, and green vegetables.

Carboyhdrates come in two basic forms: complex and simple. Simple carbohydrates, like those gotten from candy, are one, two, or at most three units of sugar linked together in single molecules. Complex carbohydrates, obtained from grains and other whole foods, are hundreds or thousands of sugar units linked together in single molecules.

Centella. *See gotu kola.*

Cerebellum is the second largest part of the brain. It coordinates balance, movement, and posture.

Cerebral cortex is the outer thin layer of the largest part of the brain, the cerebrum. The cerebral cortex is the gray matter, the site of conscious behavior, and protects the white matter, which is the inner fiber network of the deeper brain centers, the hippocampus and the limbic system.

Cerebral infarct is a loss of oxygen to the brain and can produce a stroke.

Cerebrovascular disease is any disease affecting an artery supplying blood to the brain.

Cerebrum is the largest part of the brain.

Choline is a water-soluble compound and a member of the vitamin B complex. It is essential for neurotransmitter production, aids in maintaining cell membranes, may slow down memory loss, and helps learning ability.

Cholinesterase is an enzyme that acts on the breakdown of various cholines, including acetylcholine. It occurs mostly in blood plasma, the liver, and pancreas.

Chromium picolinate is a mineral that protects the pancreas. Along with insulin, it is necessary to the breakdown of sugar and the metabolism of fat. It may help to increase muscle mass and prevent heart disease and diabetes.

Chromosomes are threadlike structures in the nucleus of cells that carry the genetic information that directs the growth and functioning of the body.

Circadian rhythm is the cycle in the body that runs approximately twenty-four hours.

Clonidine is a drug used to treat hypertension and migraine headache.

Cobalamin (Vitamin B_{12}) aids in the production of red blood cells and is essential for the normal functioning of the nervous system. It aids in the metabolism of protein and fat.

Cobalt is a mineral that enables vitamin B_{12} to do its job in the construction of red blood cells. It is necessary in very small amounts and must be obtained from foods, as it is not built into supplements.

Copper is a mineral that acts as a catalyst in concert with a broad range of enzymes in chemical reactions throughout the body. It is essential for hemoglobin synthesis and for the conversion of tyrosine into melanin (which protects the skin from sunburn). It is essential for the utilization of vitamin C and so has a strong influence on the health of the elastic tissues of the body such as ligaments and tendons. Copper is so abundant in nature that it is difficult to become deficient in this mineral. It is found in beans, whole wheat, prunes, leafy vegetables, and in high concentration from use of copper cookware.

Corpus callosum is an area of neurons in the brain at the base of the longitudinal fissure that enables the left and right hemispheres to communicate.

Corticosteroid is a class of hormone made from cholestrol produced by the adrenal glands in response to stress. It controls the metabolism. Both natural and synthetic corticosteroids are used to reduce inflammation; however, they are toxic with long-term use.

Cortisol is a type of corticosteroid made by the body's adrenal glands. It affects the metabolism of glucose, protein, and fats, and regulates the immune system, and influences other body functions. When used as a drug, it is usually called hydrocortisone.

Cortisone is a steroid isolated from the adrenal cortex that acts upon metabolism and influences the nutrition and growth of connective tissues.

Cyanocobalamin, (commonly known as vitamin B_{12}), helps maintain a healthy nervous system and prevents anemia.

Dehydroepiandrosterone (DHEA) is a hormone produced by the adrenal glands. It appears to aid in the regulation and production of steroidal hormones, may help reduce cholesterol levels and body fats, and may help increase muscle mass.

Dendrites are short multiple branches of neurons linked by impulses. They carry electrical signals toward the cell body.

Deprenyl is the trade name for a drug used for Parkinson's disease. It acts as a neuroprotective agent and enhances mental function, mood, and libido.

Dexotroamphetamine is a stronger form of the drug amphetamine.

DL-phenylalanine (DLPA) is an amino acid involved in biochemical processes related to the brain's synthesis of various neurotransmitters. It helps to increase mental alertness, promote sexual arousal, and alleviate chronic pain.

Donepezil is the generic name of the Alzheimer's drug Aricept.

Dopamine is the neurotransmitter that controls physical movement and maintains proper function of the immune system. It also stimulates the pituitary gland to secrete growth hormone. High levels of dopamine improve mood, sex drive, and memory.

Eicosanoids are tiny molecules produced by most cells from certain fats—for example, omega-3 oils—and are powerful regulators of cell functions.

Electroencephalogram (EEG) is a device that records the minute electrical impulses produced by activity in the brain. It is especially helpful in diagnosing epilepsy.

Encephalopathy is any disease or disorder affecting the brain, particularly chronic degenerative conditions.

Endocrine system consists of a number of glands scattered throughout the body that produce and release hormones directly into the bloodstream.

Endorphins are a group of substances found in the nervous system, pancreas, and testes that relieve pain and control the body's response to stress.

Epinephrine *See adrenaline.*

Ergot alkaloids are a type of fungus used to treat migraine headache.

Estrogen is a hormone produced by the pituitary gland that produces the secondary sex characteristics in women, such as breast development, distribution of body fat, and fine body hair.

Fat can be broken down into the saturated, polyunsaturated, and monounsaturated categories. A fat molecule is composed of three fatty acid molecules bound to a glycerol molecule.

Focal dystonia is a repetive movement disorder, such as a person's leg moving up and down when in a sitting position.

Folic acid (folate) is a coenzyme (an enzyme needed in combination with others to act as a catalyst for chemical reactions in the body) needed for forming protein and hemoglobin. It is available from leafy green vegetables, legumes, nuts, whole grains, and brewer's yeast. It is lost in cooking and when stored at room temperature. Your best source is a fresh green garden salad. Unlike the other water-soluble vitamins, folic acid can improve lactation, act as an analgesic for pain, promote healthy, youthful skin, and increase appetite in cases of debilitation.

Free radicals are very reactive molecules formed by normal cell processes or pollution that damage cell components unless stopped by antioxidants.

Ginkgo biloba is an herb that is rich in antioxidants. It may increase the level of dopamine in the brain, improve circulation by aiding the inhibiting plaque deposition in arteries, inhibit coagulation in blood vessels, and improve memory.

Ginseng is an herb that may help improve mental performance. It contains antioxidants that prevent cellular damage from free radicals. It may inhibit the growth of cancer cells, increase and enhance energy, and help the body cope with stress by normalizing body functions.

Glial cells support nerve cells by providing them with nutrients or by attacking invading bacteria.

Glucagon is a hormone manufactured by the pancreas that plays a vital part in monitoring sugar levels in the blood.

Glucocorticoid refers to a group of steroids produced by the adrenal cortex that regulates the body's metabolism of carbohydrate, fat, and protein. They also affect muscle tone, blood pressure, and gas secretion; inhibit inflammation, allergies, and immune responses; and affect the function of the central nervous system.

Glucose is a sugar substance found in the blood that is the source of the body and brain's energy supply.

Glutamine is the precursor of glutamic acid, which serves the brain by neutralizing excess ammonia, thus creating a clearer space for brain activity. Glutamine may improve IQ, alleviate fatigue, depression, and impotence as well as speed healing.

Glutathione peroxidase is an enzyme that has an important role in protecting against free-radical oxidating damage.

Glycine, a nonessential amino acid, aids in the treatment of low pituitary gland function and is useful in the treatment of muscular dystrophy.

Glycocyamine is a derivative of glucose and essential to the maintenance of soft tissue structures such as cartilage, tendons, ligaments, joint fluid, heart valves, and blood vessels.

Gotu kola (centella) is an herb that may fight fatigue, stimulate memory, strengthen and tone blood vessels, and help prevent circulatory problems.

Hippocampus is the area of the brain that controls learning and memory.

Human growth hormone (hGH) is responsible for maintaining the tissues of the body in a state of vitality. It diminishes as you grow older until age sixty, when it is usually absent. Many of the aches and pains of aging are a result of diminishing levels of this hormone.

Hypertension is abnormally high blood pressure, which increases the risk of heart attack or brain hemorrhage.

Hypervolemia is a condition in which an abnormally increased volume of blood is present in the body.

Hypothalamus is an endocrine gland in the brain that coordinates hormone production and influences food intake by sending hunger or satiety impulses and regulates body temperature.

Insulin is derived from the cells of the pancreas and is responsible for facilitating the entry of glucose into the cells. Without a sufficient supply of chromium, insulin cannot do its job.

Iodine is the mineral involved in the enzyme systems that produce thyroxin, the thyroid hormone. Two-thirds of the iodine in your body is concentrated in your thyroid gland. Sufficient iodine promotes a normal metabolic rate, proper growth, normal energy, normal mental acuity, and healthy hair, nails, skin, and teeth.

Iron is a metal that is essential for red blood cell formation and the metabolism of vitamin E. In excess, iron may be a strong catalyst in free-radical production and may aid in the deposition of plaque in blood vessels.

Isoflavones are plant estrogens that are chemically structured like estrogen and have similar effects but are weaker. Two primary isoflavones are in soybeans.

Kava (kavakava) is the root of a South Pacific herb that may help to elevate mood and reduce anxiety and fatigue.

L-arginine is a nonessential amino acid that can stimulate the release of growth hormone. It may be an effective immune enhancer and may help in the nutritional treatment of male infertility.

L-carnitine is an amino acid that transports fatty acids across the mitochondrial membrane in cardiac and skeletal muscles. It strengthens the heart and muscles, and improves stamina and endurance during exercise. It may help slow the progression of Alzheimer's disease and may help burn fat.

Lecithin is a nutritional supplement used to alleviate memory loss and manic-depression; may have antiaging benefits.

L-glutamine is an amino acid that helps control alcohol cravings, energize the mind, inhibit senility, and counteract depression.

Linoleic acid is an essential fatty acid that has been shown to help prevent hardening of the arteries, heart disease, high blood pressure, and multiple sclerosis. It also has a positive effect on sex hormone response, aids in lowering cholesterol levels and is important for healthy skin.

Lipids are fat chains made of fatty acids.

Luteinizing hormone stimulates ovulation and prepares a woman's body for pregnancy. In men, it triggers the testes to produce male sex hormones.

Lymphatics is a circulatory system of vessels distinct from the blood vessel circulatory system that reaches most body areas. This system contains lymph fluid and immune system cells. Lymphatics drain into lymph nodes and, eventually, the bloodstream.

Lysine is an essential amino acid found in food protein that is needed for proper growth, enzyme production, and tissue repair. It may help stimulate the immune system, appears to have antiviral properties, may inhibit herpes virus, aid in fat metabolism, and alleviate some infertility problems.

Manganese is a mineral involved in a great diversity of enzyme systems. It is important to the proper use of biotin, thiamin, and vitamin C. It is important in the production of thyroxin, normal central nervous system function, proper digestion, and sexual function.

Magnesium is a mineral involved in carbohydrate and protein metabolism. It acts as an antagonist to calcium and tends to prevent calcium stones in the kidneys and gallbladder as well as the calcium deposits of arteriosclerosis. Magnesium is also required for proper function of the central nervous system. Alcohol depletes magnesium and this is a problem in alcoholism that can lead to seizures.

Melatonin is a hormone secreted by the brain during sleep. It appears to be vital for the maintenance of normal body rhythms. It may play a role in many other body functions and may have neural antioxidant properties.

Methionine is a sulfur-containing amino acid that protects against cardiovascular disease.

Narcolepsy is a rare condition characterized by sudden uncontrollable sleep and occurs at irregular intervals.

Neurons are the cells that are the basic structural units of the nervous system. They transmit one-way electrochemical messages to and from the brain. Unlike most cells, they cannot divide and cannot be replaced.

Neuropeptide Y is an amino acid peptide. It is a vasodilator believed to help regulate feeding behavior.

Neurotransmitter is a chemical that transmits messages between nerve cells or nerve and muscle cells.

Niacin (vitamin B_3) is a potent vasodilator and may boost the effects of chromium. It enhances energy production and the normal functioning of the nervous system; helps lower cholesterol; appears to promote healthy skin and protects against sun damage; promotes healthy colon function; helps maintain balanced neurochemistry; and provides protection against the development of arteriosclerosis.

Nimodipine is a drug that acts as a calcium channel blocker and is used to treat high blood pressure.

Norepinephrine. *See dopamine.*

Omega-3 fatty acids contain two polyunsaturated fats. They may prevent the formation of blood clots leading to heart attacks and protect against cancer. They are found in fish oils.

Oxytocin is a pituitary hormone that stimulates muscle contractions during birth.

Pancreas is one of the glands of the endocrine system. It controls blood sugar (glucose) by producing insulin, which decreases glucose levels, and glucagon, which increases them. Digestive enzymes are also produced in the pancreas.

Pantothenic acid (vitamin B_5) is a precursor to cortisone in the adrenal gland. It is necessary for the conversion of fat and sugar into energy, although its mechanism of action is not known. It appears to aid in steroid synthesis, aids in energy metabolism, and acts as an antistress and antioxidant vitamin. Also called calcium pantothenate, pantothenol.

Parkinson's disease is a disorder in which brain cells degenerate, affecting muscle control, causing tremors, stiffness, and weakness. The cause is unknown.

Peptide is a compound of two or more amino acids.

Perimenopause is a period of some five years before the onset of menopause when some menopausal symptoms, such as hot flashes and irregular bleeding, occur sporadically.

Pernicious anemia is a chronic progressive disease of older adults thought to result from a defect of the stomach so that vitamin B_{12} cannot be absorbed and levels of red blood cells drop.

Phenylalanine is an amino acid that is used by the body to produce the neurotransmitters norepinephrine and dopamine, which promote alertness. It can reduce hunger, increase sexual interest, improve memory and mental alertness, and alleviate depression.

Pheromones are substances secreted externally by one individual and perceived by another, thus charging sexual and social behavior.

Phosphatidylcholine is a nutrient that is necessary for the production of acetylcholine, which is essential for the proper transmission of nerve impulses. Since the brain cannot manufacture choline, you must get it from diet, from choline manufactured in the liver, or as a nutritional supplement available at health food stores.

Phosphatidylserine is a phospholipid essential for maintaining healthy cell membranes throughout the body, and especially in the brain. The brain normally manufactures sufficient phosphatidylserine; however, with aging and nutrient deficiencies, efficiency of PS utilization may decline. A PS-enriched phospholipid complex made from soy lecithin is sold as a dietary supplement that proved helpful in retarding or even reversing the progression of age-associated memory impairment.

Phosphorus is a mineral widely distributed in the enzyme systems of the body. It is a component of bone. Phosphorus is present as phosphate in many food preservatives such as those in colas.

Pineal gland is a pine-cone-shaped structure in the brain that regulates the body's response to light.

Piracetam is a kind of drug believed to improve thinking and memory.

Pituitary gland is located in the brain and receives instructions from the hypothalamus to release hormones that target other endocrine glands. Human growth hormone is produced in the pituitary, as is thyroid-stimulating hormone.

Potassium is a mineral found primarily inside the cells and is particularly important in glucose metabolism, water and fluid balance, muscle (including heart muscle) action, transmission of impulses along nerves, and in kidney function.

Progesterone is a hormone that aids in placenta function and helps prevent ovulation during pregnancy and lactation.

Prolactin is a hormone that stimulates the production of breast milk.

Proline is a nonessential amino acid that enhances fat metabolism and aids in the production of connective tissue.

Prostaglandins is another, older name for eicosanoids.

Proteins are large molecules made of amino acids, of which there are twenty. Eight of these amino acids are "essential," meaning that they cannot be synthesized in the body even though they are necessary for life. Essential amino acids must be consumed from sources outside the body.

Pyridoxine (vitamin B_6) is necessary for the metabolism of amino acids and aids in the synthesis of nucleic acids and the formation of blood cells. It appears to be an important factor in many cellular reactions.

REM (rapid eye movement) sleep is the period in the human sleep cycle when the brain is most active but the body is still, save for rapid eye movements. This is when we dream. It lasts for ten to sixty minutes.

Riboflavin (B_2) found in organ meats and plant sources such as almonds, whole grains, and green leafy vegetables; is an important supplier of the enzymes of energy production.

Selegiline is the active ingredient in a drug (trade name Deprenyl or Eldepyrl) used to treat Parkinson's disease.

Selenium is a mineral that works with glutathione peroxidase to prevent damage by free radicals. It appears to be involved in the metabolism of eicosanoids and to protect cell membranes from attack by free radicals; it may also protect lipids from oxidation, which helps to prevent cardiovascular disease; aid in the production of thyroid hormones; and protect against environmental pollutants.

Serotonin is the brain's primary "feel good" neurotransmitter, second only in importance to acetylcholine.

Sleep apnea is the condition of cessation of breathing during sleep, for a few seconds or even minutes.

Synapse is the functional membrane-to-membrane contact of one nerve cell with another so that electrical impulses may travel from one cell to another.

Tau is a protein that is the main component of the neurofibrillary tangles of Alzheimer's disease.

Taurine is an amino acid that modulates neurotransmitters. It aids in maintaining clear blood vessels and in stablizing heart rhythm.

Testosterone is the most active androgen, the male sex hormone.

Thiamine (vitamin B_1) is involved in the metabolism of carbohydrates to glucose. It also appears to be necessary for the normal functioning of the nervous system, heart, and muscles, aids in energy production, and helps to alleviate symptoms of stress.

Thyroid gland is located at the base of the throat and controls metabolism, the rate at which the body uses energy.

Thyroxine is a hormone produced in the thyroid gland and is responsible for maintaining a normal metabolic rate in all the cells of the body. It is responsible for the healthy growth of hair, nails, skin, and teeth.

Tocopherol (vitamin E) is a fat-soluble potent antioxidant that works synergistically with selenium. It may reduce the susceptibility of low-density lipoproteins to oxidize, prevent the formation of blood clots, help maintain normal blood glucose levels, and help prevent cancers of the gastrointestinal tract by inhibiting the conversion of nitrates to nitrosamines (carcinogens).

Tryptophan is used by the brain along with niacin (B_6) and magnesium to produce serotonin, a neurotransmitter. Tryptophan can help induce natural sleep, reduce sensitivity to pain, act as an antidepressant, reduce anxiety, and aid in the control of alcoholism.

Tyrosine is an amino acid involved with neurotransmitters. It helps to alleviate depression and stress.

Valerian root is an herb with effective antispasmodic properties and may act as a nerve tonic.

Vanadium is a trace mineral that aids in the regulation of insulin metabolism.

Vasopressin is a hormone released from the pituitary gland that helps to control the body's overall water balance.

Vitamin B_1. *See thiamin.*

Vitamin B_2. *See riboflavin.*

Vitamin B_3. *See niacin.*

Vitamin B_5. *See pantothenic acid.*

Vitamin B_6. *See pyridoxine.*

Vitamin B_{12}. *See cobalamine.*

Vitamin C. *See ascorbic acid.*

Vitamin E. *See tocopherol.*

Zinc is an essential trace mineral and a component of over two hundred enzymes. It may increase the level of T cells in individuals over seventy; be involved in cellular division, growth, and repair; help prevent prostate gland dysfunction in older men; help prevent vision loss due to macular degeneration and cataracts; and stabilize cell membranes against free-radical damage, thereby boosting immunity.

Appendix B

NUTRITIONAL NOOTROPICS

You can find mind-enhancing supplements at nutrition stores, health food stores, and even sporting goods stores. Sometimes the array of offerings can be confusing. The following products contain the kinds of components I look for in a nutritional brain booster.

Cerebro-Gain Longevity Age Erasers
(Bodyonics, 140 Lauman Lane, Hicksville, NY 11801. 800-527-7965)

St.-John's-Wort (Hypericum)
5-HTP (Elemental)
Panax Ginseng (American)
Synephrine
Yerba Mate
Pregnenolone
Ginkgo Biloba
DMAE
DHA
L-Glutamine

SomatoPlus HGH Enhancer
Medical Center Pharmacy (800-723-7455)
Alpha-GPC
Phosphatidylserine
L-Glutamine
L-Arginine
L-Ornithine
L-Lysine
Vinpocetine
Ginkgo Biloba
Pituitary & herbal extracts

Leci-PS®
(Lucas Meyer, Inc. P.O. Box 3218, Decatur, IL 62524. 217-857-3660.)
Raw material manufacturers of Phosphatidylserine and Alpha-G
Phosphatidylcholine.

Appendix C

SPECIAL BRAIN NUTRIENT PROGRAMS

The following is a series of specially designed Super Mind Power Brain Nutrient Programs for specific health conditions you may be experiencing. You should always try to take your supplements with meals and always consult your personal physician before beginning any aggressive nutritional program. The dose variations depend on your body weight, gender, and absorption capacity.

Memory-Enhancing Brain Nutrient Program

Probably the second thing to go (after sexual potency) is one's memory. This can be very frustrating and can result from being overworked, overstressed, or sleep-deprived. However, sometimes it may be an early warning sign of organic disease. Best advice is to arm yourself with supernutrients for peak brain memory function to go with your mind-training memory exercises.

Choline, 50–100 mg/day
Folic Acid, 500–800 mcg/day
Ginkgo Biloba, 50–150 mg/day
Lecithin, 1–2 g/day
Magnesium, 5–10 mg/day
Phosphatidylcholine, 250–500 mg/day

Phosphatidylserine, 300–500 mg/day
B Vitamins (B_1, B_2, B_3, B_6, B_{12}), strong antioxidant formula
Vitamin C, 1–2 g/day
Zinc, 30–50 mg/day

Mental Alertness/Antifatigue Brain Nutrient Program

The brain is like an exercising muscle and requires the right power fuel to keep it alert and humming along on all turbines. The proper ratio, combination, and levels of brain-powering nutrients are key for this. By following this program you may also boost your adrenal and immune system functions.

Glutamine, 1–2 g/day
Tyrosine, 1–2 g/day
Acetyl-L-Carnitine, 50–100 mg/day
Choline, 100–200 mg/day
Deprenyl, 50 mg 3x/week
Ginseng, 200–500 mg/day
Ginkgo Biloba, 50–100 mg/day
Licorice, 50–150 mg/day standardized extract (Do not use if hypertension or depression is existing condition)
Magnesium, 100–500 mg/day in divided doses
Pantothenic Acid, 50 mg/day
Phosphatidylcholine, 50–100 mg/day
Phosphatidylserine, 300–500 mg/day
Vitamin C, 3 g/day in divided doses
Zinc, 30 mg/day

Antistress Brain Nutrient Program

Stress robs the body of amino acids and important nutrients. It is important to have protective levels of critical free-radical scavenging nutrients to protect the brain and keep it at maximum function.

Glutamine, 1–2 g/day
Isoleucine, 1–2 g/day
Leucine, 1–2 g/day

Lysine, 500–1,000 mg/day
Choline, 50–100 mg/day
Coenzyme Q10, 60–180 mg/day
Folic Acid, 800 mcg/day
Garlic, 250–500 mg/day
Ginkgo Biloba, 30–60 mg/day
Ginseng, 3–6 g/day
Inositol, 50–100 mg/day
Magnesium, 5–10 mg/day
Pantothenic Acid, 100–500 mg/day
Phosphatidylcholine, 100–300 g/day
Vitamin A, 5,000 IU/day
Vitamin B_1 (Thiamine), 50–100 mg/day
Vitamin B_2 (Riboflavin), 50–100 mg/day
Vitamin B_3 (Niacin), 50–100 mg/day
Vitamin B_6 (Pyridoxine), 50–100 mg/day
Vitamin B_{12} (Cobalamine), 50–100 mg/day
Vitamin C, 500–2,000 mg/day
Vitamin E, 400–800 IU/day
Zinc, 30 mg/day

Alzheimer's Protection Brain Nutrient Program

There are lots of exciting developments in pharmaceutical research toward a cure for Alzheimer's disease. In the meantime, an aggressive nutritional preventative program is a good first line of defense. Aside from evaluating the use of hormone replacement programs of DHEA, estrogen, and such, some natural nutritional approaches should also be considered.

Acetyl-L-Carnitine, 1–2 g/day on empty stomach
Antioxidants, high-dose complex daily
B Vitamins, high-dose multiple B complex
Choline, 1–4 g/day
Coenzyme Q10, 100–200 mg/day
Ginkgo Biloba, 100–250 mg/day
Lipoic Acid, 100–200 mg/day

N-Acetyl-Cysteine, 1 g/day on empty stomach
Phosphatidylserine, 200–300 mg/day

Antidepression Brain Nutrient Program

To keep brain at peak function, depression must be staved off. You want to restore optimum levels of mood-elevating neurotransmitters such as norepinephrine and serotonin.

Glutamine, 1–2 g/day
Glycine, 40 mg
Tyrosine, 1–2 g/day
Tryptophan, 500 mg at bedtime
Gamma-Aminobutyric acid (GABA), 100 mg
Kava, 100 mg at bedtime
Lecithin, 1 g
Phosphatidylserine, 300 mg/day
Inositol, 6–12 mg/day in divided doses
St.-John's-Wort, 300 mg loading dose, then 200 mg/day
Flaxseed, 1 tbsp/day

Appendix D

MEDICAL CENTERS SPECIALIZING IN TREATMENTS FOR COGNITIVE ENHANCEMENT AND ANTI-AGING

Alzheimer's Prevention Foundation
Dharma Singh Khalsa, M.D.
11901 E. Colorado
Tucson, AZ 85749
502-749-8374

Cenegenics
Alan Mintz, M.D.
851 S. Rampart Blvd., Suite 210
Las Vegas, NV 89128
888-YOUNGER

Thierry Hertoghe, M.D.
Avenue de l'Armée 127
1040 Bruxelles, Belgium
011-32-2-736-6868
Fax: 011-32-2-732-5743

Longevity Institute International
Vincent Giampapa, M.D.
89 Valley Rd.
Montclair, NJ 07042
201-783-6868

Optimum Health
Stephen Sinatra, M.D.
483 W. Middle Turnpike, Suite 309
Manchester, CT 06040
860-643-5101

Princeton Associates for Total Health
Eric Braverman, M.D.
212 Commons Way, Building 2
Princeton, NJ 08540
609-921-1842

Binyamin Rothstein, D.O.
2835 Smith Ave., Suite 208
Baltimore, MD 21209
410-484-2121

Appendix E

SUGGESTIONS FOR FURTHER INFORMATION AND SUPPORT

Alzheimer's Disease

Alzheimer's Disease Education and Referral Center
National Institute on Aging
P.O. Box 8250
Silver Spring, MD 20907–8250
800-438-4380
www.cais.com/adear

Alzheimer's Association
919 N. Michigan Ave., Suite 1000
Chicago, IL 60611
800-272-3900
www.alz.org

Attention Deficit Disorder

ADD Warehouse
800-ADD-WARE

ADD/LD Online Resource Center
www4.interaccess.com/add/

Brain Aging and Memory

American Academy of Anti-Aging Medicine
1341 W. Fullerton, Suite 111
Chicago, IL 60614
773-528-4333
www.worldhealth.net

Exercise

National Academy of Sports Medicine
123 Hodencamp Dr., Suite 204
Thousand Oaks, CA 91360
800-656-2739
www.worldhealth.net

Impotence

WWW Impotence Information Page
www.ypn.com/topics/3385.html

Geddings Osbon Sr. Foundation
800-433-4215
www.impotence.org

Menopause

Important Menopause Resources on the Internet
www.meditopia.com/menopause

Menopause News Newsletter
2074 Union St.
San Francisco, CA 94123

Menopause Support Group
7136 West McNab Rd.
Tamarac, FL 33321

Mental Health

National Institute of Mental Health
5600 Fishers Lane, Room 7C-02
Rockville, MD 20857
888-8-ANXIETY
www.nimh.nih.gov

Anxiety Disorders Association of America
1190 Parklawn Dr., Suite 1000
Rockville, MD 20852
301-231-9350

National Alliance for Research on Schizophrenia and Depression
208 LaSalle, Room 1431
Chicago, IL 60604
312-641-1666

American Psychological Association
750 First St. NE
Washington, DC 20002
202-336-5500

Migraines

National Headache Foundation
128 St. James Place, 2nd Floor
Chicago, IL 60614-6399
800-843-2256
www.headaches.org

American Council for Headache Education
875 Kings Highway, Suite 200
Woodbury, NJ 08096-3172
609-384-8760
www.achenet.org

Sleep Disorders

Sleep Medicine Home Page
www.cloud9.net

National Sleep Foundation
729 15th St. NW, 4th Floor
Washington, DC 20005
www.websciences.org/nsf

Narcolepsy Network
P.O. Box 42460
Cincinnati, OH 45242
513-891-3522

Traumatic Brain Injury

Brain Injury Association
1776 Massachusetts Ave. NW, Suite 100
Washington, DC 20036-1904
202-296-6443

Appendix F

KIDS' BRAIN FITNESS

New brain development research is providing clinical insight into what many parents and child-care givers have known for years: (1) proper prenatal care, (2) consistent loving and caring interactions between young children and adults, (3) positive stimulation from the time of birth really do make a difference in children's development for a lifetime.

A recent conference of the Families and Work Institute held at the University of Chicago focused on what has been learned. Participants included professionals from the neurosciences, medicine, education, human services, the media, business, and public policy.

Their findings have been compiled into a document entitled *Rethinking the Brain: New Insights into Early Development,* by the Families and Work Institute.

The following is taken from this work and summarizes its conclusions.

1. Human development hinges on the interplay between nature and nurture.
    - The impact of environmental factors on the young child's brain development is dramatic and specific, not merely influencing the general direction of development but actually affecting how the intricate circuitry of the human brain is "wired."
    - How humans develop and learn depends critically and continually on the interplay between an individual's genetic endowment and the nutrition, surroundings, care, stimulation, and teaching that are provided or withheld.
2. Early care has a decisive and long-lasting effect on how people

develop and learn, how they cope with stress, and how they regulate their emotions.

- Warm and responsive early care helps a baby thrive and plays a vital role in healthy development.
- A child's capacity to control its own emotional state appears to hinge on biological systems shaped by its early expressions and attachments.
- Strong, secure attachment to a nurturing adult can have a protective biological function helping a growing child withstand the ordinary stress of daily life.

3. The human brain has a remarkable capacity to change, but timing is crucial.

- The brain itself can be altered or helped to compensate for problems with appropriately timed intensive intervention. In the first decade of life, the brain's ability to change and compensate is remarkable.
- There are optimal periods of opportunity—"prime times"—during which the brain is particularly efficient at specific types of learning.

4. The brain's plasticity also means that there are times when negative experiences, or the absence of appropriate stimulation, are more likely to have serious and sustained effects.

- Early exposure to nicotine, alcohol, and drugs may have even more harmful and long-lasting effects on young children than was previously suspected.
- These risk factors are frequently associated with or exacerbated by poverty. For children growing up in poverty, economic deprivation affects their nutrition, access to medical care, the safety and predictability of the physical environment, the level of family stress, and the quality and continuity of their daily care.

5. Evidence amassed by neuroscientists and child development experts over the last decade point to the wisdom and efficacy of prevention and early intervention.

- Well-designed programs created to promote healthy cognitive, emotional, and social development can improve the prospects and the quality of life for many children.

- The efficacy of early interventions has been demonstrated and replicated in diverse communities across the nation.

Fascinating studies completed at the University of California at Irvine and the University of Konstanz in Germany demonstrate how classical music (both listening to and learning to play at an early age) develops the brain dendrite connections needed for higher forms of thinking.

Companies are organizing to develop products and services that deliver the necessary information for better early childhood education. One such company, The Academy for Early Childhood Education of Chicago, Illinois, has compiled a remarkable product including a curriculum for learning centers and schools, learning materials, teachers/parent/caregiver training programs, and a lab school that delivers a comprehensive program for accelerated early childhood development. The program has been refined over several years of experimentation and is based upon Montessori's outstanding academic and socialization program and carefully substantiated by current early childhood brain research. It includes a unique integration of select aspects of Howard Gardner's Multiple Intelligences, Glenn Doman's program for neurological stimulation, Italy's Reggio Emilia concepts of emergent curriculum, Stanley Greenspan and Daniel Goleman's work in emotional intelligence. It also incorporates social skills, hemispheric integration techniques and divergent thinking. Of special note is its successful reading program for preschoolers, which has been getting wonderful results. The Academy is currently operating its lab school in conjunction with the Creative Care Children's Center of Barrington, Illinois. Its educational program is called the Heartpath Learning System.

For additional information, contact the Academy for Early Childhood Education (773-528-0091).

The effects of early play [illegible] has been [illegible] and [illegible] in diverse [illegible].

Fascinating studies [illegible] at the University of [illegible] and the University of Konstanz in Germany [illegible] must [illegible] learning to [illegible] needed for higher [illegible].

Community [illegible] the necessary information [illegible] early childhood [illegible] [illegible] The [illegible] [illegible] [illegible] [illegible] [illegible] [illegible] early childhood [illegible]. The program [illegible] over several years [illegible] [illegible] by current early childhood brain research [illegible] [illegible] Stanley Greenspan and Daniel Goleman's [illegible] emotional intelligence [illegible] [illegible] successful reading program for preschoolers which has [illegible] the wonderful results. The Academy is currently [illegible] [illegible].

For additional information contact the Academy [illegible] Education [illegible]

Appendix G

THE AMERICAN ACADEMY OF ANTI-AGING MEDICINE

"The surest way to predict the future is to create the future."

THE FUTURE OF HEALTH CARE

Twelve pioneering clinicians and scientists met in Chicago in August 1992. This meeting was convened to establish a not-for-profit organization addressing the rapid growth in the new science of longevity and anti-aging medicine. The outcome of this meeting was the founding of the American Academy of Anti-Aging Medicine (A4M), which today has over 5,300 members in 44 nations worldwide. The mission: to promote the development and dissemination of medical practices, technologies, pharmaceuticals, and processes that retard, reverse, or suspend deterioration of the human body resulting from the physiology of aging. A4M was founded on the premise that many of the consequences of aging that are considered diseases are biophysical processes that can be altered by medical intervention.

A4M's goals are to actively develop, support, and encourage educational and scientific programs concerned with the advancement of scientific knowledge and the application of anti-aging and brain fitness techniques for the benefit of the community and the common good of all mankind. A4M's goals are to:

1. Facilitate expeditious advances in areas of longevity and brain fitness medicine.
2. Make available to practicing physicians information about the multiple benefits of lifesaving, mind-enhancing, and life-extending technologies.
3. Facilitate the dissemination of biomedically and scientifically proven information in longevity science to physicians, scientists, and the public.
4. Assist in developing therapeutic protocols and innovative diagnostic tools to aid physicians in the implementation of effective longevity treatment.
5. Act as an information center for valid and effective anti-aging medicine protocols.
6. Establish a medical protocol review process in anti-aging medicine.
7. Administer Board Certification programs for the American Board of Anti-Aging Medicine.
8. Develop funding for scientifically sound and innovative research in anti-aging medicine and biomedical technology.

A4M members reside in all fifty states of the United States and in forty-four countries worldwide. Eighty-five percent of its members are physicians and surgeons, with the remaining membership consisting of scientists, researchers, health care providers, educators, and individuals interested in longevity science, brain fitness, and wellness. Members include health care decision-makers from the highest levels of academia and government, with affiliations from prestigious institutions such as Harvard University, Stanford University, the University of California, and the University of Chicago, along with prominent members of the United States Senate, the House of Representatives, and administrators and researchers at the National Institutes of Health, the National Institute of Aging, and the U.S. Department of Defense.

Because of the diversity of its membership, A4M is making a significant impact on a wide range of medical arenas simultaneously. Shared accurate information about the prevention, early diagnosis, and treatment of age-related diseases is permitting effective changes in the way medicine is being practiced today. A4M's declaration that "aging is not inevitable" has become the working philosophy of the leaders in medicine for the next millennium.

For more information, contact:

American Academy of Anti-Aging Medicine
1341 W. Fullerton, Suite 111
Chicago, IL 60614
773-528-4333
Fax: 773-528-5390
Web site: *http://www.worldhealth.net*

WORLD HEALTH NETWORK HTTP://WWW.WORLDHEALTH.NET

World Health Network (WHN) is the primary Internet resource for breakthrough, life-enhancing information and products that promote health, longevity, well-being, and proper nutrition.

Co-developed by the American Academy of Anti-Aging Medicine (A4M), the leading association for resources in anti-aging and longevity, WHN is a forum for addressing key issues in the enhancement of people's lives.

A4M recognized the value of the Internet as the perfect medium for distributing health-related information to the world. WHN envisioned an area of the Internet where people could easily access information about longevity, anti-aging, and similar topics. And the World Health Network was born.

WHN is dedicated to making a difference for all of mankind. Combining the discoveries and resources of A4M and the technology of the World Wide Web, WHN delivers breakthrough information on topics such as human growth hormone, DHEA, melatonin, estrogen, and testosterone; provides the opportunity to learn about traditional and alternative health care practices, practitioners, and associations; offers authors the chance to contribute their works for public display and the general public the chance to communicate directly with leaders in the health and longevity field; and much more.

The World Health Net is now hosting:

- Anti-Aging Medical Therapeutics
- *Advances in Anti-Aging Medicine*
- The Science of Anti-Aging Medicine
- *Stopping the Clock,* clinical updates
- National Academy of Sports Medicine
- American Longevity Research Institute
- High Technology Research Institute
- American Board of Anti-Aging Medicine
- Mothernature.com

For more information, contact:

American Academy of Anti-Aging Medicine
1341 W. Fullerton, Suite 111
Chicago, IL 60614
773-528-4333
Fax: 773-528-5390
Web site: *http://www.worldhealth.net*

Appendix H

NEW BRAIN FITNESS RESEARCH

ALPHA-GLYCERYLPHOSPHORYLCHOLINE (Alpha-GPC)

An interesting natural compound developed by the European pharmaceutical community, Alpha-GPC has been well researched as a brain-enhancing nutrient. It has served as a stand-alone ingredient and in combination formulas. Research in animal and human models have shown increases in HGH (Human Growth Hormone) levels, and the compound seems also to serve as an acetylcholine precursor, improving neuromuscular enervation and stimulation of cognitive function. Increases of choline blood and tissue levels enhance liver lipotrophic function and support the cell membrane phospholipid synthesis.

The compound has been shown to increase GH responses to GHRH (Growth Hormone Releasing Hormone) in young and elderly subjects. In multicenter clinical trials, Alpha-GPC provided high levels of choline for the nerve cells of the brain and protected cell walls tested in 2044 patients suffering from recent stroke or transient ischemic attacks.

HGH secretion is a complex series of neurotransmitter hormonal interactions within our body. The hormone Growth Hormone Releasing Factor (GHRF) is released from the hypothalamus, which in turn stimulates HGH secretion from the pituitary. On the other hand, the hypothalamic hormone Somatostatin inhibits HGH release. When our body is under increased stress, such as that which occurs with aging, there is a widened gap between "beneficial" (stimulatory GHRF) and "bad" (inhibitory Somatostatin) activity on HGH secretion. The end result typically appears to be enhanced Somatostatin action and decreased HGH release, which is not good for anti-aging purposes, or for clear, sharp, brain fitness.

This imbalance occurs due to the concurrent decrease in levels of the neurotransmitter acetylcholine, that has been shown to play an important role in the control of HGH secretion from the pituitary. Compounds that decrease acetylcholine activity diminish HGH release, while those that increase acetylcholine transmission, enhance the stimulatory effect of GHRF, thus increasing HGH release.

This compound shows promise as not only a HGH secretagogue, but as a brain enhancement compound that may combat some of the neurologic deficits noted with aging brains such as memory loss, and decreased concentration and alertness. This may also be of significant impact with pre-Alzheimer's patients in the mild Stage 1 of the disease.

SELECTED SOURCES

Barbagallo, Sangiorgi G., et al. "alpha-Glycerophosphocholine in the mental recovery of cerebral ischemic attacks. An Italian multicenter clinical trial." *Ann. NY Academy Sci.*, 717, 253–69, June 30, 1994.

Ceda, G. P., et al. "alpha-Glycerylphosphorylcholine administration increases the GH responses to GHRH of young and elderly subjects." *Hormone Metabolic Research*, 24 (3), 119–21, March 1992.

Ceda, G. P., et al. "Androgens do not regulate the growth hormone response to GHRH in elderly men." *Hormone Metabolic Research*, 21 (12), 695–96, December 1989.

Chamberlain, S., et al. "Effect of lecithin on disability and plasma free-choline levels in Friedreich's ataxia." *J. Neurol. Neurosurg. Psychiatry*, 43 (9), 843–45, September 1980.

Das, I., et al. "Determination of free choline in plasma and erythrocyte samples and choline derived from membrane phosphatidylcholine by a chemiluminescence method." *Anal. Biochem.*, 152 (1), 178–82, January 1986.

Greenwald, B. S., et al. "Red blood cell choline. I: Choline in Alzheimer's disease." *Biol. Psychiatry*, 20 (4), 367–74, April 1985.

Rennick, B., et al. "Choline loss during hemodialysis: homeostatic control of plasma choline concentrations." *Kidney Int.*, 10 (4), 329–35, October 1976.

Schettini, G., et al. "Molecular mechanisms mediating the effects of L-alpha-glycerylphosphorylcholine, a new cognition-enhancing drug, on behavioral and biochemical parameters in young and aged rats." *Pharmacol. Biochem. Behav.*, 43 (1), 139–51, September 1992.

Trabucchi, M., et al. "Changes in the interaction between CNS cholinergic and dopaminergic neurons induced by L-alpha-glycerylphosphorylcholine, a cholinomimetic drug." *Farmaco*, 41 (4), 325–34, April 1986.

Zeisel, S. H., et al. "Choline, an essential nutrient for humans." *FASEB J.*, 5 (7), 2093–98, April 1991.

DEMENTIAS AND AGE-RELATED COGNITIVE DECLINE: RISK FACTORS AND MANAGEMENT WITH PS (PHOSPHATIDYLSERINE)

(contributed by: Parris M. Kidd, Ph.D.)

Severe, disabling memory loss and related symptoms of cognitive degeneration have become epidemic in North America. The main diagnoses include Vascular Dementia (VD) and Alzheimer's Disease (AD), which have a great degree of overlap, and Age-Related Cognitive Decline (ARCD). The prevalence of diagnosable dementia in North America is 12–20 percent in subjects sixty-five years and older,[1] and some experts have estimated that Alzheimer's will strike one in two of all persons who live to age eighty-five.[2] Alzheimer's is now the third-highest cause of death in the United States, after cardiovascular disease and cancer, but in a majority of the younger population memory loss becomes measurable as early as age forty-five to fifty.[2,3] The condition Age Related Cognitive Decline was developed to classify individuals aged fifty and over who are healthy but are at the lowest levels of cognitive performance in comparison with the age-matched general population.[3] Over the remainder of their life span such individuals can lose as much as 50 percent of their ability to perform cognitive tasks. Those in the lowest fifth percentile may be at increased risk for dementia.[3]

Many factors may increase the risk of abnormal memory loss linked to aging. Genetic factors and especially high apolipoprotein E4 load undoubtedly can increase susceptibility to AD. Major exogenous influences likely to interact with the genetic and other endogenous susceptibilities to dementia include previous head trauma, alcohol abuse, pro-inflammatory agents, and pharmaceutical side effects.[4] As much as 10 percent of all apparent Alzheimer's cases may be misdiagnoses of pharmaceutical-induced dementias.[5] These are often reversible, at least to some degree. The profitability of dementia risk from aluminum antiperspirant use continues to be hotly debated in the literature.[6]

Depression often precedes Alzheimer's and may be a risk factor for the severe memory loss that is characteristic of the disease. Brain tissue, with its high metabolic rate and high content of polyunsaturated lipids, is particularly susceptible to peroxidative toxic attack. Environmental pollutants are implicated in the causation of Parkinson's disease, which is itself a risk factor for dementia. This plethora of risk factors is consistent with the necessity of an integrative strategy for the clinical management of dementia, pre-dementia, and ARCD.[3,7,8] No one nutrient, herbal preparation, or pharmaceutical will cure memory loss, but to date the single agent proven most consistently effective is phosphatidylserine.

Phosphatidylserine (PS) has been validated for its benefits to memory and other cognitive functions from eleven double-blind trials conducted in Europe and the USA.[8] Seven other double-blind trials and a total sixty-plus human studies affirm its global benefits for human brain functions. The Leci-PS® phosphatidylserine prepared from soy is safer for human intake than PS prepared from bovine brain, and clinically is just as effective.[3] PS is a key building block for membranes, the dynamic structures upon which most life processes occur. The membrane systems of the nerve cells make up the synaptic connections of the brain circuits and facilitate the production, release, and action of all the brain's chemical transmitters. PS is essential to the integrity, renewal, and functional adaptability of these key synaptic membranes, and is utilized within the mitochondrial membranes to facilitate energy generation for the nerve cells.[8]

PS is clinically effective against a variety of cognitive deficits. Under double-blind conditions it benefits the lowest-functioning ARCD subjects and early-stage dementia patients.[3,7,8] Within this continuous "window" of dementia progression, PS improves memory, learning, concentration, and sociability. ARCD subjects experience recovery of as much as twelve years' worth of recall function.[3] In non-demented, aged subjects PS improves mood, anxiety, and overall hypothalamic-pituitary-adrenal integration.[8] In young, healthy athletes subjected to exhaustive exercise regimens, PS reduces stress hormone production while controlling muscle soreness and other symptoms of "overtraining."[9] PS even benefits higher mental functions in children: open-label case studies by United States physicians indicate PS markedly improves the symptoms of attention deficit. PS is proven safe and well tolerated, consistent with its metabolic status as an orthomolecule.[8]

Effective PS intakes range from 100 mg per day (for smaller children and for maintenance in healthy adults), through 300 mg per day for clinical memory loss, to 600 mg per day for mood enhancement.[3,8] The wide range of documented clinical benefits from PS and its capacity to increase glucose utilization across the entire brain, combined with its capacity to conserve brain circuitry in animal models, suggest PS has a profoundly revitalizing, trophic action in the human brain. With the recent revelations that the mature human brain can add new nerve cells, PS could be the core of an integrative strategy for the restoration of function in victims of stroke, other CNS injury, or degenerative brain disease.[10]

References

1. Hendrie, H. C. "Epidemiology of dementia and Alzheimer's disease." *Am. J. Ger. Psychiatry,* 6 (2, Supplement 1), S3–18, 1998.
2. Khalsa, D. S. *Brain Longevity.* Warner Books, New York, 1997.
3. Crook, T. H. "Treatment of age-related cognitive decline: effects of phosphatidylserine." Klatz, R. M., and Goldman, R., eds. *Anti-Aging Medical Therapeutics,* 2. Health Quest Publications, Chicago, 1998.
4. Skoog, I. "Status of risk factors for vascular dementia." *Neuroepidemiology* 17, 2–9, 1998; Small, G. W. "The pathogenesis of Alzheimer's disease." *J. Clin. Psychiatry,* 59 (Supplement 9), 7–14, 1998.
5. Wolfe, S. M., and Hope, R. E. *Worst Pills, Best Pills II.* Public Citizen Health Research Group, Washington, D.C., 1993.
6. Forbes, W. F., Hill, G. B., and Munoz, D. G. "Is exposure to aluminum a risk factor for the development of Alzheimer's disease? (Comments)." *Archs. Neurol.,* 55, 737–39, 740–41, 742, 1998.
7. Crook, T. H., and Adderly, B. *The Memory Cure.* Simon & Schuster, New York, 1998.

8. Kidd, P. M. *PhosphatidylSerine, Number One Brain Booster.* Keats Publishing, New Canaan, Conn., 1998.
9. Burke, E. R., and Fahey, T. D. *PhosphatidylSerine: Promise for Athletic Performance.* Keats Publishing, New Canaan, Conn., 1998.
10. Klinkhammer, P., et al. "Effect of phosphatidylserine on cerebral glucose metabolism in Alzheimer's Disease." *Cognitive Deterioration* 1, 197–201, 1990; Nunzi, M. G., et al. "Dendritic spine loss in hippocampus of aged rats. Effect of brain phosphatidylserine administration." *Neurobiol. Aging,* 8, 501–10, 1987.

SPHERONS AND THE CAUSE OF ALZHEIMER'S DISEASE

Spherons are small balls of protein found in neurons of every human brain after the age of one. They steadily grow in size (but not in number) from age one, when they are about one to two microns in diameter, until by age eighty they reach a size of eight to ten microns. It is believed that beginning around age sixty, they begin to fall out of the protective dendrites that have safely housed them for all those years and burst, becoming the senile plaques that are the defining characteristic of Alzheimer's disease.

Discovered, described, and isolated by Dr. Paul Averback in the 1970s and '80s, spherons represent the first new, normal brain entity found in over a hundred years. Although they are readily visible under the light microscope, spherons had escaped the scrutiny and description of the great neuroanatomists and neuropathologists who charted the anatomy and histology of the brain in the nineteenth century. This was probably because spherons do not stain with the usual stains used to examine brain tissue, and, even if properly stained, look for all the world like a stray blood cell, with their circular profile and red staining, rather than like a part of normal brain structure.

During the course of his work to characterize spherons, Dr. Averback noticed a puzzling feature. He had assumed the number of spherons would steadily increase over time as the same biological processes that gave rise to them in infant brains would presumably continue to operate as the person grew older. Instead, he found the opposite: the number of spherons stayed constant until around age sixty-five, when their number began to drop. The drop was most noticeable in the brains of elderly patients with Alzheimer's disease.

The distribution of spherons in the brain was also unusual. They were sparsely and randomly distributed through the sections of brain tissue he observed, unlike most other cellular features in the brain, which have a distinct order and pattern to their occurrences. The only other features of a similar size and distribution were the senile plaques characteristic of Alzheimer's disease. Examination of brains of patients with Alzheimer's revealed that in those brains spherons were very difficult to find; instead, in the same areas of the brain where the spherons once were, now were senile plaques.

Counting the numbers of spherons and senile plaques in normal brain tissue and that of patients with Alzheimer's disease led to the discovery that the total number of spherons and senile plaques remained constant: the decline in the number of spherons found in the brains with Alzheimer's disease was offset by a corresponding increase in the number of senile plaques. Dr. Averback's conclusion was that spherons were the precursors of senile plaques and hence the cause of Alzheimer's disease.

The isolation of individual spherons from brain tissue proved beyond any doubt their existence in all human brains. The subsequent analysis of the proteins contained in spherons provided another link to senile plaques: amyloid proteins, just like those found in abundance in senile plaques, were a major constituent of spherons. Injecting the isolated spherons into rat brain produced the distinctive signs of amyloid protein for the first time in an animal that does not normally have spherons nor suffer from Alzheimer's disease.

All in all, the theory that spherons lead to the senile plaques of Alzheimer's disease satisfies some twenty criteria of validity in explaining many of the characteristics of senile plaques and Alzheimer's. It is thought that the bursting of spherons sets off a cascade of neural damage that in turn leads to the release of more spherons and the death of still more nerve cells, until the destruction begins to manifest itself in the first signs of the cognitive decline and dementia of Alzheimer's.

Spherons offer more than a theory of the cause of Alzheimer's disease; they also offer the hope for the first effective treatments of this dread illness. Experimental drugs have been found that stop the conversion of the burst spheron into the massive area of destruction associated with a senile plaque. Instead the burst spheron remains relatively intact and able to be removed from the tissue by the body's normal housekeeping processes before it can

become a deadly plaque. The early results look promising, but full-scale trials with these drugs on patients with Alzheimer's have not yet started.

THE AD7C™ TEST

The AD7C™ Test measures the level of Neural Thread Protein (NTP) which is elevated early in Alzheimer's disease as reported both in the peer-reviewed literature [(1–9)] and at scientific conferences.[10–19] Researchers at the Massachusetts General Hospital led by Suzanne de la Monte and Jack Wands first found NTP in the brains of patients with AD in large amounts associated with one of the hallmarks of the disease, neurofibrillary tangles. There is evidence that NTP promotes neuritic growth and sprouting,[1,20] and accordingly may be the body's response to the neurodegeneration that occurs with AD. Subsequent research led to the characterization of the protein,[1,20–23] and an immunoassay was developed to detect its presence not only in brain tissue[1,4,5,7] but also in CSF[1] and urine.[3]

For the urinary version of the test, a first-morning, midstream urine sample of 50 to 100 ml is required. A reading of more than 1.5 ng/ml in urine or more than 2.0 ng/ml in CSF is strongly indicative of AD. Based on ten out of ten independent coded double-blind clinical studies, the AD7C™ Test has been proven to be a highly sensitive and specific test for AD. Based on studies using postmortem-verified cases reported in the literature, the AD7C™ Test in CSF had a sensitivity of 87 percent and a specificity of 90 percent;[1,3] in urine, it is 80–85 percent sensitive and over 90 percent specific.[3]

Its accuracy compares favorably with other standard tests, such as routine urinalysis for urinary tract infection[26] or PSA for prostate cancer. Even the gold standard for the diagnosis of AD—postmortem histopathologic examination of the brain by a certified specialist—is only between 84 percent to 92 percent reliable, based on comparisons between postmortem diagnoses by different specialists.[27] There is no other antemortem biomarker for AD that has the accuracy, sensitivity, or specificity of the AD7C™ Test.

From a clinical standpoint, the AD7C™ Test is a valuable aid to a physician because it is an early[1,2,4] and accurate marker of AD. Previously, the diagnosis of AD was one of exclusion, and typically took on the order of three years[28] from the time initial symptoms were first noticed until a diagnosis was reached. This exclusionary process was often time-consuming,

expensive, and frustrating to the patient and his or her family, who faced the prospect of making difficult social, economic, and legal decisions but without any hard answers to help them. The delays also made effective treatment with the new drugs like Aricept™ and Cognex™ more difficult. Once the dementia had progressed to the stage that a diagnosis of possible or probable AD could be made with confidence, much of the damage may have already become irreparable.

The advent of the urinary version of the AD7C™ Test has dramatically changed this picture. Now a safe, painless, easy, and accurate test is available to aid the physician in the early stages of the investigation of this disease. This allows the physician to focus his or her investigation on other causes of dementia and other cognitive changes, such as adverse drug reactions, depression, and metabolic disorders. This makes for better health care for the patient and avoids unnecessary and expensive tests.

The AD7C™ Test also correlates with the severity of the dementia during the early stages of AD,[1] making it a potential means of tracking the effectiveness of treatment and of better managing the patient's care. It is the only biological marker for AD that correlates with cognitive decline.

The test is meant as an aid to clinical diagnosis and not as a substitute for a physician's clinical judgment based on the relevant medical history and examinations of the patient.

References

1. De la Monte, S. M., et al. "Characterization of the AD7C-NTP cDNA expression in Alzheimer's disease and measurement of a 41-kD protein in cerebrospinal fluid." *J. Clin. Invest.*, 100: 3093–3104, 1997.
2. Ghanbari, H., et al. "Specificity of AD7C-NTP as a Biochemical Marker for Alzheimer's Disease." *Contemp. Neurol.*, 4: 2–6, 1998.
3. Ghanbari, H., et al. "Biochemical Assay for AD7C-NTP in Urine as an Alzheimer's Disease Marker." *J. Clin. Lab. Anal.*, 12: 285–88, 1998.
4. De la Monte, S. M., et al. "Profiles of neuronal thread protein expression in Alzheimer's disease." *J. Neuropath Exp. Neurol.*, 55: 1038–50, 1996.
5. De la Monte, S. M., et al. "Developmental patterns of neuronal thread protein gene expression in Down Syndrome." *J. Neurol. Sci.*, 135: 118–25, 1996.
6. De la Monte, S. M., et al. "Increased levels of neuronal thread protein in cere-

brospinal fluid of patients with Alzheimer's disease." *Ann. Neurol.*, 32: 733–42, 1992.

7. De la Monte, S.,M., et al. "Neuronal thread protein over-expression in brains with Alzheimer's disease lesions." *J. Neurol. Sci.*, 113: 152–64, 1992.
8. De la Monte, S. M., et al. "Enhanced expression of an exocrine pancreatic protein in Alzheimer's disease and the developing human brain." *J. Clin. Invest.*, 86: 1004–13, 1990.
9. Ozturk, M., et al. "Elevated levels of an exocrine pancreatic secretory protein in Alzheimer's disease brain." *Proc. Natl. Acad. Sci. USA*, 86: 419–23, 1989.
10. Kahle, P., et al. *Soc. Neurosci. Abstr.*, 24,1,1222, October 1998.
11. Ghanbari, H., et al. *Soc. Neurosci. Abstr.*, 24,2,1270, October 1998.
12. Ghanbari, H., et al. American Psychiatric Association Institute on Psychiatric Services, Los Angeles, October 3, 1998.
13. Beheshti, I., et al. American Association for Clinical Chemistry, Chicago, August 6, 1998.
14. Kahle, P., et al. Sixth International Conference on AD & Related Disorders, Amsterdam, July 21, 1998.
15. Ghanbari, H., et al. Sixth International Conference on AD & Related Disorders, July 20, 1998.
16. Ghanbari, H., et al. American Psychiatric Association, NR 347, Toronto, June 2, 1998.
17. Ghanbari, H., et al. American Geriatric Society, Seattle, May 9, 1998.
18. Averback, P., et al. American Association for Geriatric Psychiatry, San Diego, March 1998.
19. Ghanbari, H., et al. International Conference of AD & Related Disorders, Osaka, July 29, 1996.
20. De la Monte, S. M., et al. "Modulation of neuronal thread protein expression with neuritic sprouting: relevance to Alzheimer's disease." *J. Neurol. Sci.*, 138: 26–35, 1996.
21. Xu, Y. Y., et al. "Ethanol inhibits insulin receptor substrate-1 tyrosine phosphorylation and insulin-stimulated neuronal thread protein gene expression." *Biochem. J.*, 310: 125–32, 1995.
22. Xu, Y. Y., et al. "Insulin-induced differentiation and modulation of neuronal thread protein expression in primitive neuroectodermal tumor cells is linked to phosphorylation of insulin receptor substrate-1." *J. Mol. Neurosci.*, 6: 91–108, 1995.
23. Xu, Y. Y., et al. "Characterization of thread proteins expressed in neuroectodermal tumors." *Cancer Res.*, 53: 3823–29, 1993.
24. Ghanbari, K., et al. "A Sandwich Enzyme Immunoassay for Measuring AD7C-NTP as an Alzheimer's Disease Marker: AD7C Test." *J. Clin. Lab. Anal.*, 12: 223–26, 1998.

25. Chong, J. K., et al. "Automated microparticle enzyme immunoassay for neural thread protein in cerebrospinal fluid from Alzheimer's disease patients." *J. Clin. Lab. Anal.*, 6: 379–83, 1992.
26. Wallach, J. *Interpretation of Diagnostic Tests*, fifth ed., Little, Brown, Boston, p. 85, 1992.
27. Chui, H. C., et al. "Neuropathologic Diagnosis of Alzheimer's Disease: Interrater Reliability in the Assessment of Senile Plaques and Neurofibrillary Tangles." *Alzheimer's Disease and Associated Disorders*, 7 (1): 48–54, 1993.
28. Jost, B. C., et al. "The natural history of Alzheimer's disease: a brain bank study." *J. Am. Geriatr. Soc.*, 43: 1248–55, 1995.

HUPERZINE A

One of the new and promising compounds available for improving brain function is huperzine A. This herbal compound has recently received a significant amount of attention from biochemists and neurologists but is just now beginning to reach consumers in the form of a dietary supplement. Huperzine A, a purified compound derived from the herb club moss *huperzia serrata,* was indicated in the *Journal of the American Medical Association* as a treatment for memory loss and dementia. By binding to the enzyme that breaks down acetylcholine, purified huperzine A effectively prohibits the breakdown of the neurotransmitter necessary for memory. The standardized, purified form of huperzine A has been clinically proven to enhance focus, memory, and concentration, especially in time of "mental overload," when it is important to be able to perform at peak mental capacity and alertness. However, the whole, crude herb, unlike the purified form, has been shown to exhibit toxicity.

Clinical trials in the United States have shown huperzine A to be safe to use as recommended. With no side effects, huperzine A is a useful alternative to tacrine and donepezil, prescription drugs for Alzheimer's that are both accompanied by unpleasant side effects. Recently, a thirty-patient study found that more than half of the patients showed either an improvement in their mental capacities, or the pace of their mental decline slowed to a halt.

In addition to aiding memory, huperzine A also promises other health benefits. It may help to reduce neuron damage from stroke, epilepsy, and other disorders. Surprisingly, it may also protect you against chemical weapons and pesticides. Scientists at the Walter Reed Army Institute of Research in Washington, D.C., are currently studying the neuroprotective effects of huperzine A in more detail. Additionally, huperzine A appears to improve muscle weakness and alleviate symptoms of glaucoma.

SELECTED SOURCES

1. Ashani, Y., et al. "Mechanism of inhibition of cholinesterases by Huperzine A." *Biochem. Biophys. Res. Commun.*, 184, 719–26, 1992.
2. Cheng, D. H., et al. "Huperzine A, a novel promising acetylcholinesterase inhibitor." *Neuroreport*, 8, 97–101, 1996.
3. Geib, S. J., et al. "Huperzine A—a potent acetylcholinesterase inhibitor of use in the treatment of Alzheimer's disease." *Acta. Cryst.*, C47, 824–27, 1991.
4. Grunwald, J., et al. "Huperzine A as a pretreatment candidate drug against nerve agent toxicity." *Life Sci.*, 54, 991–97, 1994.
5. Hao, X. Y., et al. "Effects of Huperzine A on cholinesterase isozymes in plasma of dogs and mice and dogs." *Acta. Pharmacologica Sinica*, 9, 312–16, 1988.
6. Kozikowski, A. P., et al. "Synthesis of Huperzine A and its analogues and their anti-cholinesterase activity." *J. Org. Chem.*, 56 (15): 4636–45, 1991.
7. Laganiere, S., et al. "Acute and chronic studies with the acetylcholinesterase Huperzine A: Effect on central nervous system cholinergic parameters." *Neuropharmacology*, 30, 763–68, 1991.
8. Raves, M. L., et al. "Structure of acetylcholinesterase complexed with the nootropic alkaloid, (-)–huperzine A." *Nature Structural Biology*, 4 (1): 5–63, 1997.
9. Skolnick, A. A. "Old Chinese herbal medicine used for fever yields possible new Alzheimer's Disease Therapy." *JAMA*, 277 (10): 776, March 1997.
10. Tang, X. C., et al. "Cognition improvement by oral Huperzine A: A Novel acetylcholinesterase inhibitor." *Alzheimer's Therapy: Therapeutic Strategies*. Giacobini, E., and Becker, R., eds. Birkhauser Boston, 113–19, 1994.
11. Xu, S. S., et al. "Efficacy of tablet Huperzine A on memory, cognition and behavior in Alzheimer's disease." *Acta. Pharmacologic Sinica*, 16, 391–95, 1995.

INDEX

Acetaminophen, 279
Acetyl-l-carnitine (ALC), 41, 67, 194, 217
Acetylcholine, 58, 62, 76, 122, 193, 208–9, 215, 216
ACTH. *See* Adrenocorticotropic hormone (ACTH)
ADD. *See* Attention deficit disorder (ADD)
Adrenaline, 143, 167, 178
Adrenocorticotropic hormone (ACTH), 143, 161
Advil, 206
Age/aging, 7, 10–15, 52–55
  Alzheimer's and, 193–94
  hGH and, 100–1, 102, 119
  melatonin and, 128, 129
  sleep and, 96, 98–99, 118–20, 128
  stress and, 155–58, 179, 194
Albert, Marilyn, 20–21
ALC. *See* Acetyl-l-carnitine (ALC)
Alcohol, 83, 84, 89, 171, 179, 196, 238, 245, 251, 253, 274
  headaches and, 276, 277, 283
  sleep and, 97, 104, 106, 108, 127
Aluminum, 84, 193, 197–99, 260
Alzheimer's disease, 6, 41, 54, 59, 85, 166, 185–225
  depression vs., 260
  drugs for, 86, 87, 193–94, 195, 206–13, 216–23
  piracetam and, 66
Amino acids, 57, 76, 126, 219–20, 249, 262, 274
  stress and, 141, 165, 169, 171, 180
Amitriptyline, 271
Ampakine, 86, 220, 222
Ampalex, 86 , 220, 222
Amphetamines, 271
Anacin, 107
Analgesics, 84, 220
Androgen, 72
Antagonic Stress, 222
Antiarrhythmics, 220
Antibiotics, 84, 157, 220
Anticonvulsants, 220
Antidepressants, 84, 220, 251, 254, 261, 266, 271
  for brain trauma, 286
  exercise as, 268
  for headaches, 278

Antihistamines, 129–30, 220, 279
Antihypertensives, 84, 220
Anti-inflammatories, 83, 84, 195, 206–7, 279
Antioxidants, 42, 88, 194, 203, 204, 205–6, 216, 221, 275
sex life and, 249, 251
stress and, 144, 168
Antiparkinsonian drugs, 220
Antistress compounds, 222
Anxiety, 273–76, 286
Arginine, 76
Aricept, 215
Art, 3, 34, 35
Ascorbic acid, 62–63, 249–50
Aspirin, 132, 133, 171, 206, 207, 279
Associative learning/memory, 50, 54, 67, 69–70, 81, 90
Asthana, Sanjay, 209
Attention, 146, 258, 285
memory and, 49, 50, 89
Attention deficit disorder (ADD), 268–73, 286

Bengtsson, Bengt-Ake, 75
Benson, Herbert, 154, 161, 172
Benton, David, 62
Bergner, Paul, 170
Berliner, David, 246
Berman, Allison, 35
Beta-amyloid, 191–93, 206
Beta blockers, 107, 278
Beta-carotene, 167–68, 205
Beta-endorphins. *See* Endorphins
Biofeedback, dreaming and, 124
Birth control pills, 261, 280
Body, mind linked to, 1, 174, 227
Bono, Edward de, 27
Booth, Alan, 233
Boron, 59, 60, 90
Brain, 9–11, 21, 39, 48, 66, 71, 79, 156, 163, 192, 231–32, 239–41
electrical reactions in, 50, 82
male vs. female, 228–31, 239–41, 242
plasticity of, 11, 15, 52
tumors of, 281
Brain cells, 53, 82, 84, 144–45, 156, 179, 216
Alzheimer's and, 193–94, 212, 214
Brain chemistry, 50, 51, 57, 84, 193–94, 231–32, 273–74, 277
hGH in, 74, 102
mental disorders and, 258
sleep and, 97, 104, 125
Brain Cooling Device, 9, 22, 24, 28
Brain food, 40, 42, 55–58, 90
Brainpower, 2–8, 10–15
Brain Resuscitation Device, 9, 21, 22
Brain trauma, 9, 281, 284–86
Brain waves, 98, 102–3, 122
Brannon, Linda, 153
Breathing, 26, 78, 89–90
sleep and, 98, 104–8, 132
stress and, 159, 172–80
Bronchodilators, 107
Buckwalter, Galen, 209
Bunching technique, 33

C-PAP, 108
Caffeine, 41, 84, 272–73, 274
depression and, 261, 269
headaches and, 278–79
sleep and, 107, 125, 130
stress and, 166–67, 171, 179
Calcium, 83, 126, 129, 144, 171, 194, 216
Calcium channel blocker, 66–67, 216, 278
Carbamazepine, 220
Carbohydrates, 40, 55, 57, 60, 89, 196, 212, 263, 272
sex life and, 251, 252
sleep and, 97, 125, 126, 127
stress and, 141, 165, 166
Carnitine, 60
Carvacrol, 216
Chamomile, 126, 127
Chinese gung fu, 2, 174
Chocolate, 249, 251, 263, 276, 280
Cholesterol, 168, 203
Choline, 58, 60, 76, 90, 171, 216, 249, 251
Cholinergic system, 76, 85–86, 216
Cholinesterase inhibitors, 193, 215
Circadian rhythms, 98, 106, 119, 128
Citicoline, 58, 60, 86–87
Clonidine, 67, 68, 90, 107
Codeine, 220
Coenzyme Q10, 171
Cognex, 87, 215
"Cognitive cocktail," 41–42

Cognitive exercise, 159, 175, 180
Colgan, Michael, 244
Computers, 7
Concentration, 2–6, 57, 84, 89, 174, 212, 242, 268, 270
  ADD and, 268
  brain trauma and, 285, 286
  muscles and, 26
  sleep and, 96, 118
  sleep apnea and, 108
  stress and, 146, 161
  vasopressin and, 244
Congeners, 277
Copper, 171
Coren, Stanley, 116
Corticosteroids, 143, 220
Corticosterone, 72
Cortisol, 82, 143, 145, 157, 161, 166, 173, 245
  sleep and, 102
  sugar and, 275
Cortisone, 107, 143, 167
Cottman, Carl, 39
Creativity, 2, 3, 6, 17, 19, 27, 29, 35, 214
Crick, Francis, 122–23
Critical thinking, 27
Crook, Thomas, 58
Cross-training, 158
Crystal, Billy, 5
Culture, 16
Cylert, 271

Dabbs, James, 233
Deanol, 67
Decision making, 26, 28, 29, 103, 115, 146
Decongestants, 107
Dehydroepiandrosterone (DHEA), 42, 69, 71–74, 90, 111, 141, 244–45, 253
  Alzheimer's and, 210–11
Dementia, 83, 86, 189, 199–200, 202, 204, 205, 210
Dendrites, 36, 68, 85
DeNiro, Robert, 5
Deprenyl, 206, 249, 251
Depression, 61, 108, 109, 170, 258–68, 286
  ADD vs., 268–73
  brain trauma and, 285
  exercise and, 161
  prolactin and, 243
  stress and, 146
Desipramine, 271
Details, 20, 36, 45–93
Dexedrine, 271
Dextroamphetamine, 271
DHA. *See* Docosahexaenoic acid (DHA)
DHEA. *See* Dehydroepiandrosterone (DHEA)
Diapid, 244
Diazepam, 220
Diet, 89, 132, 154, 203, 234, 238, 250–52, 254, 274–76
  Alzheimer's and, 195–96, 211–12, 221
  stress and, 159, 164–72, 179, 180
Diet pills, 107, 262, 271
Dimethylaminoethanol (DMAE), 130
Diphenhydramine, 220
Discipline, 6, 55, 139, 174
Disease, vitamins and, 60–63
DL-phenylalanine (DLPA), 219, 263, 269
DMAE. *See* Dimethylaminoethanol (DMAE)
Docosahexaenoic acid (DHA), 264
Donepezil, 193, 215, 222
Dopamine, 74, 249
Dream diary, 38
Dreaming, 98, 102–3, 120–24
  memory of, 54, 122, 124
  problem solving and, 104
  vasopressin and, 244
Drinks, 89, 125, 274
Drugs, 8, 107, 261
  Alzheimer's and, 86, 87, 193–94, 195, 206–13, 216–23
  for memory, 49, 64–68, 83, 86–88
  See also Medications
Drug testing, 138, 151–52
Dustman, Robert, 77

Edison, Thomas, 4
Eicosanoids, 264
Eldepryl, 206, 249
Emotional disorders, 257–58
Emotions, 36, 47, 84, 112, 124, 146, 155, 227–55, 276
  Alzheimer's and, 188
  brain trauma and, 285
Empirin, 107

Endorphins, 74, 163, 173, 267
Energy, 6, 56, 102, 103, 143, 144, 168, 179
Engel, Peter, 212
Environment, 197–99, 276
Epinephrine, 143, 145
Ergotamine, 278, 283
ERT. *See* Hormone/estrogen replacement therapy (ERT)
Estrogen, 69, 71–72, 85–86, 90, 236–39, 243, 250, 254, 260
  Alzheimer's and, 207–10, 221
  LHRH and, 242
  SDN and, 231
  sex life and, 250, 251, 252
  sleep and, 110–11, 119
Excedrin, 107

Faith, 6
Farrell, Peter, 163
Fats, 55, 56, 60, 84, 90, 196, 211–12, 250–52
Fatty acids, 56, 83, 264–65, 269, 273
Feist, Jess, 153
Feverfew, 279
Fight-or-flight, 90, 143–44, 275
Fish, 212, 264, 265, 273
Fluoride, 222
Focus, 2, 4, 6, 19, 174, 242
  memory and, 89, 90
Folic acid, 41–42, 60, 261
Food, 261–65, 249–52
  brain, 40, 42, 55–58, 90
  headaches and, 276, 280, 282
  sleep and, 125–26
Food additives, 274
Ford, Harrison, 4
Frye, Cheryl, 72

GABA. *See* Gamma-aminobutyric acid (GABA)
Gable, Dan, 2
Galanthamine, 222
Gamma-aminobutyric acid (GABA), 127, 274
Gardner, Howard, 15–17
Garlic, 55, 60, 88, 90
Gates, Bill, 5
Genes, 7, 187, 209
Genetic engineering, 8
Geula, Changis, 192
Ginkgo biloba, 67, 171, 194, 217, 219
Ginseng, 67, 169–70, 171, 179, 180
Glial cells, 52
Glucagon, 145
Glucocorticoids, 72, 82, 143, 157, 194
Glucose, 41, 42, 56, 60, 76, 82, 194, 209, 263, 275
  stress and, 144, 168
Glutamate, 194
Glutathione, 76
Goal-setting, 175
Gold, Paul, 55–56
Goldberg, Whoopi, 5
Gottschalk, Louis, 104
GPI-1046, 223
Grant, William, 195–96, 211
Greenough, William T., 39
GTS-21, 213

Habits, 37, 50
Hallowell, Edward, 271
Hassles Scale, 153
Hayflick, Leonard, 14, 52
Headaches, 276–82, 283–84, 286
  brain trauma and, 285
  migraine, 277, 278, 279, 281, 282, 283
  tension, 278, 279, 282, 284
Hearing, 228, 241, 242
Herbs, 126–27, 133, 216, 279
  depression and, 265–66
  stress and, 159, 169–70
Hertoghe, Thierry, 68, 69, 208
hGH. *See* Human growth hormone (hGH)
Hobson, Allan, 122
Holmes, Thomas, 152
Hormone therapy, 68–76
Hormone/estrogen replacement therapy (ERT), 70–71, 85–86, 111, 207–10, 243, 254
Hormones, 26, 42, 90, 168
  breathing and, 89–90
  depression and, 260
  emotions and, 227–52
  growth. *See* Human growth hormone (hGH)

headaches and, 276, 280
"love," 246, 249
sex, 228–41
sleep and, 98–102, 107, 110–12, 119, 128
stress. *See* Stress hormones
"youth," 141
Horse balm, 216
Howe, Elias, 123
Human growth hormone (hGH), 69, 74–76, 90, 145, 193
sleep and, 100–2, 112, 119
Huperzine A, 87, 216
Hydrocortisone, 143, 220
Hypericum, 265, 266

I.Q., 10, 15
Ibuprofen, 83, 84, 206, 277
IGF-1. *See* Insulin-like growth factor 1 (IGF-1)
Imagery, 175–76, 181
Imagination, 2, 3, 6
Imipramine, 220, 271
Imitrex, 278
Immune system, 103, 207
stress and, 144, 167, 168
Information (capturing), 37, 29–35, 50, 54, 68–70
Innovation, 20
Inositol, 171
Insomnia, 98–99, 103, 104–12, 118, 119, 128, 170
Insulin, 145, 275
Insulin-like growth factor 1 (IGF-1), 208
"Intellectual profile," 16
Intelligence, 9–43
exercise and. *See* Mental/brain exercise; Physical exercise
food and. *See* Food; Nutrients
hormones and. *See* Hormones
studies in, 10–21
types of, 15–21
Intuitive thinking, 27, 38

Jessel, David, 240
Jet lag, 96–97, 105, 128, 129
Jordan, Michael, 4, 5, 149

Karate, 1, 174, 284–85
Kava, 126, 127, 274
Kawas, Claudia, 209
Khalsa, Dharma, 166
Killer T cells, 103
Klatz, Ronald, 7, 9
Kobasa, Suzanne, 147–48, 149

LaBerge, Stephen, 104, 124
Language/linguistic ability, 16, 71, 201, 242
Lavender oil, 126, 127
Lavie, Peretz, 96, 97
Lawrence, Ron, 23, 40, 141, 265
Lazarus, Richard, 152, 153
Learning, 23–26, 36, 48, 50, 51, 56, 82, 83, 84, 214
aging and, 54
associative, 54, 67
boron and, 60
estrogen and, 208, 209
intelligence and, 16
perceptual, 104
REM sleep and, 103–4
sensory memory and, 79–80
sleep and, 115
Leathwood, Peter, 126
Lecithin, 58, 216, 249, 251
Lemon balm, 126, 127
Levi-Montalcini, Rita, 85
Levodopa, 107, 220
LHRH. *See* Luteinizing hormone releasing hormone (LHRH)
Life Events Scale, 152
Life span, 7
Light, 119, 127–28, 242, 261, 269, 276, 280, 281
Listening, 29, 33–34, 268, 272
Lithium, 84
Little, Tony, 88
Logic, 15, 16, 19, 58, 285
Lombardi, Vince, 139
Long-term memory, 23, 49–50, 53, 69, 75, 83, 103
Long-term potentiation (LTP), 51
Lorimer, Jim, 51
LTP. *See* Long-term potentiation (LTP)
Luteinizing hormone releasing hormone (LHRH), 242, 252
Lykken, David, 247, 248
Lynch, Gary, 220

Magnesium, 59, 60, 90, 141, 144, 166, 167, 171
Manganese, 171
Map reading, 13, 37, 231, 242
Martial arts, 2, 159, 161
Math ability/calculating, 16, 29, 32–33, 37, 115, 240, 242
Mayeaux, Richard, 209
Medications, 6, 7, 8
  for brain trauma and, 286
  for headaches, 278, 279, 283–84
  memory and, 84
  sleep and, 127–30, 133
  See also Drugs
Meditation, 41, 159, 173, 174–75, 181, 245
Melatonin, 98–99, 119, 126, 127–28, 129
Memorization, 20
Memory, 2, 5, 6, 16, 36, 49, 50, 75, 83, 84, 89, 212, 268
  aging and, 52–55, 54
  associative, 50, 69–70, 81, 90
  categories of, 25–26
  drugs and, 49, 83, 84, 86–88
  education and, 21, 48
  estrogen and, 208, 209
  explicit (flashbulb), 147
  fats and, 56
  hormones and, 68–76
  improving, 13, 38, 81–82, 90
  kinds of, 49–51
  learning and, 25, 50
  long-term. *See* Long-term memory
  neurotransmitters and, 52
  numbers and, 33
  physical exercise and, 76–79, 88, 90
  poisons for, 82–85
  practice and, 51
  sensory, 54, 79–80
  short-term. *See* Short-term memory
  sleep and, 103, 115
  smell and, 79–80, 90
  sound and, 79
  spatial, 54, 68, 69, 70
  stress and, 82–83, 85, 88, 146, 147
  tests of, 45–46, 53, 87
  vasopressin and, 244
  verbal, 16, 25, 57–58, 60, 69, 70, 83, 115
  visualization and, 81
  vitamins for, 60–63
  vocalization and, 81, 90
  "working," 49–50, 54, 61
  writing and, 47, 81, 90
Memory loss, 8, 45–93
  tip-of-the-tongue, 53, 54, 81–82
"Memory pills," 49, 64–68, 88
Memory response time, 53, 54
Men, 153, 228–41, 242–54
  Alzheimer's in, 186, 210, 211
  DHEA and, 71–74, 111
  exercise and, 160, 161
  sleep and, 98, 105, 107, 110, 112
Mental agility program, 21–42
Mental deterioration, 14
Mental disorders, 6, 36, 257–58
  insomnia and, 109–10
Mental/brain exercise, 13, 20, 36–41, 49, 214, 222
  stress and, 159
Merzenich, Michael, 11–12
Methocarbamol, 220
Methylphenidate, 271, 286
Metronidazole, 220
Midler, Bette, 3, 4
Mind, 3–4, 6, 257–87
  ADD and, 268–73
  anxiety and, 273–74
  linked to body, 1, 174, 227
  Super Powers of, 3, 4–8
Minerals, 59–60, 85, 90, 141, 180, 197–98, 222, 274
Miracles, 6
Moir, Anne, 240
Monosodium glutamate (MSG), 68, 90, 274, 280
Morrison, Ann, 209
Motrin, 206
MSG. *See* Monosodium glutamate (MSG)
Mullan, Michael, 206
Muscle relaxants, 220, 279

Naps, 6, 96, 113, 131–32, 133
Narcolepsy, 112–13
Naylor, Cecile, 240
Nerve growth factor (NGF), 71, 85–86, 223
Nervous system, 17, 85, 143
Neural connections, 36, 39, 48, 52
Neurons, 11, 39, 71, 144, 194, 208, 211, 212, 264, 285
Neuropeptide Y, 141, 166

Neurotransmitters, 52, 76, 168, 169, 173, 251, 274
depression and, 260
NGF and, 85
nicotine and, 212
nutrition and, 166, 249
Neurotrophins, 86
Nicklaus, Jack, 123, 130
Nicotine, 107, 130, 212–13
Nimodipine, 66–67, 90
Nitrites, 280
Nitrone, 87–88
Nonsteroidal anti-inflammatory drugs (NSAIDs), 83, 84, 206–7
Nootropics, 65, 87, 90, 222
Noradrenaline, 143, 193
Norepinephrine, 143, 219
NSAIDs. *See* Nonsteroidal anti-inflammatory drugs (NSAIDs)
Null, Gary, 261
Nutrients, 6, 9, 41–42, 58, 60–63, 76, 86–88, 203
anxiety and, 274
depression and, 261–64, 269
stress and, 159, 166–71, 180

Oils, 56, 60, 90, 126, 127, 264
Omega-3, 264, 269, 273
Omega-6, 264
Oral contraceptives, 107
Ornithine, 76
Other-handedness, 37
Overweight/obesity, 108, 167
DHEA and, 245
estrogen and, 209, 237
exercise and, 76, 90
Oxytocin, 243

Pacino, Al, 5
Painkillers, 83, 163, 279
Paired-associates, 54, 69–70
Panex, 169–70
Panic, 90
Pasta, 57, 60, 90
PEA. *See* Phenylethylamine (PEA)
Pemoline, 271
Peptides, 50
Perceptual learning, 17, 51, 75, 104, 242
Personality, 47, 61, 190, 284, 286
Perspective, 19–20
Petruzzello, Steven, 162
Phenobarbital, 220
Phenylethylamine (PEA), 246, 249, 280
Pheromones, 245–46
Phosphatidylcholine, 171
Phosphatidylserine (PS), 58–59, 60, 90, 171
Phosphorus, 144
Physical comfort, 26
Physical exercise, 39–40, 76–79, 160, 245, 281
breathing and. *See* Breathing
depression and, 261, 266–68, 269
estrogen and, 238, 251
guidelines for moderate, 161
memory and, 88, 90
sleep and, 119, 120
stress and, 157, 158, 159–64, 180–81
testosterone and, 234, 251
walking as, 160, 161, 164, 173, 267, 268
Physical fitness, 4, 96
Physostigmine, 216
Phytoestrogens, 238, 250
Picasso, Pablo, 35
Piracetam, 65–66, 90
PMR. *See* Progressive muscle relaxation (PMR)
Positive thinking, 27
Potassium, 144, 203, 274
"Power naps," 96, 131–32, 133
Prednisone, 220
Pregnenolone, 41, 42, 74
Presley, Priscilla, 4
Problem solving, 13, 16, 19, 268
sleep and, 103, 104
thinking style and, 26, 28, 29
Procedural learning/memory, 25, 36, 50, 51
Progesterone, 107, 111, 237–38, 243
Progressive muscle relaxation (PMR), 176
Prolactin, 243, 253
Propanolol, 220
Protein, 55, 57, 85, 144, 165, 166, 169, 212, 263, 272
sleep and, 97, 125
Prozac, 261–63
PS. *See* Phosphatidylserine (PS)
Psychological disorders, 106, 108, 114
Psychological Skills Training, 175

Pyridoxine, 261
Pyritinol, 67

Quinidine, 107, 220

Rahe, Richard, 152
Raloxifene, 71
Rapid eye movement (REM) sleep, 98, 102, 103–4, 121, 152
  acetylcholine and, 122
  age and, 118
  hGH and, 112
  MSLT and, 113
  progesterone and, 111
  vasopressin and, 244
Reading, 29–31, 37, 38
Redux, 262
Rehearsal, mental, 50, 83, 88
Relaxation, 159, 163, 172–78, 179, 180
Religion, 6
REM sleep. *See* Rapid eye movement (REM) sleep
Repetition, 50, 51, 174
Reserpine, 107
Restless leg syndrome, 106, 109
Retrospect/prospect game, 158–59, 179–80
Riboflavin, 60, 169
Richardson, Dot, 21, 121
Rikli, Roberta, 39
Ritalin, 271, 272, 286
Roberts, Eugene, 72
Rosemary, 216
Routines, 90

SAD. *See* Seasonal affective disorder (SAD)
St.-John's-wort, 265, 266, 269
Salt, 166, 171, 179, 196
Sapolsky, Robert, 157, 194
Scanning, 29–30
Schaie, K. Warner, 13, 14
Scheibel, Arnold, 36
Schreiner-Engle, Patricia, 235
Schwarzenegger, Arnold, 5, 51, 147, 247
SDN. *See* Sexually dimorphic nucleus (SDN)
Seasonal affective disorder (SAD), 119, 261
Sedatives, 220
Selective Combination/Encoding Insight, 19–20
Selective Comparison Insight, 20
Selective comprehension, 29, 30–31
Selective estrogen-receptor modulators (SERM), 71
Selegiline, 193, 206, 217
Selenium, 171, 274
Self-knowledge, 17
Self-monitoring thinking, 27
Selye, Hans, 140–41, 142, 144, 145
Sensory memory, 54, 79–80
Sensory variations, 232, 241, 242
SERM. *See* Selective estrogen-receptor modulators (SERM)
Serotonin, 57, 60, 125, 126, 193, 251, 252
  depression and, 260, 261–63
  headaches and, 277, 278, 279
Sex hormones, 110–12, 228–41, 252, 253–54
Sex life, 249–52, 253, 276
Sexually dimorphic nucleus (SDN), 231
Sherwin, Barbara, 69, 70, 237
Short-term memory, 14, 23, 49–50, 69, 75, 81, 228
  drugs for, 64–68
Sleep, 6, 95–135
  depression and, 261
  headaches and, 282
  insomnia and, 98–99, 104–12
  narcolepsy and, 112–13
  paradoxical, 10
  stress and, 152
Sleep apnea, 104, 106, 107–8
Sleep debt, 113–15, 116, 117
  overeating and, 125
Sleep diary/log, 110, 132
Sleep hygiene, 130, 133
Sleeping pills, 127–30, 220
"Smart drug," 42
"Smart foods," 49
Smell/odor, 79–80, 90, 241, 246, 276, 280
Smith, Carlyle, 103
Smith, David C., 80
Smith, Katy, 262
Smoking, 250, 251, 253, 283
  insomnia and, 106, 130

Snoring, 108
Snowdon, David, 201, 202, 204
Somatostatin, 193
Sound, 79
Spatial memory, 54, 60, 68, 69, 70
Spatial skills, 13, 37, 242
Spielberg, Steven, 3, 4
Steinfeld, Jake, 3, 4, 38, 79, 130, 155
Stern, Yaakov, 213
Sternberg, Robert, 17, 19
Steroid hormone precursor, 42
Stevens, Charles, 48
Stevenson, Robert Lewis, 123
Streep, Meryl, 5
Stress, 6, 41, 137–83, 253
  acute vs. chronic, 179–81
  alarm reaction and, 144
  Alzheimer's and, 194
  DHEA and, 245
  eustress and, 141–42
  exercise and, 157, 158, 159–64
  learning and, 82
  LHRH and, 242
  memory and, 82–83, 85, 88, 146, 147
  nutrition and, 165–72
  occupations and, 140
  quiz on, 181–82
  scales for, 152–54
  signs of, 150, 152, 153–54
  sleep and, 96, 105
  testosterone and, 234, 251
  triggers for, 180
Stress diseases, 144, 147, 148, 153, 160
Stress hormones, 72, 143, 156–59, 173, 194
  exercise and, 161, 162
Stress Inoculation Training, 175
Strokes, 9, 52, 156, 199–205, 221
Sturgis, Jodi, 72
Sugar, 40, 55–56, 60, 90, 275
  anxiety and, 274–76
  depression and, 261, 263, 269
Sumitriptan, 278
Synapses, 11, 26, 52, 64
  ampakine and, 220
  estrogen and, 208–9
Synder, Solomon, 223
Synergy, 1

Tacrine, 193, 215, 222
Tai chi breathing, 78, 161, 173
Talents, quiz on, 18–19
Tau, 193
TBI. *See* Traumatic brain injury (TBI)
Tea, 41, 42, 126, 127
Testosterone, 69, 72, 90, 210, 233–36, 237, 254
  DHEA and, 245
  LHRH and, 242
  progesterone and, 243
  prolactin and, 243
  SDN and, 231
  sex life and, 251, 252, 253
  sleep and, 110, 111, 119
  vasopressin and, 244
Thiamine, 60, 168–69, 171
Thinking, 26–28
  ALC for, 41
  alcohol and, 83
  brain trauma and, 285
  breathing and, 89
  creativity and, 27
  deterioration in, 13
  developing styles of, 28
  drugs that impair, 220
  estrogen and, 210
  hGH and, 75
  neurotransmitters and, 52
  stress and, 146
  training in, 13
Thinking disease, 268
Thyroid, 68, 107, 143
Thyrotropic hormone (TTH), 143
Thyroxine, 143
Tranquilizers, 220
Traumatic brain injury (TBI), 281, 284–86
Tryptophan, 57, 126, 127, 252
  depression and, 262–63, 269
TTH. *See* Thyrotropic hormone (TTH)
Tubman, Harriet, 123
Type A behavior, 246
Tyrosine, 76, 169, 171, 249, 251

Valerian root, 126, 127
Vasopressin, 143, 244
Verbal learning/memory, 16, 25, 57–58, 60, 69, 70, 83, 115
Verbal skills, 15, 71, 240, 241, 242
  exercises for, 13, 38
Visual learning/memory, 25, 60, 242
Visual sense, 232, 240, 242

Visual-spatial response, 54
Visualization, 81, 82–83, 88
Vitamin A, 167–68, 171, 180, 203, 205
Vitamin B complex, 41, 49, 60–62, 76, 90, 129
  depression and, 261, 262
  stress and, 144, 168–69, 171, 180
  sugar and, 275
Vitamin C, 62, 63, 88, 90, 203, 249–50, 251
  headaches and, 277
  stress and, 144, 166, 168, 171, 180
Vitamin E, 144, 166, 168, 171, 180, 277
  Alzheimer's and, 203, 205, 206, 217
Vitamins, 41, 49, 60–63, 76
  sleep and, 129
  stress and, 144, 159, 165, 167–71, 180
Vocabulary, 14, 16, 242
  enhancing your, 29, 31–32

Water (as drink), 84–85, 89, 97, 197–98, 199, 277
Weider, Ben, 151
Weil, Andrew, 126, 262
Wellbutrin, 249
Williams, Robin, 5
Willis, Sherry, 13
Winfrey, Oprah, 5
Women, 39, 62, 228–54
  Alzheimer's in, 186, 208–10, 221
  depression in, 259–60, 261, 267
  DHEA and, 71–74
  exercise and, 160, 161
  headaches in, 280, 282
  memory in, 49, 82
  sleep and, 98, 105, 110–11, 112
  stress in, 153
  See also Estrogen; Hormone/estrogen replacement therapy (ERT)
Woods, Tiger, 5–6
Word association, 32, 54, 81, 90
Word games, 37
Word recall, 84
Writing, 47, 81, 90, 201, 214
Wurtman, Judith, 262
Wurtman, Richard, 57, 262

Yaeger, Don, 21, 121
Yankner, Bruce A., 192–93
Yoga, 173–74, 177

Zinc, 59, 60, 90, 171, 198, 199, 234, 251

ABOUT THE AUTHORS

Robert M. Goldman, M.D., D.O., Ph.D.

Dr. Goldman has spearheaded the development of numerous international medical organizations and corporations. A physician and surgeon, Dr. Goldman received medical degrees from Midwestern University, the Chicago College of Osteopathic Medicine and Surgery, and Central American Health Sciences University School of Medicine. He has also received Ph.D.s in androgenic anabolic steroid biochemistry from the Institute D'Études Superieures L'Avenir (Belgium), Honolulu University (U.S.A.), and Akademie Fur Internationale Kulturund Wissenschaftsforderung Accademia (Germany). Dr. Goldman has an Affiliate appointment and is a visiting lecturer at Harvard University's Philosophy of Education Research Center, Graduate School of Education, a Senior Fellow at Tufts University, and an assistant professor at Oklahoma State University's Department of Internal Medicine. He is a Fellow of the American Academy of Sports Physicians and a Board Diplomat in Sports Medicine and Anti-Aging Medicine. He cofounded and serves as Chairman of the Board of Life Science Holdings, which is a biomedical research company with over 100 medical patents under development in the areas of brain resuscitation, trauma and emergency medicine, and organ transplant and blood preservation technologies. He has overseen cooperative research agreement development programs in conjunction with such prominent institutions as the American National Red Cross, NASA, the Department of Defense, and the FDA's Center for Devices and Radiological Health.

As an inventor, Dr. Goldman was awarded the "Gold Medal for Science" (1993), the "Grand Prize for Medicine" (1994), the "Humanitarian Award" (1995), and the "Business Development Award" (1996) from the International Invention New Products Exposition competing against hundreds of inventors from around the world.

A black belt in karate, Chinese weapons expert, and world champion athlete with over 20 world strength records, he has been listed in the *Guinness Book of World Records.* Some of his past records were 13,500 consecutive situps and 321 consecutive handstand pushups. Dr. Goldman was an All-College athlete in four sports, a three-time winner of the JFK Physical Fitness Award, was voted Athlete of the Year in 1981 and 1982, and was the recipient of the 1983 Champions Award. In 1980 he was inducted into the World Hall of Fame of Physical Fitness, and in 1995 was awarded the Healthy American Fitness Leader Award from the President's Council on Physical Fitness and Sports and U.S. Chamber of Commerce.

Dr. Goldman has served as Chairman of the International Medical Commission overseeing sports medicine committees in over 170 nations since 1985 and serves as a Special Adviser to the President's Council on Physical Fitness and Sports. Aside from the numerous books he has authored, he has also published over 200 articles, and has appeared in hundreds of national and international media presentations.

He founded the National Academy of Sport Medicine (International President), American Academy of Anti-Aging Medicine (Chairman of the Board), and High Technology Research Institute. His main hobbies aside from sports and academic pursuits are expanding the fine art collection of the museum he founded, the Institute Museum of Chicago, and visiting an average of twenty countries annually to promote brain research and sports medicine programs.

Ronald Klatz, M.D., D.O.

Dr. Klatz is a graduate of Florida Technological University and the College of Osteopathic Medicine and Surgery in Des Moines, Iowa. He is board-certified in both family practice and sports medicine and, along with Dr. Goldman, is cofounder of the American Academy of Anti-Aging Medicine. He is the author of *Grow Young with HGH* (HarperCollins), *Stopping the Clock* (Keats), and numerous other books. Dr. Klatz served as Senior Medical Editor for *Longevity* magazine and as a contributing editor to *The Archives of Gerontology and Geriatrics*. He serves as President of the American Academy of Anti-Aging Medicine and dedicates significant time to the organization and promotion of anti-aging medical concepts and seeking treatment protocols for the diseases of aging.

Lisa Berger

Lisa Berger is a professional writer whose books include *The Healthy Company* (with Dr. Robert Rosen), *Under Observation: Life Inside the McLean Psychiatric Hospital* (with Dr. Alexander Vuckovic), and *Dying Well* (with Dr. Ira Byock). She lives in Washington, D.C.